Advance Praise for *It's Not About the Money*

"The Buddha taught about the dangers of the wanting mind in all of us, and here Brent Kessel applies that wisdom to the modern challenge of people and their emotional relationship with money. All aspects of our lives are interconnected, so ignoring this important relationship usually leads to self-deception and suffering. Applying Eastern wisdom to a very Western concern, Kessel shows how being mindful of our relationship to money can free one of anxiety and even turn money into a tool for compassion."

> —Thich Nhat Hanh, Zen Buddhist monk and bestselling author nominated for the Nobel Peace Prize by Dr. Martin Luther King Jr.

"What's your heart's desire—spiritual fulfillment, or wealth? The good news is that it's not an either/or proposition—you can have both. This magnificent book will show you how to get your ego out of the way so you can align your financial decisions with your heart and soul."

> —Ken Blanchard, coauthor of *The One Minute Manager®* and *Lead Like Jesus*

"This book is clear, kind, helpful, and empowering. It offers a psychological and spiritual lens to observe your confusions, obsessions, aversions, and passions all playing out on the movie screen of money and investing. It can help everyone from the timid to the extravagant get more sane, solvent, and secure. Brent has done his pragmatic as well as his inner homework, and his advice and exercises can help readers approach investing wisely."

> —Vicki Robin, coauthor with Joe Dominguez, *Your Money or Your Life*

"Brent Kessel is one of the smartest financial planners I've ever encountered and also the most soulful. Not only does he have the financial acumen to guide even the most sophisticated investor, but he has an unusually deep understanding of the emotional, psychological, and spiritual effect of money in our lives.

"Now he's written a book that is a must-read for anyone who has anxieties about money —which is pretty much all of us. If you can't figure out how to make peace with your finances, read *It's Not About the Money* and I'll bet you'll find the answers you need."

> —Liz Pulliam Weston, columnist for MSN Money and author of *Easy Money: How to Simplify Your Finances and Get What You Want Out of Life*

"Money is one of the most confusing, anxiety-producing topics for almost everyone, regardless of income level. This book does a beautiful job at helping us make peace with money and our relationship to it. Bringing together Eastern and Western thought creates the perfect balance and gives us an incredible dose of perspective and wisdom to deal with money for the rest of our lives. I highly and enthusiastically recommend *It's Not About the Money* for anyone with any amount of money!"

 —Richard Carlson, author of *Don't Sweat the Small Stuff . . . And It's All Small Stuff*

"Brent's compassionate guidance speaks to the spirit and helped me to navigate the complex world of finances and investing with confidence, empowering me to make financial choices that are in alignment with my soul's purpose. I highly recommend Brent's work to anyone interested in understanding the power of money, its relationship to spirit, and how one doesn't have to exist without the other."

 —Seane Corn, author of the video series *Vinyasa Flow Yoga*

"Brent Kessel combines some of the most sophisticated knowledge of financial planning and investment strategies with a sincere and grounded practice in the meditation arts. He has written the deepest and most comprehensive book about money in some time. I applaud him for it. It calls for a serious reading."

 —George Kinder, author of *The Seven Stages of Money Maturity*

"Brent Kessel is one of the financial planning profession's true thought leaders around what may be the most important issue of our time: How can each of us find personally fulfilling strategies that will lead us toward a life of happiness and spiritual prosperity?"

 —Bob Veres, editor, *Inside Information*

"Brent Kessel is one of the most thoughtful, thorough, and knowledgeable investment professionals that I've met. His advice on blending the personal and financial aspects of life have served him well in doing an outstanding job for his clients."

 —Jim O'Shaughnessy, author of *What Works on Wall Street* and *How to Retire Rich*

"Brent Kessel will change your relationship with money in a way that may also enhance the richness of your life."

—Tom Bradley, president, TD AMERITRADE Institutional

"Kessel has a unique perspective on money. He is able to open people's eyes to the financial world and at the same time show them how to look inward for value. Anyone who wants to not only be rich but lead a rich life should read this book."

—Thomas M. Kostigen, Dow Jones MarketWatch columnist and author of the *New York Times* bestseller *The Green Book: The Everyday Guide to Saving the Planet One Simple Step at a Time*

"It's rare that a book on personal finance succeeds equally well on both sides of the coin. Brent Kessel has pulled it off. This is one that's rich in solid, practical advice—but not at the expense of the human spirit."

—Lee Eisenberg, author of *The Number: A Completely Different Way to Think About the Rest of Your Life*

"Most books on the subject of money are usually deadly boring, address a part of a person that should not be encouraged, or give you the feeling that the author is trying to sell you something you will later regret having bought. Brent Kessel has written something far more sophisticated, psychologically accurate, and helpful to a person trying to live at the center of all this constant getting and spending. This is a book that establishes a larger context that we so desperately need and succeeds admirably in helping us to understand ourselves, our goals, and our relationship to money."

—David Whyte, author of *The Heart Aroused* and *Crossing the Unknown Sea: Work as a Pilgrimage of Identity*

It's Not About the Money

It's Not About the Money

UNLOCK YOUR MONEY TYPE TO ACHIEVE SPIRITUAL AND FINANCIAL ABUNDANCE

Brent Kessel

HarperOne
An Imprint of HarperCollinsPublishers

This book is designed to provide information on the subject of personal finances. It is not intended to provide investment advisory, legal, tax, accounting, or financial planning services. Individual financial situations are unique, and therefore, any and all financial, tax, legal, or investment questions must be addressed by the appropriate professional. Information contained herein is gathered from sources deemed reliable as of the date of publication, but accuracy cannot be guaranteed. The figures shown are not intended to represent potential future performance of actual or hypothetical clients, portfolios, models, or asset classes. Future results may vary substantially from past results due to a wide variety of uncontrollable and unpredictable factors. The author and publisher specifically disclaim any liability, loss, or risk that is incurred as a consequence, directly or indirectly, of the use and application of any of the contents of this book.

The stories and anecdotes included are based on true experiences. However, all names are pseudonyms, some stories are compilations, and some situations have been changed slightly for educational purposes or to protect the privacy of and confidential relationship with those involved.

Printed on paper containing 15 percent postconsumer and 5 percent preconsumer recycled fiber.

Printed using soy-based ink.

The author is donating 25 percent of the net income from sales of *It's Not About the Money* to charity.

FIRST EDITION

Library of Congress Cataloging-in-Publication Data

Kessel, Brent.
    It's not about the money : unlock your money type to achieve spiritual and financial
abundance / Brent Kessel. —1st ed.
        p. cm.
    ISBN: 978–0–06–123406–4
    1. Finance, Personal—Psychological aspects.   2. Typology (Psychology).   3. Self-perception.
4. Money—Psychological aspects.   5. Peace of mind—Religious aspects.   I. Title.
II. Title: Unlock your money type to achieve spiritual and financial abundance.
HG179.K494   2008
332.024—dc22   2007018380

08 09 10 11 12 RRD(H) 10 9 8 7 6 5 4 3 2 1

CONTENTS

Introduction xiii

    It's Not About the Money xv

    Financial Planner by Day, Yogi by Dawn xvi

    Why This Book? xviii

    Financial Freedom for Your Soul xx

Part 1: The Nature of Mind

Chapter One: You Will Never Have Enough 3

    The Wanting Mind 4

    Wired to Want 6

    If Only 7

    In the Flow 9

    But It Feels Good! 10

    The Financial Toll of Wanting 11

    Diminishing Returns 12

    The More We Want, the More We Want 12

    Financial Planning and Great Investment Advice Won't Get You "There" 13

    Wanting Better Investment Returns 16

    At War with Yourself 17

    Not Wanting 20

Chapter Two: The Unconscious Wins Every Time 23

    We Get What We Think We Deserve 24

    Your Core Story 25

The Script Is Written 26

The Seeds of the Core Story...30

Understand Your Story..31

To the Very Core 33

No Quick Fix...35

Part 2: The Eight Financial Archetypes

Introducing the Archetypes..39

Our Stories Change 42

Chapter Three: The Guardian

Chapter Three: The Guardian...45

The Guardian's Core Story...49

What the Guardian Feels 51

Seeds of the Guardian: Survival Mode..51

What the Guardian Thinks 55

The Payoff...55

Breaking the Guardian's Death Grip 57

Chapter Four: The Pleasure Seeker 61

The Pleasure Seeker's Core Story 62

Seeds of the Pleasure Seeker—"Why Suffer?" 64

The Payoff: Death-Defying Buying 65

What the Pleasure Seeker Fears 66

The Dark Side of Pleasure-Seeking: Buy Now, Pay (Big) Later 68

A Different Kind of Pleasure 72

My Hands Are Empty 74

Chapter Five: The Idealist..77

The Idealist's Core Story...78

Seeds of the Idealist—"The Eye of a Needle" 80

"Money Just Sucks"..81

Heads in the Sand 82

Hippies with Money 84

The Payoff..85

Breaking Free...86

Chapter Six: The Saver..89

The Saver's Core Story 90

The Dark Side of Saving..93

The Payoff 95

Breaking the Saver's Death Grip 95

Chapter Seven: The Star 99

The Star's Core Story 100

Seeds of the Star—Bring on the Bling 101

The Payoff 103

A Painful Chasm 104

Freeing the Star..105

Chapter Eight: The Innocent..109

The Innocent's Core Story 110

What the Innocent Believes..111

Seeds of the Innocent 113

The Payoff 114

Get Comfortable with Money 115

Chapter Nine: The Caretaker..119

The Caretaker's Core Story..120

What the Caretaker Believes..121

Seeds of the Caretaker: "He's Not Heavy ..." 122

The Payoff 123

The Dark Side of Caretaking..125

A Different Kind of Caretaking 128

Chapter Ten: The Empire Builder..135

What the Empire Builder Believes..137

The Wanting Mind and the Empire Builder 138

The Payoff 139

Treat Yourself Like You Treat Your Business........................140

Removing the Blinders 141

Part 3: In the World and of It

Chapter Eleven: The Middle Way with Money 151

    Think More 154

    A Four-Year-Old Runs Your Financial Life 156

    Your Money Mask 159

    Your Innate Financial Wisdom 161

    Hold Both 163

    This Is Depressing! 165

    The Middle Way for Each Archetype 165

    Heart Racing? 175

    Opposites Attract 175

    Go Slowly 177

    Play! 178

    Your Divine Nature and Your Human Nature 178

Chapter Twelve: The Conscious Investor 181

    Holy Investing! 183

    What Investing Is 183

    Interconnected Versus Isolated Wealth 184

    Investing as Though We're All One 187

    Does It Really Work? 188

    When the Past Does Not Equal the Future 189

    Doing Good and Doing Well 190

    The Middle Way for Investors 191

    True Diversity 193

    So How Does a Diversified Portfolio Perform? 196

    Unearthing the Hidden Fees and Costs of Investing 198

    Time Is on Your Side 202

    Prepare Yourself 205

Chapter Thirteen: The Yoga of Money 211

    Self-Centeredness 213

    It's Not Just for Saints 216

    Right Motivation 219

    If Not Now, When? 220

    How Much Should You Give? 221

Three Buckets 224

What Can You Give? 226

What's Your Cause? 229

Teach a Man to Fish 231

So You Want to Leave a Legacy 232

Don't Wait until You're Dead and Gone 233

Chapter Fourteen: You Have Arrived 237

Don't Do, Be 239

As Good as It Gets 241

Appendix: The Nuts and Bolts 245

Ready-to-Go Investment Strategies 246

Cash Flow 249

Debt and Mortgage Management 250

Retirement Planning 253

Taxes 254

Annuities 255

Insurance 256

Estate Planning 260

Financial Planners 263

Socially Responsible Investing (SRI) 263

Smart Philanthropy 263

Debt Reduction Services 264

Donor-Advised Funds 264

Characteristics of and Practical Recommendations for Each Archetype 264

The Guardian 264

The Pleasure Seeker 267

The Idealist 269

The Saver 271

The Star 273

The Innocent 275

The Caretaker 277

The Empire Builder 279

Resources 283

Acknowledgments 289

Index 293

LIST OF EXERCISES

Knowledge Is Power xix

Detach 9

What Are Your Heartfelt Goals? 15

Letting Go...18

What You Want..22

Look Within..29

Your Story at Work...32

My Money History..33

Inquire...35

How to Relax...53

The Worst-Case Scenario 56

Creating Safety for the Guardian 58

What Has Motivated My Recent Purchases? 67

Pleasure Redefined 73

A Day of Rest 74

One Thing at a Time...75

The Skeptic's Lens..83

Some Things to Try...87

The Number 95

Breaking the Saver's Death Grip 96

Freeing the Star...106

Freeing the Innocent 116

Truthfulness...127

Not Doing...128

Caring for the Caretaker...131

Removing the Blinders 142
Finding Your Financial Archetypes 146
Your Dominant Archetypes.. 153
Let the Four-Year-Old Speak 157
Uncovering Your Mask... 160
Your Innate Financial Wisdom 162
Holding Both... 164
Buying Low and Selling High 197
Hidden Fees 200
What's the Right Mix of Stocks and Bonds for You? 205
I'm Going to Lose It All! 208
When Have You Been Touched by Your Own Generosity?......... 213
Share the Pain. Share the Gain. 218
Obligation or Inspiration? 220
How Much Have You Given, and Why? 223
Give It Away.. 224
Create Your Personalized Giving Policy 230
Will They Remember Me? 232
Write Your Own Obituary.. 233
Loving-Kindness Meditation 234
Be Still.. 238
"Who Am I?".. 240
Presence and the Contemplation of Death............................... 241
You Have Arrived.. 243

INTRODUCTION

"Wealth is not his that has it, but his that enjoys it."

—Benjamin Franklin

Regardless of your net worth, if you are like most people in our society, you would probably like to change something about your relationship to money. Maybe you have a healthy nest egg built up, yet you still worry about having enough for the future. Maybe you're struggling with the basics of sound financial management, with bank balances and assets that aren't anywhere near what they should be, given the amount you've earned over time. Or maybe you become paralyzed with indecision anytime you need to make a major financial decision.

You are not alone. When it comes to money, most of us have experienced one or more of the following:

- Feelings of anxiety and fear

- A sense that money is separate from the more sacred or spiritual parts of our lives

- Endless wants, or the feeling that we'll never have enough money to be happy

- Frustration with a spouse or family member regarding spending habits

- The belief that our finances are beyond our control

In my twelve years of running one of the nation's top financial planning and money management companies, I've worked with people who have hundreds of millions of dollars, as well as people who are a hundred thousand in debt. I've counseled captains of industry who are driven to ever higher levels of financial success and social activists one paycheck away from eviction. I've led workshops for seasoned students of meditation and yoga and for affluent entrepreneurs enjoying the good life. While there's no denying that in many ways it is easier to be rich than poor, I have found that without exception it makes little difference what people's outer life circumstances are—everyone struggles with some aspect of their relationship to money.

I've seen it all, from the middle-aged owner of a successful software company who frets over buying a new couch, to the single mother anguished by her $25,000 in credit-card debt but unwilling to say no to her sixteen-year-old son's plea for a new car, to the young fashion designer who is so ashamed of her substantial inheritance that she lives in an unsafe neighborhood so that she can afford the rent on her salary alone. The darkest emotions evoked by money often have absolutely nothing to do with objective security. I know people who live on $20,000 per year with no fear and others who live on millions with unrelenting anxiety. I've also encountered many people who consider themselves self-aware and conscious, perhaps having gone through great personal transformations with the help of psychotherapy, twelve-step programs, or religious or spiritual practice, but who have extremely unconscious and unsatisfying relationships to money. Millions who came of age in the 1960s and '70s, for example, though outwardly successful, have great distrust in, if not utter disdain for, Wall Street and corporate America, and are often trapped in unhealthy, self-sabotaging money behaviors. Finally, for so many of us, no matter which generation we come from or what we believe about money, rich or poor, there can never be enough. We crave more money, material possessions, or investment success, even when our financial needs don't warrant it. We might know that we're caught up in our desire but feel impotent to do anything about it.

Many people find themselves stuck in a pattern with money regardless of whose advice they follow or how much time goes by. To make matters even more challenging, they may end up with a partner or family member whose values, fears, or financial tendencies irritate them. Old habits die hard. The person who has always felt poor goes on feeling poor and making decisions from a poverty mindset; the penny-pincher remains frugal, perhaps to the point of deprivation.

IT'S NOT ABOUT THE MONEY

The predominant message in our culture is that it's all about the money—that more money or a different set of financial circumstances will bring us the freedom to stop worrying and just enjoy life. But many people remain stuck in the same financial predicament, even though they've tried everything they know to get ahead. No matter what your balance sheet looks like, you probably already suspect that there has to be a way to make the lasting, profound changes in your financial life that you crave, or you wouldn't have picked up this book.

One reason most people aren't happy with their financial lives is that the ways we have traditionally been taught to deal with money simply don't work. We are told to spend less, to save more, to think positive thoughts that will create the abundance we want, or to find the perfect career. We set goals, create budgets, put all the right insurance in place, write updated wills and estate plans, and invest in a certain way. Though important, these actions aren't enough. The reason? They approach money from the outside in, rather than from the inside out.

Whether we hoard, splurge, or give it all away, we perpetually repeat ineffective behavior patterns with money because we are accustomed to specific states of being where money is concerned. We are used to a particular level of anxiety or calm, craving or avoidance, scarcity or abundance. And no matter what changes occur in our outer circumstances, the unconscious mind, if it remains unexamined, untrained, and unconnected to our spirit, will recreate those old, familiar circumstances in our financial life.

This is the reason I've seen people sell a business for many millions of dollars and then, through bad decision-making, either spend, loan, or poorly invest their nest egg, ending up in exactly the same financial condition they were in prior to their windfall. Their unconscious mind was so used to striving to make it that they literally couldn't cope with the abundance and freedom that was thrust upon them, so their unconscious manifested the old, familiar financial conditions in their outer lives again. Americans as a whole enjoy a higher standard of living than most of the world, at least in financial terms. Yet even when people achieve the financial success that's so highly valued by our culture, they aren't necessarily content. We've all heard about people who receive a huge windfall but are still unhappy or anxious all the time. The business press is filled with stories of workaholics who have built one business after another, at times even alienating their loved ones or destroying their marriages. There are wealthy inheritors and divorcées who are among the most tormented souls I know.

Don't get me wrong. I am by no means saying that you can't be both wealthy and happy. But whether you have a seven-figure trust fund or a pile of unpaid bills on your kitchen table, the path to freedom requires that you focus more on your inner life than on your outer financial circumstances.

Those of you facing a stack of bills with no means to pay them may balk at the notion that you can change your outer circumstances by going within, but the fact is that I have seen it happen in countless people's lives. And though it's easy to tell you to go within for answers, this book will show you how to do just that. I've successfully used the tried-and-true strategies you'll find in these pages for myself and for hundreds of clients and workshop participants. The insights you'll find here grow out of my own experience of having a foot in two distinct worlds.

FINANCIAL PLANNER BY DAY, YOGI BY DAWN

From a very young age, I've been fascinated with making money, yet I also always knew that there was more to life. I studied economics and psychology in college and began my professional career in the commercial mortgage business. But I wanted to provide much more holistic financial advice to people than the mortgage business would allow. In 1996 I founded Abacus Wealth Management, which I later merged with my partner, Spencer Sherman, to create Abacus Wealth Partners, a fee-only® financial planning business that focuses on the internal and external factors essential to creating a satisfying financial life, primarily serving very affluent clients. Later, as Abacus grew, we saw how poorly served most investors were, regardless of their net worth. In an effort to reach a larger, less affluent population, we established Kubera Portfolios for clients who wanted a low-cost but professionally managed way to invest. By this time, I had begun a daily two-hour practice of the ancient Ashtanga system of yoga postures and, for many years before this, had immersed myself in Eastern spiritual practices. As a Certified Financial Planner® professional by day and a yogi by dawn, I went from yoga studio to office, from client meeting to meditation cushion, and from financial conference to weekend retreat. I began to notice a profound difference between how financial planning approached our everyday challenges and complaints and how the world's oldest wisdom traditions approached them. In the financial planning world, when a problem arises in a client's life, there is always a better financial strategy that will solve the problem and bring greater fulfillment and happiness. The solutions exist primarily in the outer, tangible world. There is an implicit assumption that something must change "out there" in order to be happier "in here."

By contrast, in the yoga and meditation worlds, most of our attention is directed inward, toward gaining a better understanding of who we really are, why we behave in certain ways, and what the root causes of our suffering are. We are then encouraged to integrate our outer actions with that inner understanding. Financial planning is most concerned with the future, whereas yoga and meditation are most concerned with the present moment and suggest that we cannot hope to be free in the future if we're not inquiring deeply into what it takes to be free right now. Whereas financial advice compels us to action, spiritual inquiry compels us to awareness.

I was seeing many clients who had their financial planning house in order, were doing all the right things with their money, had achieved most or all of their most important personal goals, but still were uneasy about money and usually believed that there was some external change that could bring them inner peace. Some of them had more money than they could possibly spend in a lifetime, and yet they felt insecure about having enough money in a culture that says, "More is better."

There was the retired college professor and her husband who had significant assets, including a TIAA-CREF pension, various mutual fund accounts, and two IRA accounts—enough to cover their standard of living forever as well as pay for the education of their kids, grandkids, and great-grandkids too. Still, they battled constantly over money. She felt guilty and ashamed of any spending they did beyond bare necessities, calling it "extravagant" and "showy." He constantly second-guessed their stockbroker's advice and spent hours reading the many financial publications to which he subscribed.

They weren't the only ones who wanted something more from their relationship to money than outer abundance could deliver. This was a common theme with my clients and my colleagues' clients. And the people in my life who were not affluent also craved more peace of mind. It became clear that I needed a new way to help people who wanted more peace and happiness with their money, whether they already had ample resources or not. The traditional tools of financial planning just weren't enough.

In 1999 I began to seek specific training from financial planners and meditation teachers who specialized in matters of the heart and spirit, especially those focused on the causes of suffering and the path away from it. I voraciously read every book, listened to every tape, and attended every workshop I could find that had something to say about money and spirituality. I began integrating the insights from these teachings into my daily financial planning practice. The response was overwhelmingly positive, with many clients saying that they understood more than they ever had about their relationship to money. I also noticed a marked increase in requests for press interviews and invitations to speak at financial conferences on this subject. My client base began to grow dramatically. It seemed people yearned for this merging of money and spirit.

In addition to the training I was doing with other professionals, I began blending the practices and insights of yoga and meditation with my financial expertise. I read the ancient texts of yoga philosophy looking for teachings about greed, attachment, self-observation, and desire, and was surprised by the many overt references to money and wealth that I found. Out of this research, I created a workshop called "The Yoga of Money," which I presented in the United States and Europe for clients, yoga students, and the general public. Not only did the participants begin to realize their financial dreams—doubling their net worth, leaving their jobs to start their own businesses, or simplifying their lives to focus on creative endeavors—but people from varying socioeconomic backgrounds told me that they were beginning to experience more understanding, peace, and ease in their relationship to money than ever before.

WHY THIS BOOK?

There are numerous books about money, and you may well be familiar with them. Maybe you've read the ones about the ins and outs of financial planning, or those that tell you how to become a millionaire by investing in real estate or giving up your daily latte, or still others that help you visualize abundance or play the stock market more effectively. Many train you to "think like a millionaire" or even help you embrace a more simple way of life so that you can get out of the rat race. Depending on personal preference, any one of these approaches may be right, yet most of them are essentially offering external solutions to a problem whose real answer lies within.

KNOWLEDGE IS POWER

If you want to make lasting changes in your relationship to money, you must first observe your experience exactly as it is, without trying to change it. So settle in, take a deep breath, and ask yourself these simple questions: What are you feeling about money right now, in this moment? Which of the following words capture your mood? Feel free to add your own to the list:

Worry	Fear	Greed	Panic	Hope
Contentment	Happiness	Boredom	Anger	Gloom
Frustration	Excitement	Neutrality	Enjoyment	Peace
Confusion	Envy	Sufficiency	Serenity	Overwhelm

At first, just observe. Don't judge or try to change what you're aware of. Without talking yourself out of the feelings or trying to justify them, observe these feelings as if they were a weather system, separate from yourself. Is it raining or sunny, cloudy or cold, when it comes to your ideas about money? Notice the quality of the emotions you are experiencing and notice too when the emotions begin naturally to shift on their own, when the weather begins to change and into what. This technique of observation without judgment and without forcing change is the basis for the radical alterations you will be making in your relationship to money in the pages to come. Make a habit of the techniques taught in this book and you will be amazed at what begins to happen in your financial world.

This book will help you access and increase inner and outer wealth. Inner wealth means:

- Freedom from the feeling of never having enough

- A sense of financial choice instead of constraint

- The sensation of abundance that inspires us to use money for the greater good

- The knowledge that we are connected, that our individual well-being is related to the well-being of our fellow humans

Though outer wealth rarely leads to inner wealth, inner wealth often does lead to outer wealth. By embracing the ideas and following the practices I set forward in the coming pages, you can have all of the above and a thriving financial life too.

It's Not About the Money draws on my expertise as a financial advisor to people from a wide variety of socioeconomic backgrounds, interviews with many of the world's top spiritual teachers, and two decades of yoga and meditation practice to bring you a completely different perspective on your financial life. You will get the same cutting-edge financial planning advice that has created tens of millions of dollars in wealth for my clients and enabled them to feel relief and happiness, whatever their level of financial abundance. You will also find insights and exercises that I've gleaned from the world's ancient wisdom traditions to optimize awareness, growth, and financial fulfillment.

This body of work has been informed by my middle-class upbringing as well as my financial advisory practice, which in recent years has primarily focused on very affluent clients. The stories of their struggles (identities and personal details changed to respect privacy, of course) confirm the truism that money alone will not bring happiness. But I've also helped people who have overwhelming credit-card debt, trouble holding down a job, or a hopeless sense of confusion about all matters financial, and their stories appear here too. As you read, remember that the same basic advice holds true for everyone, no matter what his or her net worth.

FINANCIAL FREEDOM FOR YOUR SOUL

Though this book will teach you about investment, cash flow, tax, and other strategies that can help you realize your financial dreams, it is not a financial how-to book in spiritual clothing. Rather, it is a profound inner journey in which money is the primary focus. It is not a philosophical tome, but an intimate, practical resource for coming to know yourself through money. In part 1, "The Nature of Mind," I explore the way our minds work (and don't work!) when it comes to money. In part 2, "The Eight Financial Archetypes," I offer detailed descriptions of typical ingrained behaviors and beliefs about money that prevent us from being truly financially free. In part 3, "In the World and of It," I show you ways to move beyond old patterns with money, as well as providing cutting-edge investment advice and a new approach to philanthropy. The appendix offers a concise but comprehensive collection of practical financial planning advice and three ready-to-go investment solutions that you can implement immediately. Throughout the book, there are exercises to help you delve more deeply as you read. You might even want to have a notebook and pen handy so you can keep track of your responses, you might create a special folder on your computer for this purpose, or you can visit www.BrentKessel.com, where several of the exercises are duplicated.

As you embark on this path with me, I ask only that you be willing to look honestly into your own mind and heart and to suspend what you already think you know about money and happiness. Looking deeply into your relationship to money will help you gain:

- An abiding sense of financial fulfillment

- A clear understanding of the powerful forces that have shaped your financial life

- A real sense of security and confidence about your future

- Improved financial relationships with your life partner, parents, and children

- A greater ability to reach your most important financial goals

It's not about the money. Join me now as we explore what it is about.

It's Not About the Money

PART I

The Nature of Mind

CHAPTER ONE

YOU WILL NEVER HAVE ENOUGH

"Just a little bit more."

—JOHN D. ROCKEFELLER,
WHEN ASKED HOW MUCH IS ENOUGH

A friend of mine recently handed a homeless person on the street a dollar. The man looked at the money in his hand, looked up into my friend's eyes, and then quite matter-of-factly stated, "It's not enough." Though that dollar was probably not enough to meet the needs of this unfortunate person, even those with abundant financial means tend to approach money from this same "not enough" perspective. Why is it that so many of us feel such a deep sense of scarcity when it comes to money?

Compared not only to a person who relies on handouts for income but to a nineteenth-century monarch, you're probably relatively wealthy. You probably have a warm home and your clothes are comfortable. You can travel most anywhere you want at fifty times the speed of the monarch's fastest team of horses, and you can visit a modern health care facility for treatment if you become ill, a place where no one will try to bleed you or apply leeches as a cure.

Of course, some of you may answer that the reason you feel you don't have enough is that you simply don't. Indeed, you may be struggling.

You might not be able to be admitted to that modern hospital due to a lack of insurance coverage or financial resources. You may have to choose between paying your heating bill or your car insurance or hesitate about investing in real estate for fear of not being able to pay the property taxes. If you face this kind of dilemma, I acknowledge that you are in a very difficult position, one that my own experience with finances makes it difficult for me to fathom.

But no matter what our circumstances, our minds tend to promise us, falsely, that happiness is tied to getting more of what we want—better food, housing, transportation, recreation, health, and travel, to name just a few possibilities. If that were really true, though, wouldn't we all be happy beyond belief by now?

Over the last several decades, economic growth in almost all developed societies has been accompanied by a very modest rise in subjective well-being. In the United States between World War II and 1995, the increase in income has been dramatic and the amount of work time required to buy most goods has fallen substantially. Yet according to almost all of the scientific evidence, there has been little or no change in how happy Americans say they feel. And this is true the world over. In 1958, Japan had an average per capita income of about $3,000, an amount well below the present poverty level in the United States. By the end of the twentieth century, Japan was one of the wealthiest nations in the world, but still there was little discernible change in subjective well-being (a mere 3 percent increase over forty years). And in a survey of members of the Forbes 400 "richest" list, the world's wealthiest individuals rated their life satisfaction exactly the same as did the Inuit people of northern Greenland and the Masai of Kenya, who have no electricity or running water. Obviously, we're not that much happier despite our collective material progress. Why is that?

THE WANTING MIND

Most of us would not consider ourselves greedy. Yes, we might want a bigger house in a better neighborhood, but we want it for our expanding family. Yes, we want a nicer, newer car, but it's because of its safety features or fuel efficiency, or because the reality is that our position in our company depends in part on how others perceive us. We may not want a specific material item, but instead want a better salary or a higher quality of life, the ability to take more vacations and enjoy time with our spouse or friends. But even when we crave something intangible like security or time off, there's no denying that most of us spend a lot of time just wanting. What's more, we often act on these desires in ways that leave us less than free financially. It's as if there's a force outside of us compelling us to squander our capital, be it financial or spiritual. This force is known in several Buddhist traditions as the *Wanting Mind.*

The Wanting Mind is always craving an experience different from the one it currently has. Whether we want money, love, that great new sweater, a 20 percent investment return, or a more equitable world, the Wanting Mind insists that things need to change in order for us to be happy, and money is one of its favorite objects to focus on. The Wanting Mind's whole reason for existence is to strategize and fight for a different future. It exists on the premise that what we have right here, right now, can't possibly be enough. The Wanting Mind continually takes us out of the present moment in its attempts to make us happy in some better tomorrow. And unless we inquire into the subtle and often hidden workings of the Wanting Mind, including whether its promises of happiness are actually true, we remain its slave and will likely spend a lifetime chasing its images of freedom.

The broader evidence shows how pervasive the Wanting Mind really is. In *The Overspent American,* Juliet Schor writes that between 1975 and 1991, the number of people who said that a vacation home was a key component of the good life increased 84 percent. During the period from 1987 to 1994, the income people said they needed to "fulfill all [their] dreams" increased from $50,000 to $102,000, much more than the rate of inflation. According to another psychological study, the majority of those people in industrial nations want more than they possess: 61 percent of those surveyed said they always had something in mind that they were looking forward to buying.

We all like to point fingers at the overspenders and insatiable materialists as the culprits, the real money addicts. However, in my experience, the Wanting Mind plagues everyone, from people on the lowest rungs of the socioeconomic ladder to the most aware spiritual teachers and the wealthiest members of society.

WIRED TO WANT

All beings in nature have a biological imperative to survive. Without this imperative, they die. A tree grows toward whatever available sunlight is piercing through the forest canopy. Whales migrate thousands of miles to birth their calves in the warm Sea of Cortez. A human baby screams with hunger until she is fed. Without this inherent drive for survival, living organisms would die and evolution would cease altogether.

This drive is the very core of our wanting. Our physiology is wired to constantly deliver messages about what threatens us and what will make us more likely to survive, more secure. We naturally want to eat until we are no longer hungry, and usually a fair way beyond that. Our skin senses a drop in temperature, and we want to be warmer. Pain and suffering, or even mild discomfort, are taken as warning signs that our very survival may be threatened.

Nothing in modern society is as closely tied to our survival as money. Is it any surprise that when we find ourselves wanting to buy a new pair of jeans, a portable DVD player, or a vacation we've been longing for, we exclaim, "I've just got to have it!" as though our very survival depended on that one purchase? Even though our rational minds know it isn't the case, the Wanting Mind attaches a certain life-or-death urgency to objects we crave. In fact, we often can't get something we want out of our minds until we've bought it. This is the same kind of focus and intention that was biologically programmed into us over millions of years. But today, this physiological, reflexive response is carried over into all but the most mundane purchases we make.

> "When you begin to really understand how wired you are to want pleasure and to want to avoid pain, that sort of basic instinctual wiring—when you start to see through that clearly, you begin to take it less personally."
>
> —WES NISKER,
> MEDITATION TEACHER

Wanting more is a universal phenomenon. If you pay attention, you'll find that there isn't a whole lot you can do to stop this desire—you just go on and on wanting material things or better emotional states, wishing the people around you were different or that the weather were a bit better, or wishing you were less stressed out, more generous, or kinder. There is no way out when we are seduced by our mind's endless chatter for more, better, bigger, faster.

I recall a retired dentist who sat at our conference room table at Abacus. Sporting a polo shirt and khaki pants, he looked down through gold-rimmed reading glasses at his portfolio report. It clearly showed that his original $4 million net worth had grown to almost $8 million in just under five years. He looked up at me and said matter-of-factly, "I know that I'll feel truly financially independent when I have $15 million. That's my number."

To those who have less money than this dentist, his statement probably seems absurd. "I wouldn't be saying that if I had eight million!" you might retort. It is quite easy for us to peg others as having extreme desires. But in labeling others, we may miss the ways in which our own interactions with money are almost always motivated by a desire to move beyond our innate sense of scarcity and insecurity.

The numbers really don't matter. The truth is that we all have the experience of "not enough" thousands of times every day. In fact, many of the thoughts that arise in your mind have a component of "not enough," and each of these thoughts wants you to do something, to change your experience in some way. Our thoughts are constantly telling us, "This moment, just as it is, is not enough, and so I want _____." Underscoring every thought is an outcome that the mind believes will make us happier or more secure.

> "There is never enough in the world to satisfy the dissatisfied heart."
>
> —CHRISTINA FELDMAN,
> MEDITATION TEACHER

IF ONLY

Almost everyone I've ever met, whether rich or poor, has at one time in their life had an experience of not having enough money. For some people, the most horrific experience of their life involved the family running out of money just before the rent was due and going through the trauma of being evicted. For others, there were feelings of social inferiority in school in the face of kids who could afford better clothes, vacations, or cars. Because these experiences are so painful, many people compensate by making sure they will always have more than enough money in their lives. Even people who seem to have enough money find their inner thoughts focused on their finances, on how things could be even better. Just like all our thoughts, those that concern money are almost always targeted at rejecting our present experience. Do any of the following examples sound familiar?

- If I inherited or won $_____, I'd be able to quit my miserable job and do what I want.

- If my raise had just been a little bit higher, we'd have been able to afford _____.

- If I could get my spouse to stop spending all our money on _____, we wouldn't have so much pressure each month to pay our bills.

- If I could sell my company for $_____, I'd be set.

- If only I had not gained weight, I wouldn't have to be out buying new clothes and I could put that money toward _____.

- If the credit-card companies didn't charge such high interest rates, I would be out of debt by now.

- If only the stock market would go back up to its high of _____, I could stop worrying.

- Once I have $_____ in assets, I will relax and enjoy life.

If yours isn't in the above list, fill in your "if only" statement below:

- If only _____,
  then _____.

I am not saying that it is wrong to have these desires. But can you see how each of these thoughts, with its underlying foundation in "not enough," actually undermines our life right now, just as it is? Every single one of these thoughts presumes that we'd be happier or more secure if something were to change. And there would be no problem with this strategy ... *if* we actually ended up happier after fulfilling our wants. But we don't. We usually just end up wanting more.

When most people turn off the TV, lie down in bed, or try meditation for the first time, they are aghast at how many thoughts are running through their heads, how random they are and how distracting. If you remain silent and pay attention, you will find this theme of "not enough" in so many of your thoughts.

DETACH

Right now, without putting down your book, prepare to stop reading for a minute. Try not to get distracted by anything in the outside world. If it's comfortable, close your eyes for one to three minutes. Just pay attention to what thoughts arise, without trying to control those thoughts. Ready? Go.

Now reflect a little. What were your thoughts? Did you wonder what time it was or what you were going to have for lunch? Did you wish you could get to the end of the chapter without doing the exercise, so that you could learn how to solve the financial problem that prompted you to buy this book? In what ways were the thoughts you had, whatever they were, about problems to be solved? Were you fully accepting your experience, just as it is? In other words, did you simply think, "I am sitting here with my eyes closed and I feel happy and peaceful"? Or, more likely, were your thoughts focused on something that needed to change for you to be better off?

Whenever you can in the coming days, take a look at your thoughts through this lens: Is this thought happy with my life, right now, just as it is? If not, what is it trying to get me (or others) to do in order to feel a sense of "enough"?

IN THE FLOW

Most of us have been fortunate enough to experience moments of incredible connectedness, be they with a lover, in nature, in solitude, or through great art and music. Athletes sometimes achieve states of complete surrender, when mental effort has subsided and their physical exertion seems to be fueled by an outside force. Artists, poets, and entrepreneurs experience similar moments of creative "flow," when ideas seem to come from nowhere and surprise them. There is a quality of timelessness, even a sense of elation during these periods. The mind's incessant struggle with life and its desire for something better has subsided, and they feel at peace.

Regardless of what we call it or how we get there, we all know such states, in which we feel a sense of connection to something larger than ourselves.

But these states, as beautiful and pure as they feel, can also fuel the Wanting Mind if we're not careful. Why? Because all states of mind are impermanent; after a time, our thoughts return and we feel disconnected again. Often these thoughts say, "Wow! That was great. I want more of that. What would have to change so I could feel like this all the time?"

And so the Wanting Mind is back, and with it, a feeling of being disconnected from the peace and connectedness we just had. The mind is sure we should be able to get back to that state. After all, we created it once, so why can't we create it again? But the only path the mind knows is to think more thoughts and try to get what it wants—in short, to fight with our experience as it is. And this is the surest route to feeling disconnected!

BUT IT FEELS GOOD!

A few years back, I bought my first brand new car ever. Before that, I had driven an eight-year-old Toyota 4Runner. The new car was a silver Audi sports sedan, and I loved it. I had researched my purchase for a few months. I had spent some nights paging through the glossy brochure showing the Audi hugging corners in the Alps, pulling up to luxury hotels, and protecting its occupants from all the disasters that Mother Nature or other drivers might throw at it. I had test-driven the car and was amazed at its handling and its wonderful stereo. For the first time in my car-buying life, there was literally nothing wrong with my soon-to-be new car.

Driving the new car home, I was in heaven. My wanting had ceased and I felt great. My mind attributed this great feeling state to the car: I had gotten exactly what I wanted! However, this feeling of satisfaction didn't last long.

Most of the people I've worked with have their own story of money and the Wanting Mind. For some, it's buying clothes or shoes. No matter how many great pairs of shoes are home in the closet, when they see a new pair that looks great in the store display, a craving arises. This craving demands satisfaction when we're in the midst of it. It blocks our awareness of the things going on around us and focuses on the object of our desire.

In the second yoga sutra, an ancient text created long before stock markets or even paper money, the sage Patanjali explains that excessive attachment is based on the assumption that the object desired, once attained, will create everlasting happiness. When an object satisfies a desire, it provides a moment of happiness. Because of this moment, our mind makes the posses-sion of objects very important, even indispensable.

THE FINANCIAL TOLL OF WANTING

For many people in our country, the incessant demands of the Wanting Mind have created daunting personal debt, bankruptcy, and broken homes. For others, the Wanting Mind has created a feeling of being caught in a hole with no way to dig out. Some clients I've met, if not financially bankrupt, have become so imprisoned by their wants that they can't direct their money toward what's really important to them, whether it be a debt-free life, a country cabin, the time to pursue a career change or artistic dream, or even the ability to help a loved one in need. Though these more heartfelt goals are also a form of wanting, they have some notable differences from the endless parade of desires that the Wanting Mind usually offers up. We'll explore these differences a bit later in this chapter.

When we let the Wanting Mind control our financial lives, there are always tremendous costs, both financial and emotional. I recall one client who was constantly remodeling her house, doing project after project, all the while thinking the next remodel would be the last one. Her Wanting Mind craved a more beautiful environment and more living space. To her, the value of these desires was non-negotiable. I remember her saying once, "Everyone's got to have a den that's separate from their formal living room," to justify an expansion of 1,500 square feet. But financing three remodels in a five-year period had forced her to continue in a job she didn't love for an extra ten years before retiring! Another person I know, a car salesman in the San Fernando Valley, had a passion for travel. Whenever he'd lose a close sale or feel tension with his wife and kids, he'd get out of town. Sometimes it would be a several-day hike in the Sierra, sometimes a weekend in Palm Springs. His income was not high—in fact, it was not enough to support his family, even without his travels. His desire to escape the difficulties of his life led to yet more spending—spending that he couldn't afford.

Many people are in similar positions. Our Wanting Minds force us to eat out too often, buy a new car every two years, chase the newest fashion or fitness trend, or seek out the latest spa or self-help workshop, to the detri-ment of our financial well-being. Whether it is more stuff, more security, or even just more free time that we crave, too many of us fall prey to our Want-ing Mind's endless desires.

DIMINISHING RETURNS

Have you ever had the experience of eating at a new restaurant that has exceptional food, where each bite is filled with exciting new flavor and the ambience is fully experienced by your senses? We all want to repeat such pleasurable experiences, so we become focused on the idea of recreating this great happiness, usually by making plans to go back soon to the same restaurant.

Have you noticed that the next time you dine there, the food doesn't taste quite as good as it did before? You might also notice a few imperfections in the service or the décor. By the third or fourth time, the restaurant has fallen to the level of others, and the richness of the first dining experience is wholly lost. Sure, we may return again and again in the hope of recreating our first time. What we fail to see is that much of the magic of the first time happened because we were in a state of not-knowing—what Zen Buddhists call a "beginner's mind." In other words, we had few, if any, expectations because we had never been to the restaurant before. By contrast, when we return, we have many expectations. Without any conscious effort, our mind is comparing, which is not all that different from looking for problems.

It is the same with any pleasurable sensory experience, which is what we're seeking when we make most of our purchases. There are diminishing returns to almost all of our spending. When we spend on something, our mind, in its belief that it can script a happy life for us, is often trying to recreate an experience that is gone, relegated to our past. And focusing on the past means that we're not really present, not available to be surprised by this moment. Nevertheless, the mind doesn't loosen its iron grip on the belief that we can be happier than we are now.

THE MORE WE WANT, THE MORE WE WANT

The most common solution to this dilution of pleasure is to up the financial ante. If driving to Yosemite for a vacation was great last summer but is starting to get old, let's fly to New England to see the leaves change. Then perhaps we'll hit Europe next year. Is flying economy getting too crowded for you? There's always first class. How often do you see a person buy a new house or car that (even adjusting for inflation or market changes) costs more than their last one? Well, doesn't everyone like to upscale? This general upward creep in our consumption happens because a certain behavior or experience has given us enjoyment, so we long for another fix.

Those who do not see themselves as engaging in conspicuous consumption, take heed. This wanting doesn't only apply to consumption. It can be applied to any financial behavior that we think has worked for us in the past, including saving, frugality, or building a business. We might put a higher and higher percentage of our earnings into savings, make a risky investment in the hope of a big payoff, or switch jobs for a substantial raise. We might even "buy ourselves time" by making choices about what jobs to take based on how much vacation is offered or how few hours we'll have to work, at the expense of doing something we truly love in our careers. And for just a moment, we are getting what we want and we're happy. The problem? We rarely stop there.

The mind lures us into this behavior pattern by telling us that the more we want, the more we'll get, and the more we get, the happier we'll be. The truth is that the more we want now, the more we'll want in the future. Human beings are creatures of habit. The more we behave in a certain way today, the more we'll behave that way in the future. So if we water the seeds of desire now, we won't magically just wake up at some point and say, "Wow! Look at that. I suddenly have fewer desires." In reality, the amount we water the seeds of desire today will dictate how much larger and thirstier the plants of desire will be tomorrow.

Unfortunately, there are tremendous unseen financial costs to all this desire. Later chapters go into more depth about the different costs of unconscious financial behaviors and what to do about them. People have different financial wants, and so the costs of excessive wanting are accordingly very different. But I'll give you an example here:

> You're saving for college for your kids. Say your spending is now $3,000 per month and you increase that spending by 3 percent per year (the historical rate of inflation). But your neighbor, who is more caught by wanting "enough," upscales her lifestyle to the tune of a 6 percent annual increase in spending. You will have $457,000 more in eighteen years to put toward your child's education than your neighbor will (assuming you can earn 7 percent in your college savings account).

FINANCIAL PLANNING AND GREAT INVESTMENT ADVICE WON'T GET YOU "THERE"

Financial planning is an important part of creating a more balanced and spiritual relationship to money. For many people, planning is best accomplished by using the services of a Certified Financial Planner® or another trained, objective advisor. (See p. 263 for more information on how to find a competent advisor.) The process starts with the assumption that you are in your planner's office because you'd like to get somewhere—let's call it "there." In the financial planning industry, the widely used term for the beginning of this process is goal-setting. With the help of a competent financial planner, you set goals (by defining the "there" that will bring you the most fulfillment) and change some of your habits and behaviors in order to get there sooner. The idea is that, having arrived "there," you'll be happier. But if you and your planner aren't careful about how you define your destination, you won't really be as happy as you think you'll be. By understanding the differences between the Wanting Mind's desires and your more heartfelt goals, you will have a much greater likelihood of making progress toward a life that will gratify you in a more sustaining way. The following table points out some important distinctions:

THE WANTING MIND'S DESIRES	HEARTFELT GOALS
• Predominantly self-concerned	• Usually include benefits to others
• Grandiose or omnipotent, usually requiring more financial resources than you can reasonably expect to have or an unrealistically short time frame	• Realistic and achievable
• Accompanied by childlike urgency	• Characterized by patience
• Comparative or competitive: desires often feel like "shoulds" imposed by family, friends, or culture	• Originating from the inside: self-referenced
• Insatiable: as soon as one desire is satiated, the mind is onto a new one	• A sense of profound importance—"I yearn to do or have this before I die"—which creates more long-lasting fulfillment

WHAT ARE YOUR HEARTFELT GOALS?

Get a blank sheet of paper or a journal, and for the next three minutes, write down as many of your desires, goals, and dreams as you can. Don't worry about whether they're heartfelt or trivial, outrageous or reasonable. Just free-associate and write on—no one will see this list except you. Don't censor anything, and don't evaluate whether you really ought to write something down or not. If it pops into your head, write it down, no matter what it is. Do this first step before you read on.

Now, take another sheet of paper and draw a vertical line down the middle, dividing the page into two columns. Label one column "Wanting Mind's Desires" and one "Heartfelt Goals." For each desire or goal you wrote on the first piece of paper, look at it relative to the criteria shown on the prior page, and place it in one or the other column based on which attributes you think it has more of. It doesn't have to meet all of the criteria on the right to be put in your heartfelt-goals column—just more of them than those on the left.

If you don't have the paper or inclination to do this exercise in written form right now, then just take the first three goals or dreams that pop into your head, and evaluate them against the list. Keep in mind that there's nothing inherently wrong with the desires of the Wanting Mind—it's just that we are doomed to disappointment when we think they'll bring any kind of lasting fulfillment. Ask my friends—I have frequent and passionate cravings for ice cream, which certainly fall on the left side of the table. Specific goals don't inherently fall on one side or another. For one person, retiring early may fall on the left side because it's a culturally imposed dream and not something that they themselves really yearn for, while for another person it may well be a heartfelt goal.

You don't need to know how or when you're going to achieve your heartfelt goals. Instead, close your eyes for just a minute or so, and place yourself in a life where your goals have already happened. Involve as many of your senses as possible: What does the environment around you look like, what can you hear, what's the temperature, and how does it smell and taste to be there? Just enjoy the sensations of having achieved these goals. Imagining these goals as if you'd already attained them in your life should give you a palpable sense of peace and fulfillment. If not, they're more likely the cravings of the Wanting Mind. Follow the advice contained in the rest of this book and there's no reason you cannot achieve the heartfelt goals that are most important to you!

If we don't take the time to distinguish between desires and heartfelt goals, it doesn't take long after the achievement or acquisition of a desired object for your mind to spin into wanting to make even more progress. At the heart of it all, you'll still experience thoughts of "not enough," and the mind will still think it can solve those problems by wanting more. So again, though financial planning is a great tool, it's often not the solution to this dilemma. If you're not careful and conscious, what can happen with the help of your financial planner is that you end up deepening the grooves in your brain that say, "When you want a better life, set better goals, save more, spend less, invest better, and then you'll be happier."

The financial planning profession espouses this formula:

$$Goals + Resources = Happiness$$

A great financial planner will teach you how to refine your goals. He or she will help you visualize a great life, abundant in every way. An astute financial advisor can help you invest so that you accumulate wealth much faster than you would have on your own; she can aid you in curtailing your spending, cutting your tax bill, and harnessing all your resources toward the realization of your most heartfelt goals. But I would only be telling half the story if I stopped there. If you look at your own experience and the experience of your friends, no matter how wealthy, you'll find that the real formula is:

$$Goals + Resources = Bigger\ Goals + More\ Resources =$$
$$Even\ Bigger\ Goals + Even\ More\ Resources$$

And on and on it goes.

WANTING BETTER INVESTMENT RETURNS

In the financial realm, the Wanting Mind doesn't affect only our spending. It also has a tremendous impact on our investment success or lack thereof. When they find themselves in new territory, most investors don't know what's going to happen next, and so their minds latch onto what has occurred in the past as the most likely thing to happen in the future. "What if the market goes down another 25 percent?" is a common refrain immediately following a market correction. In response, many people pull their money out of the stock market. Then, when it rebounds, they're left sitting on the sidelines and wondering why they're not reaping the benefits of the now-booming market. Once you let your Wanting Mind drive your financial decisions, it's hard to stop.

One of the largest mutual fund companies in the United States studied its clients' investment returns from 1969 to 1999 and found that, though the average return of the company's mutual funds was about 16 percent, the average investor in their funds was only earning about 5 percent. The difference was attributable to the fact that money was moved in and out of funds at inopportune times. Five percent is less than the investor would have made in a simple savings account over the same time period!

Boston-based think tank Dalbar, Inc., studied the actual returns of *all* investors in equity mutual funds in the entire United States from 1987 to 2006. The QAIB®, as Dalbar's study is known, states that in those years, the average investor slowly added money to their investment accounts when the market had gone up, and took money out when the market had gone down. Over the entire twenty-year period, the typical investor grew $10,000 to $23,252. The most widely used benchmark of the U.S. stock market, the Standard & Poor's index of five hundred of the largest companies (the S&P 500®), earned 11.8 percent. Had investors bought and held $10,000 of the S&P 500, they would have ended up with $93,050. How did this happen? Most individuals are at the mercy of their Wanting Minds' constant chase for the next "hot" fund, which causes them to trade too much.

The massive increase in household debt and the dearth of retirement savings in the United States over the last twenty years is also a direct result of the Wanting Mind. Unfortunately, our collective inability to delay gratification through purchases and our inability to apply more discipline to our investment decisions have become an epidemic.

Letting the Wanting Mind control our investment decisions has literally cost us billions of dollars. But poor financial results are not the only symptom of the Wanting Mind. Our emotional state is also adversely affected when the Wanting Mind runs the show.

AT WAR WITH YOURSELF

When we are in a state of wanting, there is an inner conflict between what we have—what we are experiencing right now—and what we want. There is one part of you that is just here, taking in your present experience, whatever that experience is: "The sun is shining"; "This car is making funny sounds"; "I am feeling angry." This is the part of you that simply receives all of the information picked up by your senses without interpreting or responding to this information. At the same time, there is another part of you whose attention is sharply focused on how you'd like to change your experience: "I wish it weren't so hot"; "I need a new car"; "She shouldn't make me angry."

When you say, "It is *this* way but I want it to be *that* way," you are fighting with what is. This kind of thinking is like going to war with your own life. In addition to the negative financial consequences of this vicious circle, focusing on what you want and don't yet have takes a tremendous amount of energy away from just being. It's actually quite exhausting.

There is another way, a way that requires the courage not to follow your wanting impulses in a knee-jerk fashion. This doesn't mean that you should not buy anything ever, or that you should move to a mountaintop and give away everything you own. It doesn't mean that you need to stop saving every penny you earn. But if you really want to be free, before you take any action that involves money, you must look sincerely at the root of the behaviors your mind has always told you would make you happy. This is not easy. It requires reversing decades of programming that says you'll be happy if only you get what you want. There will be times when every cell in your body resists the practice I'm about to prescribe. But if you're reading this book because you're really interested in having more abundance, clarity, or freedom, regardless of your financial resources, you will find the resolve you need to accept this challenge.

LETTING GO

The inspiration for this exercise comes from Christina Feldman, who co-wrote *Soul Food* with Buddhist meditation teacher Jack Kornfeld.

As you go through your day, see if you can identify and let go of just one impulse of wanting. For example, you might pass by a store and admire a new pair of pants elegantly displayed in the window. Perhaps you've been longing for a wardrobe refresher, and these pants would work perfectly with other items you have.

To start with, don't walk in and buy whatever you want right now. Create a noticeable pause between sensing your want and taking action ➤

on it. This may create a small wave of grief or regret. "But, but, but ...," your inner voice might object. Back at the office, perhaps you will start fantasizing about this new purchase and even envisioning when you would first get to wear it. Notice how these fantasies are affecting you physically. Is your heart racing a little faster? Do you feel happier? Or calmer? For now, just notice how you feel when you think about this thing you want. Don't try to make decisions or even judge yourself. What does wanting feel like? Does it cause your stomach to tighten or your heart to constrict? Do you get a nice burst of adrenaline from it? Is the energy it creates moving through you, changing, or staying in the same place? Is it increasing or decreasing? Let several hours go by. Do you still want the new pants, or has your attention shifted? A day or two later, having refrained from buying what you wanted, are you more or less fulfilled?

Do this exercise at least once a day for a week—it will take less than a minute each time. Do it no matter how small the item: a donut, a new CD, a gift for someone else, or even an impulse to check on or make a change to your investments—anything that involves money. Just notice the impulse of wanting, and jot it down. A sample entry might look something like this:

Wanting Impulses 2/10

- a spinach and cheese croissant from the bistro on the corner

- a raise for the extra hours I'm putting in at work

- the new iPhone

- to sell my biotech mutual fund that's had another losing month

Simply note but don't act on any of the impulses. And then watch how your experience changes and shifts in the coming hours and days. In time, whether you end up giving yourself what you initially desired or not, you'll become aware of how much your actions are driven by this habit of leaping to satisfy every impulse you possibly can. (Go to my Web site at www.BrentKessel.com to download a free guided meditation on observing your mind, as well as a list of practices, teachers, and courses that I have found particularly helpful.)

NOT WANTING

Many spiritual teachers have spent their lives examining how the Wanting Mind functions. Adyashanti, a California-bred teacher and author steeped in the Zen meditation tradition, says that the primary pleasure we experience from getting something we want is that in the moment we get it, our wanting stops. For once, we are just enjoying something as it is, be it a new piece of art, a remodeled house, or a new dress. Confused, the mind focuses on the object itself as the source of our happiness. After all, it's the great meal, the beautiful vista, or the new watch that holds our conscious attention. But in giving the credit for our contentment to the object itself, we miss the point. If we really look at what's creating our happiness, it's not the meal, the vista, or the new watch; it's actually the temporary power these objects have to keep us from wanting anything else.

> "The simple act of reflecting, the simple act of pausing to consider, to reason, can have an impact."
>
> —HIS HOLINESS THE DALAI LAMA AND HOWARD CUTLER, MD, *The Art of Happiness at Work*

For a brief moment, we've stopped wanting anything other than what we have. Another way to say this is that we have given up trying to change our experience. We are consumed by our enjoyment of the meal, the vista, or the watch. They just happen to be the key that unlocked the door to desirelessness in that moment. A blueberry can accomplish this just as well as a Rolex. So can the laugh of a young child. A great movie or a symphony or a novel would also hold our attention and relieve us from wanting.

But as most of us know all too well, no matter what brings us to this state, the desireless state is itself impermanent. It doesn't take long for something to arise in our life that is not ideal, something the mind feels could be slightly improved or needs to be completely overhauled.

Remember my new Audi? Well, about a month after buying it, I began to notice the first blemishes. When I took a corner on the way home at about 40 mph, the tires squealed a little, which I was convinced hadn't happened on the test drive. And the alloy wheels protruded beyond the tires by about half an inch, a fact I didn't realize until I was parallel parking one day and heard the harsh scraping of aluminum on a concrete curb. Finally, at a party one weekend, a friend wondered why, given my growing family, I hadn't bought the next larger model. I wondered too.

I had been convinced that this car was perfect because it satisfied many of the wants my mind had come up with based on prior cars I'd had. However, after some time had passed, I wanted more—oh, just a few small changes, nothing major. But my mind was used to thinking that getting what it wanted would make me happy. Even though it had firmly believed that the car was perfect just as it was, my mind now had a new set of wants related to cornering, wheels, and what other people thought of the car.

Because we focus on objects or experiences as the source of our happiness, there is nothing to stop the mind from focusing on similar objects or experiences as the source of our future happiness. This is why so many people continue acquiring more of what has made them happy in the past, be it cars, clothes, or exotic travel. Obviously, there is some enjoyment in these acquisitions, and we should enjoy them. But if our wanting is out of balance, trying to fill a void that nothing in the external world can ever fill, the financial consequences can be disastrous.

If we look carefully and honestly, we are able to see that the happiness we feel when we get what we want comes from the absence of wanting. If we could experience the same absence of wanting regardless of whether we buy something we crave or not, we would be able to fully accept our present experience and not seek happiness from the objects or experiences we crave. That way, our deepest selves and not our Wanting Minds would be in control of the important financial decisions that will either contribute to or undermine our true freedom.

When we don't chase the object our Wanting Mind is craving, our attention can remain on ourselves, the subject, rather than the thing we want, the object. When we go within in this way, our deepest fulfillment comes from just being, unfettered by desires that propel us to do something other than what we're already doing.

See what happens if you let the mind be just as it is, without indulgence or resistance. Look truthfully and with a humble curiosity, and see what you find. Without the perspective that this simple practice brings, you will be forever caught up in wanting and never have enough, perhaps literally and certainly emotionally. On the other hand, if you are willing to look truthfully and consistently at your own mind, you can stop unconsciously following its promises of a better future. You will make smarter, more self-supporting decisions and be well on your way to a newfound peace and clarity with money.

WHAT YOU WANT

When it comes to your finances, what exactly do you want? Set a timer for two minutes and begin making a list, where each item on the list begins with "I want …". Your list need not be limited to material possessions. It can include nonmaterial yearnings like a desire for early retirement, more childcare, or time to write a novel, anything affected by money. Of course, it can also include your desire for a new plasma flat-panel TV, a fashionable pair of boots, a remodeled kitchen, or a sleek new laptop computer. Write down anything you want, uncensored. No one will see your list.

At the end of two minutes stop writing. Now go down your list and imagine that you actually have every one of the things you listed, whether it is $10 million in tax-free bonds, a college fund for all the children in your family, or the freedom to never have to handle or think about money again. That's right, imagine I've waved a magic wand and you have everything on your list. In fact, you have had it all for years.

Close your eyes and notice how it feels to have each of these things. Does your pulse calm? Do the muscles in your stomach relax? Are you breathing a little easier? It's an amazing feeling, isn't it? A feeling that you have arrived.

However, that wonderful sense of contentment is impermanent. That amazing feeling has the tendency to do only one thing: fuel more wanting. If you are like most people, this list is only the beginning. Your financial desires over time could probably fill pages.

What's the point? It's not the stuff on your list you want. It's that feeling you want—that freedom from wanting. The tragedy is that you may get everything you listed and more, but that delightful, peaceful feeling of having arrived won't last if your Wanting Mind remains in charge.

In the pages to come, you will learn more techniques that will enable you to experience that wonderful sensation quite independently of your external circumstances. Having made it this far, you are now well on your way to creating a more peaceful and fulfilling financial life. Just being conscious of our Wanting Mind and how it works is the first step toward breaking free of its grip. Next, we will delve more deeply into the nature of mind and how it affects our daily interactions and decisions about money. The result? You'll have even more powerful tools to help you make meaningful changes in your relationship to money.

CHAPTER TWO

THE UNCONSCIOUS WINS EVERY TIME

"One of the pitfalls of childhood is that one doesn't have to understand something to feel it. By the time the mind is able to comprehend what's happened, the wounds of the heart are already too deep."

—CARLOS RUIZ ZAFON, NOVELIST

One of my clients is a self-employed business owner who liked but didn't love her work. When she was young, her father went bankrupt and the family suffered tremendously. In meeting after meeting, she would come into our conference room talking about how she longed for the day she could retire, but after we had shown her beyond a reasonable doubt that even if the Great Depression were to occur all over again she would have complete financial security, she couldn't stop poring over spending reports, worrying to the point of panic attacks. The situation was compounded by the fact that her husband, who was also her business partner, continuously wanted to spend lavishly on office remodels, company vehicles, vacation homes, and personal wardrobes. His argument, hard to refute, was that these outer signs of success drew even more wealth in the form of impressed clients. Because of her anxiety, his wife felt compelled to continually increase their net worth. And his beliefs about money and status, no doubt formed from his own childhood experiences, kept him locked in a cycle of excessive spending. Their very different belief systems about money kept them working for many more years than they needed to.

I see these entrenched behaviors all the time. Good savers tend to keep right on saving, even after they've amassed more than enough money for their own and their family's needs. Those who struggle to make ends meet seem to continually find themselves in that same predicament. Those who tend to spend excessively or give it all away keep right on doing that. And those who are anxious about financial security seem to worry, no matter what external financial changes occur.

Most of us have seen or heard stories of financial folly before. We may even be aware of some ways in which we ourselves repeat the same financial mistakes over and over again. And yet we have failed to ask why it is that regardless of our financial situation, we constantly find ourselves in a familiar relationship to money.

WE GET WHAT WE THINK WE DESERVE

Most people say they want a different financial life than the one they have. They may want more money, more peace of mind, more possessions, an easier time communicating with family about money, or more tools with which to manage it. However, I contend that we actually have the relationship with money that our unconscious mind wants, right now.

"CHAPTER ELEVEN"

Consider the following statistics:

- Seventy-eight percent of NFL players are bankrupt, divorced, or unemployed within two years of their last game.

- Estimates show that about one-third (33%) of lottery winners file for bankruptcy at some point after their windfall.

- Despite their tremendous financial success, entertainers Burt Reynolds, Kim Basinger, Gary Coleman, Mike Tyson, Debbie Reynolds, Michael Jackson, and MC Hammer have all filed for bankruptcy.

You might say, "How can this be? How can you tell someone who is bankrupt that they 'want' that? Or someone who hasn't been able to make ends meet for years? Or someone who is always stressed out about money?"

My answer is that we get what we think we deserve. And in order to change these patterns, you need to understand your financial Core Story. Applied to our financial lives, our Core Story represents the deepest-held feelings and beliefs we have about money, what we are unconsciously telling ourselves we are like, what we can and can't have, and what we must or must not do. The power of the unconscious mind is so strong that despite our considerable efforts to improve our financial situations on the outside, very little usually changes on the inside. In the real world, the unconscious mind holds us back financially, even as we're desperately seeking a different relationship to money. Until you can identify and examine your Core Story, your outer financial life will be a mirror of your unconscious expectations. It is only when you understand what your unconscious mind believes about your financial lot in life, and what it believes is going to make you happy or safe, that you have a chance to change the tale you're constantly replaying in your head.

YOUR CORE STORY

This idea of the Core Story is explained in slightly different terms by Thich Nhat Hanh. This prominent Vietnamese Zen Buddhist monk says it's as if each of us had a basement in our mind in which we'd stored hundreds of movies. Most people replay those same movies over and over again in their minds: movies about how things should change to make us happy, about who is to blame for our pain, about what's wrong with our life. The astounding thing is that the more we replay each movie, the more the events in our life begin to resemble the plot of that movie.

We find many examples of this when it comes to people's relationship to money. The more someone who is prone to worry and anxiety, for instance, replays the scene of her family losing their home during her childhood, the more likely she is to create a life of worry and anxiety for herself, and possibly even lose a house herself. Or she may replay the foreclosure scene and, to avoid repeating that pain, latch onto workaholic behavior or penny-pinching. In both cases, her response to her distressing experience, coupled with deep and difficult feelings, puts her into an unquestioned, unconscious, and unbalanced set of financial behaviors.

For many, the replaying of movies does not happen by choice or even in the conscious mind. It is often just the subliminal track that accompanies our life. But conscious or not, you won't change your overall relationship to money unless you learn to watch your most-played movie with the objectivity of a film critic rather than the inherent biases of the film's producer, writer, director, and main character.

THE SCRIPT IS WRITTEN

This movie, our Core Story, is so powerful that it leads us to manifest the outer financial circumstances with which our unconscious is most comfortable. This is probably why Donald Trump, whose father was also a real-estate mogul, keeps working to build and expand his vast empire, even though he has earned more than enough money to support his lifestyle forever. Trump is known to have said, "I like thinking big. If you're going to be thinking anything, you might as well think big." This kind of Core Story can create tremendous wealth and prosperity, but if its aims are pursued in an unbalanced way, the fruits of success often come at the expense of close personal relationships, physical health and well-being, or a balanced, integrated life.

Another example of how our script influences us is billionaire fund manager and philanthropist George Soros, who finds unusual ways to give away his vast wealth. Soros values creative, sophisticated ways of making money rather than predominantly emphasizing the building of a larger and more public empire. A Hungarian refugee of World War II, he was moved by the plight of the people whose suffering he witnessed. In response, he became driven at a very early age to make money to help others, as well as for his own enjoyment.

Why can't we change our financial behavior patterns and attitudes more easily? The answer is that until we understand our Core Story, it pretty much runs our financial show. If it dictates that a big business empire will make us happy and protect us, then we build our professional life around that. If the Core Story says that money should be used to buy clothes or food to make us feel loved and nourished, then we'll primarily make and spend money for those needs. If we believe one should never sell real estate, then we won't. The unconscious Core Story dictates why some people keep marrying financial "losers" over and over again, and why others spend beyond their means no matter what they earn. For almost everyone, the Core Story operates behind the scenes, out of the limelight of our conscious attention. We may have conscious desires and thoughts about the financial life we say we want, but if our Core Story is not deeply examined, the unconscious mind will get its way every time.

This is obvious to those of us who work in the financial services industry, because we constantly see people who come from apparently similar backgrounds but behave very differently with money, even siblings from the same family. As a case in point, let me tell you about two clients of mine, Lance and Bob. They are not siblings, but both are in their mid-fifties and had similar upbringings and similar economic prospects when they left college. But because their Core Stories are different, they have ended up in drastically different financial situations.

Lance lost his father to a heart attack when he was fifteen. His mother, who had a teaching degree she'd never used, began teaching elementary school and tutoring after school to supplement her income. Lance was left to make dinner for and take care of his two younger siblings until his mother got home. His mother became more and more anxious about money, so Lance took a job in a bicycle store stockroom to help with the family's bills. These early experiences led him to his core belief: "Money should be used to take care of others who are struggling and need it more than I do." Lance eventually became a pediatrician. When he came to me as a client, he was earning $75,000 per year, but had no savings to show for it. I knew that Lance was single and lived modestly, so I inquired as to where all the money had gone. As we sifted through his spending reports and tax returns, I found that he had given or lent over $20,000 to family members, friends, and charities, while denying himself a vacation he badly wanted and saving nothing for his future.

In contrast, Bob has over $2 million in savings and spends less than $35,000 per year. This ratio of spending to assets means that Bob will never run out of money as long as he follows a basically prudent investment strategy. But he admits to being beset by irrational fears when it comes to his money—fears that have led Bob, unlike Lance and much to his wife's chagrin, to shy away from giving. Bob was raised in western Pennsylvania. His father worked in a factory, and his family, like Lance's, always struggled with money. He distinctly recalls his parents sharing one plate of food so that he and his three siblings could have more. But Bob had cousins who were well off because their parents owned a uniform supply business.

When he was about eight years old, during one of those lean weeks when his parents were curtailing their meals, Bob visited his cousins. At their home, there was more than enough for everyone to have seconds at dinner. During the meal, he overheard his aunt and uncle excitedly discussing a new account their business had just landed and talking about how their financial situation was going to be even better.

Thinking back, Bob recalls this dinner, along with the many other meals and summer vacations he spent with his cousins, as having a pivotal influence on him. The relief he felt during these visits stood in stark contrast to the deprivation he felt at home. He unconsciously began to model his future on his aunt and uncle instead of on his own parents. By the time he was in high school, Bob knew he was going to be a business owner who would save and invest as much of his income as possible so that he would never go hungry, as his parents had. Bob's belief continues to be, "Hold on to what you have. Own your own business, save a big chunk of your income, make safe, conservative investments, and you'll be okay."

How did two people with such similar prospects end up in such different emotional and practical situations? The answer is that these two men's unconscious beliefs, which were formed very early in response to powerful emotional experiences with money, are completely different. Lance felt responsible for his emotionally stressed mother and so has grown into an adult who is the financial provider for his family and friends when they are in need. However, this giving isn't tempered by any type of financial planning to take care of his own needs, and as a result, he has given away all his excess income each year. Bob, on the other hand, saw business ownership and safe investing as the way to keep from going hungry. And though he now finds himself in much healthier shape on paper, his saving has come from extreme frugality, which separates him from family, friends, and the community in which he lives. His wife considers him a miser, and this has put stress on their relationship. His friends, too, keep their distance, having learned not to ask him to contribute to their favorite charities.

LOOK WITHIN

The following questions will prompt you to better understand your Core Story:

- What is your most painful memory related to money? If no painful memory comes easily to mind, focus on the earliest memories you can recall about money, perhaps something you saw a parent or a school friend do with money. If you could put your response to this memory into the most childlike words possible, and make it short enough to fit on a bumper sticker, what would that response be? (For example, "Save money so you won't go hungry" or "Money is for helping others.") What story did you begin to tell yourself about money early on?

- What is your biggest fear about money? Often, our fears fuel our Core Story. Think of your fear as a beacon that exists to point your attention to what is unconscious, and therefore very powerful, within you. Perhaps you had a fear of winding up in the gutter or of people hating you because you were rich. What experiences in your financial past may have contributed to your fear? If you have no obvious fear, do you feel greedy for more even though you have enough? Or do you feel just plain confused when it comes to money? Whatever your core feelings about money, ask yourself this: How have your past experiences contributed to these feelings?

- What were you taught was most important about money? What were your parents' biases and values? Did you adopt them or rebel against them?

- When have you been most positively or negatively moved by money? Was it when you bought your first toy with your own money? When the game you'd been eyeing for months was given to your sister instead of you? When your parents finally gave in and bought you that bicycle you'd been whining about for months? When you shared your ice cream money with a child less fortunate than you? Think of joyful experiences or times of incomparable pleasure, status, power, or generosity. What role did money play in these experiences?

Asking these questions will help you begin to identify and understand your particular Core Story, and to eventually loosen its grip on you.

THE SEEDS OF THE CORE STORY

Our Core Story is the mind's attempt to defend us from pain and suffering. This story is formed at a very tender age. At that age, we usually aren't cognizant that something painful is occurring, but the angst that fuels the formation of our Core Story can run very deep. We are wired to survive at all costs, and so we deal with vulnerability by unconsciously latching onto a collection of beliefs, a story about money that we hope will help us avoid pain and be happier in the future. It's as if, at pivotal times in our lives, we record the movies spoken of by Thich Nhat Hanh. As we feel or resist feeling a surge of difficult emotions, our mind tries to figure out how to prevent the experience from happening again. Similarly, when we feel pleasurable emotions, our mind tries to figure out how to repeat the behaviors that created them.

I recall a client who was always receiving hand-me-down clothing from his older brothers. He grew up in a Chicago suburb where the winters were bitterly cold, and through our work together, he realized that he had become unconsciously driven to make enough money so that he could buy whatever clothes he wanted, especially warm jackets. He admitted to me that today he has about six winter coats in his closet, even though he moved to southern California several years ago.

For some, especially those who experienced a lot of family turmoil or poverty in childhood, the Core Story often revolves around saving more in order to feel secure and stable. For others, especially those who as children felt deprived of love, ample food, or as nice a wardrobe as their friends had, the Core Story implores them: "Enjoy your money today, because it might not last."

We form our Core Story, whatever its content, with the unconscious hope that if we follow it, we'll be protected from feeling difficult or painful emotions. There is frequently great intelligence in a young child's strategy to either copy or rebel against what is being modeled for him or her. However, most adults have lived for decades by the rules and beliefs of their Core Stories, never questioning their validity, how they came to be, or whether these strategies are creating real happiness. It's as if we're living in an adult body with the financial agenda of a child. The good news is that you can learn to use your mature, adult wisdom and see the ways in which you are still following that young intelligence that so frequently no longer applies to your current situation.

UNDERSTAND YOUR STORY

With the perspective brought by understanding your Core Story, you will be able to take the steps necessary to create a more balanced approach to money.

One example of how a Core Story can run the show comes from my own life. This experience occurred when I was twenty-three, working in the commercial mortgage business, and living on about $2,000 per month. I was paid a commission for each loan I successfully closed by bringing together a borrower and a bank or commercial lender. I had been working on my first large land deal, which was likely to make me $11,000—an absolute fortune to me at the time. Out of the blue, the owner of the property told me he had shopped the loan to another broker—the loan that I had thought was virtually a done deal. Worse still, my competition was quoting a lower interest rate than my lender.

Everything went white for a split second. I felt the heat flush down my neck and back. My heart raced. The depth of feeling was incredibly intense. I calmly ended the call, but I couldn't move—I was stunned at the prospect of having to borrow against my credit cards to pay for my basic necessities. At that moment I vowed that I was going to work my tail off to make enough money so that this kind of situation would never affect me like that again.

It took a long time for me to understand that I had developed a Core Story to compensate for fears of abandonment, loneliness, and poverty that I've felt at poignant moments in my life: at the age of four, when my parents got divorced; at ten, when my family had to start over again economically after emigrating from South Africa to the United States; when I was twelve, and my stepfather left my mother, my younger sister, and me; and in my early teens, when my father lost everything he owned. With each successive trauma, the only survival strategy that made sense was that I would need to make *a lot* of money when I grew up—that is what the people who I thought were safest and happiest were doing. My Core Story, then, is that if I work hard, am smart and disciplined, don't spend frivolously, don't take success for granted, protect my money, and save and invest a substantial percentage of earnings each year, I'll get to that place of financial and emotional security. When it became clear that I wasn't going to close that land deal—even though in reality there were resources I could draw upon for survival and I wasn't going to starve—my response was greatly amplified because of my belief in that Core Story.

YOUR STORY AT WORK

What does your mind tell you to do when you're anxious about money? Think back to the most recent stressful financial event in your life. How did you get into that situation? Is it a position you have found yourself in more than once? Can you see the ways in which your Core Story with money may have contributed to getting you into or dictating your reactions to that situation?

What's tricky is that there are aspects of the Core Story that are positive and can propel you to act in healthy ways. For example, my striving to have more security has engendered good saving and financial habits. But when the going gets tough, my Core Story makes me really scared that I'm not saving enough and leaves me fearing that I'll end up in financial ruin one day. Back when I was less aware of its seeds and more of a blind follower, my Core Story led me to behave in unbalanced ways. For example, I was obsessed with work and let my ambition get in the way of nurturing other relationships and life passions. Mine is only one type of Core Story. Some people believe that the world of money is against them—that they'll never really make or save enough to be secure. Others go out and engage in "retail therapy" when the stress of life gets to be too much. In moderation, shopping is a wonderful thing and can bring great sensory pleasures. But for people who unconsciously believe they'll always just scrape by, shopping is just one of many behaviors that keeps them in the financial rut they claim they want out of.

All Core Stories have some element of wisdom and truth in them. They do work and have worked for us in the past, so they should not be dismissed out of hand. Enjoyment, frugality, innovation, generosity, recognition, and creativity are all healthy components of various Core Stories. But if we cling to them with intense, unquestioning conviction, or if we believe there is only one right way to be with money, we are likely to be governed by a force that will not bring us true financial freedom. Indeed, this clinging is what creates the most imbalanced and destructive financial behaviors in our culture, including overspending, chronic debt, workaholism, financial illiteracy, miserliness, and co-dependent relationships.

MY MONEY HISTORY

We often have more than one Core Story, so please don't feel pressured to find the one. Just write about whatever comes up for you first. You'll identify more stories as time goes on and we'll soon see which is dominant.

1. One of the most significant financial experiences of my life was when

   _____

2. This led me to feelings of _____
   (try your best to use single words such as: anger, joy, sadness, frustration, envy, rage, hopelessness, confusion, ambition, or shame).

3. After that, I told myself that I would always/never _____
   (with money).

4. I believe that one of my Core Stories with money is _____

   _____

   _____

Valerie is a thirty-five-year-old real-estate agent who answered the questions as follows: "One of the most significant financial experiences of my life was when I was nineteen. I bounced a check and my dad yelled at me that I was an idiot because I couldn't balance a checkbook. That led me to terrible feelings of inadequacy and worthlessness. Facing my finances became intolerable, and so I stopped facing them. But even though I hoped that avoiding the stack of bills would bring me peace, my adult life has been spent juggling credit-card debt, overdrafts, a repossessed car, and eviction notices. I really believe that my Core Story with money is that I'm not responsible enough to ever have any." Our relationships to money are complex, but in my experience it is often the most basic fears that drive our financial choices.

TO THE VERY CORE

Pretty much everyone's financial circumstances are determined by their conditioning—that is to say, the experiences and "movies" that have been recorded throughout their lives. Our Core Story responds to present-day situations in a knee-jerk way: with craving, desire, fear, envy, generosity, or a need for security. If we had had different conditioning—a different past—we would react differently.

Part of the reason the Core Story is able to retain so much of its power is that most people focus on external financial changes as the keys to happiness: "I need to pay off all my credit cards," "I need to sell my business and then I'll feel more relaxed," "I need my wife to stop spending so much," "I need to make a million bucks so I can quit my job," "If I just don't involve myself with money, it will take care of itself."

In and of themselves, there may be nothing wrong with any of these plans. But when you leave aside these external solutions for a moment and start to examine your Core Story, you may notice that you feel quite uncomfortable. What we believe about money is usually experienced as a set of universal laws, much like gravity. Our Core Story has served a valuable purpose, which is to give us a sense that we will survive, that we won't be annihilated. In Valerie's case, her financial self-esteem was so low that ignoring and avoiding her finances allowed her some glimmer of hope that things might somehow work out. During traumatic life experiences, especially those that are financial in nature, our very survival seems uncertain. We realize that there are no guarantees, that our bodies depend on food, shelter, medical care, and other conditions to survive, and that these things require money, either ours or someone else's.

The mind's job is to keep us alive for as long as possible, and so it jumps in with a strategy to help us survive: "If you do this, you're going to be okay." But in building our belief structure so quickly, we deny ourselves the opportunity to be truly aware of the fear or other powerful emotion that was the catalyst of our Core Story. Instead, all our energy is channeled into the thought or belief that we think will protect us. A critical first step to being released from the grip of our Core Story is to dismantle our beliefs about money and reclaim the feelings these beliefs have been protecting us from. By having the courage to face the seemingly intolerable feelings, we can start to see our irrational reactions and defenses more clearly. Our feelings are, after all, only feelings, and as I learned that awful day when that loan fell through, we are almost never in the kind of jeopardy we fear. The good news is that the process of facing the motivation *behind* our Core Story is never as scary as it seems when we are stuck *in* our Core Story.

You may be a saver, a pleasure-seeker, or an idealist about money. Don't worry if you haven't exactly identified your own Core Story. This can take time. As you read about other people's stories in the chapters to come, you may well recognize your own experience, too.

> ### INQUIRE
>
> Even if you haven't been able to succinctly state your Core Story, you may be aware of some feelings you hope you will never feel again. What are those feelings? How have you set up your financial life to avoid those feelings? To do an audio-guided self-inquiry that will help you understand your Core Story and its power, go to http://www.BrentKessel.com.

NO QUICK FIX

Because of the fierce power of the desire to survive, coming to understand your Core Story is not a quick fix. Several other personal finance self-help books discuss the need to uncover and understand one's historical relationship to money in order to become free of old patterns and money messages. In my view, however, other treatments of this subject underestimate the power of the unconscious to perpetuate unsatisfactory behavior patterns. Many authors and experts assume that just by becoming aware of your Core Story, you will be able to free yourself from it. My experience is that even after you gain powerful new insights about your Core Story, it takes great skill, intention, and perseverance to lessen the hold of our unconscious conditioning. Take heart. Change is possible and in fact well within our reach.

The trick? We must keep working to identify and retain the healthiest parts of our story's message, while at the same time letting go of the extreme and unhealthy behaviors and attitudes it has engendered in us.

We are all affected by our conditioning until we die. It's part of being human. Just like yoga, prayer, meditation, physical exercise, intellectual learning, or watering the seeds of love in a marriage, cultivating financial awareness is a lifelong practice that can yield incredible results.

But we don't have to become resigned to just being aware of and repeating the financial patterns of our past. Many people share similar Core Stories, and so there's a tremendous amount we can learn from others' experiences. Let's explore eight of the most common of these Core Stories, which I call the financial archetypes.

PART 2

The Eight Financial Archetypes

INTRODUCING THE ARCHETYPES

No matter who you are, you come to your financial life with remarkably unique life experiences, all of which have conditioned you to respond to money in particular and sometimes peculiar ways. Your life experiences caused you to develop certain financial beliefs and habits and to avoid others. The good news is that you are not alone! In my professional work with people from all financial walks of life, I have noticed that although the details of people's behaviors and problems are unique, there are great similarities among certain groups of people. Drawing on the work of various teachers, mentors, and philosophers, as well as my own observations, I've created some broad definitions of these groups, or archetypes, so that people can learn from others who have gone through similar experiences.

Archetypes can be thought of as energies within us. They are not personal but more like collective patterns that are manifested within us and recognizable in others. The value of defining these archetypes is that they give us a basis for understanding how we got the financial life we have today, as well as a plethora of tools with which to create the financial life we most want.

To this end, the coming chapters define eight of the most common sets of behaviors and beliefs about money. These Core Story archetypes can help us to identify the powerful internal forces that affect us in our daily lives. If you

> **"All of our conditioning is to get away from the hole, the abyss of being human. We avoid facing this edge in complex, myriad ways. A whole lifetime is spent in avoiding because it feels like death, and the whole organism is designed to avoid death."**
>
> —GANGAJI, SPIRITUAL TEACHER

haven't yet identified your personal Core Story, read on. These archetypal forces, which are so ingrained in our culture and personalities, can affect us in balanced, healthy ways as well as in unhealthy ways. As we'll see, there is no getting rid of our predominant archetypes, but it is certainly possible, and fundamental to a fulfilling financial life, to cultivate a healthy balance.

Coming chapters will teach you strategies that can strengthen the desirable qualities of the archetypes already present in you, and awaken dormant archetypes. Many of the most successful people I know are a combination of at least three or four types; in fact, everybody is a combination of more than one. One or two are probably dominant, perhaps even in a power struggle. Depending on our past conditioning and current circumstances, certain patterns emerge or even erupt suddenly, while others recede into the background.

In my opinion, the optimal human being would be balanced among all eight of these archetypes. Who wouldn't want to be the person whose financial life was experienced as secure and abundant, pleasure-filled and joyous, powerful and creative, self-sufficient, significant and worthy, relaxed, generous, and compassionate? Chances are you'll find yourself and your behavior when it comes to money in at least one of these archetypes:

- **THE GUARDIAN** is always alert and careful.

- **THE PLEASURE SEEKER** prioritizes pleasure and enjoyment in the here and now.

- **THE IDEALIST** places the greatest value on creativity, compassion, social justice, or spiritual growth.

- **THE SAVER** seeks security and abundance by accumulating more financial assets.

- **THE STAR** spends, invests, or gives money away to be recognized, feel hip or classy, and increase self-esteem.

- **THE INNOCENT** avoids putting significant attention on money and believes or hopes that life will work out for the best.

- **THE CARETAKER** gives and lends money to express compassion and generosity.

- **THE EMPIRE BUILDER** thrives on power and innovation to create something of enduring value.

Learning about these archetypal energies and patterns gives you the insight and power to change. This is not intended as a system to objectify, diagnose, or limit yourself or others. It's not so important that you peg yourself as one or two of these archetypes—you may recognize parts of yourself and other people in all eight. For instance, we all worry to some extent when it comes to money, so we all have some Guardian in us. We all experience the pleasure of buying things, so all of us are familiar with the Pleasure Seeker.

In real life, however, we usually lean too much in one direction. We fixate on one set of beliefs and strategies—one archetype—in response to our particular life experiences. It is most often the people who find themselves firmly rooted in just one or two archetypes who feel the least freedom to choose and create the financial lives they want.

In addition, people are imbalanced to varying degrees within each archetype. Even though behaviors may manifest in imbalanced ways in our adult lives, there is something very intelligent at the source of each archetype's coping strategy. For example, a dysfunctional Saver might be penny-pinching or saving much more than he or she needs to, but at heart this person is focused on financial self-sufficiency, which is a reasonable goal. What follows is a list for each archetype with a few words describing its lower-functioning attributes, or pitfalls, as well as its higher-functioning attributes, or gifts:

ARCHETYPES	PITFALLS	GIFTS
The Guardian	Worry, anxiety	Alertness, prudence
The Pleasure Seeker	Hedonism, impulsiveness	Enjoyment, pleasure
The Idealist	Distrust, aversion	Vision, compassion
The Saver	Hoarding, penny-pinching	Self-sufficiency, abundance
The Star	Pretentiousness, self-importance	Leadership, style
The Innocent	Avoidance, helplessness	Hope, adaptability
The Caretaker	Enabling, self-abandoning	Empathy, generosity
The Empire Builder	Greed, domination	Innovation, decisiveness

We generally understand and appreciate the way our own archetype behaves, and feel like people who exhibit other behaviors are from a different planet. We may become quite exasperated while reading about the pitfalls of our own archetype, clinging firmly to the belief that ours is the only sensible approach to money. Some other archetypes may be completely repulsive to us. This can be because a parent or lover who caused us great emotional pain exhibited the attributes of that archetype, so we reject their financial values, throwing the baby out with the bathwater. As you read the descriptions and stories that follow, don't be surprised if you find yourself saying, "No one in their right mind would think or do that with money." They do. Every example in this book occurs on a regular basis with ordinary people you might meet at a gas station, in the supermarket, or at a family reunion.

Also don't be surprised if you find yourself feeling anxious or defensive while reading. Be gentle with yourself and read on. You may just find a kernel of truth in what you most want to reject.

OUR STORIES CHANGE

The archetypes are presented not as a categorization system to be fixed in stone, but so you can tease out what might be affecting your financial life on an unconscious level. It is important to note that at different times we have thoughts, beliefs, and behaviors arising out of different archetypes. To use my own life as an example, I would say that in late adolescence I was clearly a Saver. I recall as a teenager slowly accumulating the three hundred dollars needed to buy my first ten-speed bike, and a few years later fantasizing about one day having enough so I wouldn't need to work for money. As I entered my working life, I became more of an Empire Builder, dreaming of the day when I would have enough wealth to truly not worry and to make a positive impact on the world. In my early thirties, when my business was struggling, the Guardian kicked in. I recall many sleepless nights and early mornings when I played doomsday scenarios over and over in my head and felt paralyzed by fear. Then, as the business became more successful, my Pleasure Seeker began to emerge, as we used our newfound abundance to remodel our home, travel to Europe and Hawaii, and go out to gourmet restaurants and great concerts. Interestingly, this increase in spending did not come at the expense of the Saver; throughout this time, I still saved at least 20 percent of my income each year.

To make it easy to distinguish the archetypes, the examples I use in the coming pages are extreme. Though the archetypes and their attributes are in reality not always so hard and fast, I'm betting that you will recognize yourself, your friends, and your family in the pages ahead.

Identifying the archetypes that are most active within us is an important step toward creating true financial freedom. By bringing conscious awareness to what is unconscious, we can attain balance and a sense of control over our financial destiny.

CHAPTER THREE

THE GUARDIAN

"Now that all your worry has proved such an unlucrative business, why not find a better job?"

—HAFIZ, SUFI POET

Jared is a thirty-something veterinarian in Paso Robles, California, who earns a good living from his ten-year-old practice, which is focused mostly on horses and large livestock. He is the son of a friend, a woman who asked me to see him because Jared is always worrying about money.

"Tell me how your financial life is or isn't working for you," I said, as we toured his well-appointed barn, set amid lush green pastureland replete with a view of rolling hills.

"Well, where to start?" he said, with a grimace. "I feel like I have to be constantly on guard. I'm concerned that my practice is going to drop off a cliff because so many of the smaller farms around me are going to be bought by the big agricultural corporations. They'll have their own in-house vets and won't use me anymore."

"Has this happened yet—have you already seen a drop off?"

"No, not really. Last year was a good year, a bit better than the one before."

"How much better, in dollars or percentages?" I inquired.

"About 30 percent better. But 30 percent to me is about $40,000, and after taxes, it doesn't mean anything compared to the losses that are coming down the pike."

I acknowledged that sudden changes in income do indeed occur, for both better and worse.

"To make matters worse," Jared added, "my investments have been decimated in the last few years."

"Tell me more about that. What happened?"

"Well, I had this broker—my brother-in-law had made a bunch of money with him in the nineties and I hired him in late 2000. The market began to drop just as I started with him, but he thought it was just a short-term blip that was going to turn around quickly. He called it a 'buying opportunity' and put me into a bunch of telecommunications and health care companies, which of course tanked. When my portfolio was down about 40 percent, he wanted to pull out of everything and put the money into oil, banking, and consumer staples companies, but I balked, fired him, and waited for the stocks to rebound. They never did. In all, I lost about 75 percent of what I'd given him. It was awful. At the time, my brother-in-law had convinced me that if I invested with his broker, I could double my money in a couple of years, still pay off my mortgage, and have a nice retirement nest egg on top of it."

I thought about how difficult the losses must have been and asked, "So after all that, did you pay off the mortgage?"

"Yeah," he answered. "But not without a few months of mulling it over. I would stay up at night playing with scenarios on one of those Internet calculators that help you figure out if you'll have enough to retire or not. I'd listen to business shows on the radio, and one week some expert would say, 'Keep your money out of the market, pay off your debts, stay in cash,' and the next week some other expert would say, 'Get back into the market *now* and buy the Nasdaq 100 [an index of mostly technology stocks] because it's become such a bargain.' They all seemed like bad options, and I was kind of frozen."

Jared's mother shared with me that when she visited her son on weekends, she would find him, in her words, "obsessing" about his financial situation. "It's been pretty hard on his marriage. The thing is, I'm not sure that he really has all that much to be worried about. He's always landed on his feet, and he's doing fine even now."

Jared sees things differently. "My mom thinks I'm too preoccupied with money, but I call it being vigilant. What I'm trying to do is develop a plan." He is strongly convinced that he must guard against financial disaster by making the best decisions he can. He devotes a significant amount of time and energy to analyzing his financial life in the hope that he can control it. After all, he reasons, he wouldn't be a very good husband or father if he led his family to financial ruin.

Guardians have many positive qualities that, if utilized well, can serve to protect not only themselves and their families but society as a whole. At best, feelings of worry are valid early warning signs that should be heeded. In *Maestro,* Bob Woodward's book about the famously astute then-chairman of the Federal Reserve, the author describes an incident when Alan Greenspan asked the rest of the board not to raise interest rates 0.5 percent. Greenspan urged, "I have been in the economic forecasting business since 1948, and I've been on Wall Street since 1948, and I am telling you I have a pain in the pit of my stomach." Woodward explains that Greenspan "noted that in the past he had listened to his instincts and that they had been right. This pain in the stomach was a physical awareness Greenspan had experienced many times. He felt he had a deeper understanding of the issue—a whole body of knowledge in his head and a whole value system—than he was capable of stating at the moment. If he was about to say something that wasn't right, he would feel it before he was intellectually aware of the problem. It was this physical feeling, this sense in the stomach, that he believed kept him from making dangerous or absurd statements that might appear on the front page of the newspapers."*

Jared is one type of Guardian—someone who, by objective financial planning standards, has enough money for the foreseeable future, but whose worry is debilitating. Jared can't objectively assess whether his situation is dire because he is too emotional about the stakes.

In contrast, Joan, who is also plagued by anxiety about money, is another type of Guardian. At forty-eight years of age, Joan is a nontraditional student who, never having worked outside the home, returned to school after a messy divorce. She has a much less healthy financial picture than Jared by objective standards. But Joan's debilitating worry has distracted her from making financial decisions that would have increased her wealth.

I was introduced to Joan through a mutual friend who told me that she was desperate for sound financial advice, which I provided pro bono. Joan's divorce settlement left her with the modest house she had lived in all

---

* Woodward, Bob. *Maestro: Greenspan's Fed and the American Boom.* New York: Simon & Schuster, 2000.

her life—it was her childhood home and was valued at $150,000—but she received no alimony. Indeed, her children were grown and independent, and Joan had, in her words, "absolutely nothing" saved for retirement. Although I informed her that she was eligible for a percentage of what her husband had accumulated in Social Security when he retired, she mistakenly assumed she would have to engage in a legal battle with him to get it. As she had been the one to file for divorce, she balked at pursuing this avenue. "It's not worth fighting him for it," she said, massaging her temples, her deeply lined forehead creasing with worry. "And it's such a bureaucratic nightmare that it probably wouldn't come through anyway. I couldn't really rely on it."

Despite late nights spent fretting about her very real lack of income and poring over a rapidly diminishing savings account, Joan was enjoying taking classes at the local community college and was two semesters away from earning her teaching certificate. She described herself as apprehensive but also excited about her new career. She had always volunteered at her children's schools when they were young, and she hoped the work would bring not only satisfaction but a measure of financial independence and security. As it was, Joan barely had enough to make ends meet. Her children were sending her some money when they could, but they were not exactly financially secure themselves. As is customary of many Guardians (as well as some Savers), certain expenses weren't evaluated in proportion to others. For example, Joan once fretted for forty-five minutes over whether to buy a $10 toaster at a garage sale, but wouldn't think twice about valet parking whenever it was available, which cost her about $100 per month. When Joan's federal financial aid and student loan were delayed one semester due to an error at the financial aid office, she went into panic mode. She had been expecting $7,500, enough to live on for the semester, since she had no house payment to make. When the money was not forthcoming, she couldn't eat or sleep. She frequently woke with night sweats. She was losing weight rapidly because her stomach was too unsettled for her to enjoy meals. She stuffed unopened bills into the back of a filing cabinet and suffered nightmares and anxiety that racked her body. "It was all I could do," she said, "to get myself to apply for food stamps and assistance from the state to pay my electric bill." Luckily, the car she relied on to get her to and from school was being financed through a family member's dealership. "If not for my cousin, my car would have been repossessed," Joan explained. "And then I would have been forced to drop out, because there's no public transportation where I live." The stress and fear were interfering with her ability to concentrate in school, and despite feeling that it was "her only ticket out of the poor house," she was seriously considering dropping out. "I feel like I'm going to end up living on the street," she admitted. Even though she owned her home, she worried that she might not be able to pay the property taxes.

In Joan's words, her feelings "go beyond worry—it's more like I'm frantic!" On the surface, Joan's worrying may seem more "appropriate" than Jared's. She has many fewer options, after all, and her situation is much more unstable. But whether or not we think Joan has more to worry about than Jared, the real issue is how their worry is serving them.

The answer is the same for both: it's not. If Jared can't enjoy his work and family life, all the sound financial decision-making in the world won't bring him happiness. And if Joan's anxiety prevents her from finishing school, she will be in an even worse position financially, not to mention emotionally. What's more, her initial unwillingness to investigate claiming her share of her husband's Social Security because she feared it would be "a hassle" didn't improve her financial situation either.

THE GUARDIAN'S CORE STORY

Whatever their real financial situation, Guardians are afraid, *very* afraid, of something going terribly wrong. Their Core Story often involves a doomsday scenario of one type or another. Some Guardians focus on an apocalyptic world crisis like terrorism, global warming, Y2K, nuclear weapons getting into the wrong hands, or deficits. Past fears may have been founded or unfounded, but accompanying their current fear is often the refrain "This time it's going to be even worse," whether they're focusing on the crash of 2000–2003, accounting scandals, 9/11, Enron, the war in the Middle East, or how the United States will compete with China and India. For other Guardians, like Jared and Joan, the feared crisis is much closer to home: "I might lose my job or business" or "Where are we going to find the money if one of us has a medical crisis?" or "I'm not going to be able to rely on Social Security."

Some Guardians are highly effective with money. They learned at some point in the past that the best way to deal with their anxiety is through saving, frugality, and (very conservative) investing. Jared is this type of high-functioning Guardian, as evidenced by the fact that even after losing 75 percent of his savings, he still had enough left over to pay off his mortgage. But even with coping strategies that appear prudent to the outside world, the Guardian's underlying worries don't subside.

Again, being on guard and worrying can be helpful; it can make us alert when we're proceeding down a perilous financial path. In Joan's case, her worry about her financial future had led her to the positive step of enrolling in school. I've encountered many clients who could use a bit more of the Guardian in them. However, most Guardians worry excessively given their financial situation. They experience an unhealthy amount of fear, anxiety, or trepidation about money, even though they may not consider it unhealthy, distorted, or excessive. Whether it's justified or not is not the point. This excessive worry clouds their judgment, often causing them to make poor financial decisions and to experience a great deal more suffering than necessary.

You're probably a Guardian if:

- Your financial decision-making style falls into one of two extreme camps: (1) you feel frozen, unable to make financial decisions even when you think they're best for you, or (2) you make financial decisions only after excessive analysis.

- You are focused on financial doomsday scenarios, whether for the world or yourself, hence you analyze what-if scenarios much more than most people do.

- You abide by certain fear-driven rules like never having debt or only living off your interest and other income in retirement—never your investment principal.

- Your emotional responses and level of worry are out of proportion to your actual financial circumstances. For example, you might obsessively worry about having enough to pay your bills even though you've never actually had the experience of not having enough money to pay them.

- The fear of making the wrong financial decision is more painful than the hope of making a good decision is satisfying.

WHAT THE GUARDIAN FEELS

Most of the other archetypes in this book will be described in terms of the thoughts or beliefs that make this type of person feel secure or happy with money. The Guardian, however, is identified more by what he feels than by what he thinks. Take a look at the following list of sensations. Obviously, no one feels all or even most of these at one time. In general, however, Guardians will find one or two on this list that are a significant part of their emotional experience:

> "Most people are much more afraid of living than of dying."
>
> —Adyashanti

- Fear
- Anxiety
- Doubt
- Pessimism
- Uneasiness

- Obsession
- Panic
- Loss of appetite
- Sweating
- Gloom and depression

- Fretfulness
- Tight jaw
- Neck and back pain
- Contraction of the solar plexus

- Queasy stomach
- Shortness of breath
- Nervous tick

No one can deny that there are grave problems in the world, including poverty, hunger, and unspeakable violence committed by one human being against another. It was only a few hundred years ago that most of humanity literally had to fear for their lives on a daily or at least seasonal basis, and many still do. In 1900, 9 percent of mothers died of pregnancy or birth-related complications and 10 percent of babies didn't make it to their first birthday party. There were ruthless pogroms in Europe and Russia, for example, and vicious crimes against women and children have gone wholly unpunished throughout human history. But the truth is that the majority of the Western world's population is not engaged in a daily struggle to survive (although many millions still are). Regardless of our resources, why do these base fears continue to drive so many of our behaviors with money?

SEEDS OF THE GUARDIAN: SURVIVAL MODE

Virtually everyone in Western civilization has at least one starkly painful memory related to money—what I call a money wound. In fact, the original money wound may have occurred as we were being born. In his recent, posthumously published book, *Finding Clarity,* spiritual teacher Jeru Kabbal describes the universal experience of leaving the soft, nurturing womb of our mothers and going "from paradise to shock" in just a few minutes. According to Kabbal, in moving from the comfort and security of the womb to an experience that felt almost like dying, the first thing we did was to contract, trying to save our lives by clenching our hands, our eyes tightly shut.

Even though infants have no concept of money, on a sensory level this experience may well be the seed of all financial anxiety that arises later in life. Usually before the age of fifteen, other money wounds occur. Your money wound may have been when you lost your first wallet and all the allowance money it contained, or when you first understood that without money, your parents wouldn't be able to afford food, shelter, or other life necessities. Money wounds always carry the implicit threat of taking us right back to the utter terror and dependency of our original postpartum panic. Fear about money is, at its root, the fear of not surviving. These fears may take the form of thoughts like "I'm going to wind up as a bag lady," and may have been reinforced over time by real experiences of family members or community members losing everything in economic downturns or through catastrophic life events such as illness or death.

For those who grew up in affluent surroundings, there may not have been a struggle for survival in childhood, and perhaps no experience of losing money. For these people, the difficult feelings may have been the sadness, anger, and shame that came from realizing that others hated them for having more. Though different from actually fearing for your life, this fear of being hated, rejected, abandoned, and left alone is extremely painful to children in affluent or even middle-class families. Abandonment and social rejection, especially to an adolescent, can be anxiety-inducing. And whether we fear being socially ostracized or fear annihilation, our minds blame money for the experience and therefore invest money with the power to save us or harm us.

Clearly, many people worry about money or worry about losing the financial security that cushions them from real worry about money. What separates the Guardian from other archetypes is that Guardians haven't created enough emotional safety to really thrive and enjoy their lives. They're in an anxious emotional state much more of the time than others are, or they are so "burned out" from worrying that they feel somewhat numb emotionally. For some, these fears may be well founded: they may need to take external actions (such as reducing expenses) to create more real security. For others, their fears are not well founded because they are not realistically in danger of financial failure, though they may experience a drop in social status. On an emotional level, we all panic at the thought of having to give up our house, a college education for our kids, or retirement, as though we would not survive, when in truth our survival isn't actually threatened. When we find that our fears are not based in reality and yet we can't alleviate our anxiety with more thinking, one helpful exercise is to use breath and awareness to relax the body.

HOW TO RELAX

Take a minute right now and breathe deeply into your lower abdomen. Don't force yourself to hold your breath or breathe too slowly, but relax all tension and let gravity pull the oxygen into the lowest part of your lungs. As you do this, totally relax your stomach muscles and solar plexus. If you find this particularly hard to do while sitting or standing, try lying down on your back with a pillow under your knees. It is virtually impossible to be fearful or anxious with a relaxed solar plexus and belly.

A story from my family history may help illustrate the idea of a money wound. At the turn of the twentieth century, anti-Semitism was sweeping Europe, and many Jews, including my great-grandparents, boarded boats heading for the southern tip of Africa, where I was eventually born. My ancestors did not speak the language and did not have much more than their possessions to take with them.

On any rational basis, my own relatively privileged life does not justify anywhere near the level of fear and anxiety that they must have experienced. And yet this inheritance of fear is deeply ingrained in my physiological memory, regardless of my actual circumstances.

I went through a period when the Guardian was my dominant archetype. In late 2000 and early 2001, I realized that I needed to hire another professional advisor for my financial planning practice and move to a larger office, because my business had grown threefold in two years. But in the summer and fall of 2001, fifteen months into the worst market crash since the Great Depression, two of my clients decided they couldn't stand the uncertainty of where the markets were heading and would invest their money in bank CDs instead of continuing to work with me. Sitting in my office reading that second termination letter, I felt like a failure, like I should have done a better job of communicating with these clients to keep them from leaving. My heart was racing, my head felt hot, and there was a surge of fear down my neck and the backs of my arms. The lost revenues amounted to about $20,000 per year, and the possibility that this could be the start of a larger trend among my clients was even more unnerving, although two out of fifty clients was not a high percentage. Despite these worries, I went forward with my business expansion plans.

By early 2002, I had hired a financial advisor to whom I paid a six-figure salary, and I was well into lease negotiations that would triple my monthly rent. Only four years earlier, my financial planning business had been making less than six figures, and now I had just expanded my payroll by that amount. The stock market was continuing to go down. I vividly recall my anxiety during this time. On most mornings from mid-2001 until mid-2003, I was startled awake somewhere between 3:00 and 5:30 a.m. by an adrenaline rush of terror. On the physiological level, I was truly afraid for my life and the lives of my wife and sons. As waking consciousness came, the terror would give way to endless thoughts about clients, company cash flow, whether expanding the business was the right strategy, where to lease office space, unseen liabilities the business might encounter, and how our personal cash flow was holding up.

But the thoughts that paraded through my mind were secondary to the horrendous physical sensations I experienced: my heart raced uncontrollably, I felt a hot tingling electricity jolt from my ribs and down the outermost edges of my arms to my pinky fingers. My palms were damp with sweat, my breath was shallow and rapid, and my whole torso pulsed with fear. I felt unable to get up but also unable to stop the pain I was enduring—a hot, syrupy liquid kind of anxiety that kept me lying awake for hours. The last time I'd experienced these kinds of sensations was when I failed to close that loan at age twenty-three.

What's important about this story is that my survival was not threatened in any way. In fact, to most outside observers, my situation seemed flush. My business had grown rather quickly; my wife, Britta, and I were saving over 20 percent of our income; and if it became absolutely necessary, I could always go back to being a sole proprietor in a smaller office. Yet my thoughts and physical responses were as severe as if our very next stop were the homeless shelter.

WHAT THE GUARDIAN THINKS

Remember, the mind is a problem solver, and it kicks into high gear when we are experiencing feelings that are at best highly disagreeable and at worst intolerable. When any of these negative feeling states arise, the mind initially tries to answer the question "Why am I feeling this way?" For the Guardian, the answer usually runs along the following lines:

THE GUARDIAN'S MONEY MANTRAS

- My money is going to run out because _____ .

- There is going to be a world disaster or major change that will result in _____ .

- My investments are too _____ .

- I (or my husband/wife/child) spend(s) too much.

- If I stop working, my life will fall apart.

- If I'm not vigilant, I (or someone else) might make a mistake that could ruin me.

THE PAYOFF

In fact, though Guardians feel that in worrying about their finances they exert control over the uncontrollable (and some of them have keen, useful analytical skills when it comes to their money), there is very little real payoff to all this worrying. The mind operates on the assumption that once it knows the answer to why we're feeling the way we are, it will be able to do something about it—make the feelings go away or get better. However, the action we take from a worried or anxious state rarely leads to any type of lasting inner peace. More commonly, Guardians just exhaust themselves to the point where there's no energy left with which to worry, until the next time.

THE WORST-CASE SCENARIO

The next time you find yourself feeling any of the difficult feelings or body sensations described on p. 51, take the three steps described below. Depending on your preference, you can do this exercise alone, with a friend, in a public space, or in a quiet room. The important thing is that you do it, in some form. You can do it in your mind, take notes, or simply dictate your answers to someone who can jot down the answers for you.

Ask your worrying mind to exaggerate its worst-case scenario. Really draw it out. "I think I made a terrible mistake on that report for my boss. Oh my God! I might lose my job!" What else do you think might happen? "Well, then everyone will know how incompetent I am." And what else? "I won't be able to make the mortgage payments." Keep going. "And then we'd have to move out, back into that crummy apartment." And what would happen next? "My wife will become so disgusted, she'll leave me."

Then imagine how you would optimally respond if that worst-case scenario actually occurred. What would you do? Not "I'd be a basket case," but instead "I'd move into my sister's garage with a sleeping bag and air mattress, and make money working as a shipping clerk." Be specific and realistic. You're still going to want to survive, and will call on whatever resources you have available in order to do just that.

Last, ask yourself what you think you ought to do right now. If you can't come up with anything concrete, then just as you would to a child who is telling terrifying stories to his sibling, put your foot down and tell your worrying mind to stop speaking until it thinks of something you can do about the situation in the present moment.

The only potential value of worrying is to alert us to a behavior we need to change. But if real financial behaviors aren't changed or concrete and helpful financial decisions made, then whatever circumstances we pinpoint as the cause of our feelings remain. These circumstances then justify more worrying, which is what the Guardian's unconscious is most familiar with. In other words, unless you have deeply engaged your worrying mind in a conversation like the one described above, the next time difficult feelings arise in relation to some financial part of your life, you will resort to obsessive thoughts that justify the feelings your nervous system is experiencing. It's a vicious cycle.

This hardly seems like a payoff, especially when compared with the abundant assets that, as we'll see, Savers might accrue, or the dining, travel, and spa days that Pleasure Seekers get to enjoy, or the attention that Stars garner. However, worrying without taking action can give the Guardian a feeling of being alert and sensible in the face of grave danger. Also, a fair number of Guardians do make sound financial decisions, though they torture themselves before doing so. This type of Guardian may come to link his miserable state with the good decision he ended up making, falsely assuming he can't have one without the other.

BREAKING THE GUARDIAN'S DEATH GRIP

Besides a near-death experience, a spiritual awakening, or a significant role model, any one of which can end chronic worry but over which we have relatively little control, there are several strategies I have used with great success. The first step is to recognize that all your worry is not providing you with the control you crave—far from it, in fact.

I recall a client who was constantly anxious about his family's spending. He would insist that he and his wife spend less, and dedicated countless hours to chasing pennies around their household bookkeeping system. After employing several of the strategies I'm about to share with you, he was able to calm himself greatly, take two specific actions that would create real relief (in his case, refinance their mortgage and cut travel expenses), and spend time with his wife instead of staring anxiously at numbers on his computer screen for hours on end.

> "Once you get emotional on any topic, you're probably going to make mistakes."
>
> —Joe Moglia,
> CEO of TD Ameritrade

Once you accept that you want to stop worrying, try this technique:

When I encounter particularly stubborn Guardians in my practice or workshops, I use an analogy that I don't think is too far off the mark. Imagine that you are the parent of a young child, let's say three or four years old. Your dear child wakes up one night petrified that the sound of the oak leaves brushing against the roof shingles is actually a group of giant tarantulas coming to kidnap her and eat her alive. A healthy parent would likely say something like, "Sweetheart, I see how scared you are. I can hear those sounds too, and they are a bit scary. But there are no giant tarantulas out there. It's only the big tree you love to climb in the front yard being blown by the wind. Here, let's listen closely together and see if we can hear the little leaves brushing the house." If your child persisted in her terror, you might say, "Let's go out into the front yard and check it out for ourselves. I'll be right there to protect you."

Instead of soothing their most terrified feelings as they would for a child, Guardians instead let the nightmarish thoughts continue uncensored. In the worst instances, they are allowed to morph into all kinds of wicked scenarios that have no basis in reality. Of course, most adults are not worrying about giant tarantulas; they're worrying about car payments, feeding the kids, or making smart investments. However, their responses to these thoughts need to be similar.

CREATING SAFETY FOR THE GUARDIAN

- **CHECK YOUR IDEAS AGAINST REALITY.** Get a practical read on what your worst-case scenario might be. Consider using a CFP® professional or Consumer Credit Counseling Service (CCCS) (see p. 264). How likely is it that the negative scenario will actually occur? If you don't know, tell your worrying mind there's not enough information, and commit to getting the information you need to make an accurate assessment of its probability (much like the parent would take the child outside to see whether there are really giant tarantulas there). By contrast, if the negative scenario turns out to be likely after all, take steps to respond proactively.

- **NOT UNTIL THE WORRYING CHILD FEELS DEEPLY UNDERSTOOD WILL ANYTHING CHANGE.** Speak to your inner child in the voice of your inner wise parent and maybe write down your thoughts. Let the worrying child be heard and soothed by the parts of you that are mature and centered. It is important that the parent not force the child to "see" reality correctly, but instead hold the scared child and reassure her. This does not mean just saying, "Everything will be okay"; it's more like, "It makes perfect sense that you feel this way. In fact, there is no other way you could feel." Your child may need to go deeper into what could (in a worst-case scenario) actually happen, to allow her terror to be fully felt. All the while, the parent is saying, "You are okay, you are safe, I am here for you, it is normal to be scared and it is only

➤

the old oak tree." But this reassurance will only carry weight if you've done the first step and truly know what the real risks are and what's an illusion.

- **THE GUARDIAN NEEDS TO KNOW WHEN IT'S OKAY TO FEEL UNSAFE OR HE WILL FEEL UNSAFE ALL THE TIME.** For example, in working with Jared, I helped him set the boundary that if his practice declined two years in a row, or by more than 25 percent in one year, he would sell his ranch. This made him feel better and helped free his mind to focus on family life a bit more fully. This type of clear boundary allows the Guardian to worry less when the boundary hasn't yet been crossed. (Again, you might want objective help in setting a boundary that gives ample time to change your situation before it becomes dire.)

- **DO THE RELEVANT RESEARCH AND ACTUALLY MAKE THE CONCRETE CHANGE(S)** in your life that will ease the financial pressure associated with your worry. In working with Joan, for example, I gave her the homework of checking out the Social Security option first. Because of her reluctance and lack of clarity, she asked a women's rights group to do the checking for her (many tax preparers will perform the same service). To our delight, she found that drawing a portion of her spouse's Social Security did not reduce the amount for which he would later be eligible. For Jared, it meant learning from his investment mistakes and picking a new advisor with a strategy that wasn't based on hype or predictions, as well as researching what backup vocational options he had if his practice did truly become unviable.

- **NEVER *EVER* MAKE FINANCIAL DECISIONS IN THE MIDST OF INTENSE EMOTIONS.** (See the exercise "Be Still," p. 238). The Guardian almost always feels a sense of urgency: "If I don't decide now, I never will, and _____." Write down the decisions you need to make on a three-by-five card, in a journal, or in a handheld computer or phone, and put them off until you're feeling more centered. Then you can sit quietly and make the necessary decisions, whether by using a pros-and-cons list or an advisor who can help you find the objectivity you need.

For more practical recommendations on cash flow and budgeting, investing, insurance, taxes, gifting and estate planning, and philanthropy and generosity that are specifically tailored to the Guardian, see the appendix, p. 264.

CHAPTER FOUR

THE PLEASURE SEEKER

"Nothing lulls and inebriates like money: when you have
a lot, the world seems a better place than it actually is."

—CHEKHOV

Donald sat near the back of the large, airy conference room where my work-shop was being held. He was an athletic man in his early fifties, his face tanned. He wore loose, comfortable cotton clothing, and exuded a boyish charm and a sense of ease. Earlier, Donald had shared that he just returned from a vacation on Kauai where he had taken a helicopter tour of the NaPali coastline and stayed at the area's most luxurious resort hotel.

During a section of the workshop when we discuss the financial behav-iors that are most persistent in each participant's life, Donald revealed that he loved spending his money on vacations, clothes, home theater equipment, and other electronic gadgets.

"Most people live to work. I work to live!" he said enthusiastically. "I put a lot of time and effort into my job as a real estate agent, and when I earn a handsome commission, I feel I deserve to treat myself, and I do! You can't take it with you, so you might as well enjoy it as much as possible now."

"That sounds like a life philosophy that's been working well for you," I responded, smiling. "Is that true?"

"Well, I guess it works most of the time. I really enjoy my approach when I have money, because then I can afford to buy and do the things that I love. I recently bought some new home theater speakers, and I couldn't have been happier standing in the listening room of that high-end audio place trying out different speaker configurations." He paused, and his expression grew serious. "When it doesn't work so well is when I don't have any money left over at the end of the month. What comes in just ... goes out."

THE PLEASURE SEEKER'S CORE STORY

More than anything else, the Pleasure Seeker believes that money is to be used to enjoy life. In the extreme, Pleasure Seekers may even feel that you should aim to die broke. Their financial role models may be parents who were Pleasure Seekers themselves, really enjoying the good life. Or equally often, the Pleasure Seeker is reacting to a more spartan upbringing. Many boomers, raised by a generation of parents who remembered the Great Depression and responded by becoming Savers, vowed to partake of the good things in life when they grew up, instead of being "slaves to money" like their parents.

Above all, the Pleasure Seeker's purchases are for sensory enjoyment. They want to see, hear, taste, touch, and smell the fruits of their money. They tend to reject intangible assets like savings accounts in favor of tangibles like vehicles, homes, and gadgets. Though others might spend a lot of money, no one enjoys the things they spend money on more than the Pleasure Seeker.

As with every archetype, there are wonderful gifts that go along with being a Pleasure Seeker, which many people would do well to emulate. Pleasure Seekers are often described by their friends and family as people who "really know how to enjoy life." Admirably, they avoid the common pitfalls of workaholic behavior that plague our society. However, I'd like to turn your attention to what is imbalanced or may not work well for this archetype. As we all know, the sensory pleasure we derive from things we can buy is fleeting. Remember the cycle of the Wanting Mind? We yearn not really for what we buy but for the inner freedom from wanting. A few days after a great vacation, we no longer feel the relaxation or exhilaration we had while we were lying by the pool with a good novel. A month after we buy that flat-panel TV, we no longer notice the differences between it and the older model it replaced. And yet the next time we buy something that brings a new rush of sensory enjoyment, the mind latches onto the purchase itself as the cause of our happiness. As they go through life, Pleasure Seekers in particular become hard-wired to believe that:

more money = more pleasure = more happiness

I've worked with many adult children of wealthy parents who struggle to effectively manage their trusts or inheritances and to achieve financial independence. These trust-fund kids have become accustomed to a higher standard of living than they are able to afford as adults. They were raised with vacations on Martha's Vineyard and educations at Exeter or Andover followed by Ivy League colleges. In their young life, they could fly on Dad's corporate jet to Europe or, if time was of the essence, to summer camp across the state. They drove expensive cars, ate at the best restaurants, and wore designer clothes, and they came to expect those things in their adult life, regardless of their financial wherewithal.

I've also worked with more than a few wealthy families in which the parents are incredulous—and angry—that their children continue to spend beyond their means even as adults. Their frustration with their spendthrift offspring often causes these parents to tighten their purse strings, which leads to more financial hardship for the adult kids, as well as feelings of unfairness and entitlement. Pleasure Seekers who are children of wealthy parents may feel that they ought to be able to live in the same neighborhoods, drive the same cars, and otherwise enjoy life as they did in their formative years. These beliefs may mask an inner sense of not being worthy or entitled, uncomfortable feelings that lead the Pleasure Seeker to seek solace by spending on items or experiences that bring temporary pleasure. In response to this cycle, Pleasure Seekers often become more adamant than ever that money is to be enjoyed, not hoarded, and may perceive all those who save like their parents as "tightwads."

Certainly, not all Pleasure Seekers grew up wealthy. Plenty seek the good things in life because they never had them. But whether a Pleasure Seeker was raised in conditions of wealth or scarcity, or somewhere in between, his or her fundamental story is that money is to be used for personal enjoyment. No other use brings the same level of gratification.

You're probably a Pleasure Seeker if:

- You save less than 5 percent of your income. When you're feeling flush, you tend to buy things that aren't necessary to your basic lifestyle.

- Your debts exceed your assets, perhaps because you've purchased multiple items on credit. You opt to postpone payments until next year to satisfy your desire to enjoy something new sooner rather than later.

- Your investments, if you have them, tend to be in vacation homes, art collections, fine wines, jewelry, restaurants, or other collectibles.

- You regularly engage in "retail therapy" when you're feeling low, spending beyond your budget on items that are not necessities.

- Your spending on luxury items creates tension in your relationship with your spouse or partner.

SEEDS OF THE PLEASURE SEEKER—"WHY SUFFER?"

For Pleasure Seekers, money exists primarily for experiencing pleasure in life. Another way to describe this archetype is hedonistic. Although *hedonist* is somewhat of a dirty word today, the term originally arose from the Greek word for pleasure and designated a group of philosophers, followers of Socrates, who believed that the only way we can really be sure of anything is through our sensory perceptions. This is manifested in modern-day Pleasure Seekers by their delight in tangible purchases as opposed to more abstract uses of money, like saving or investing in the stock market. Common beliefs of the Pleasure Seeker run something like this: "Why suffer?" or "It's just money. What's it for, anyway, if not to enjoy?" or "You can't take it with you," or, last but certainly not least, "I deserve it."

This last idea is key. On some level, the inner voice of the Pleasure Seeker is saying, "I've worked so hard (or suffered so much) that I deserve this." I once had a client who saved for many years to be able to buy his first home. When he finally did, he spent an amount equal to half his down payment to furnish the house—all on layaway credit. Five years later, he and his wife are still bearing the financial burden of that decision. With the inheritors I've worked with, there is often initially some guilt when parents bequeath a substantial sum. But inevitably, most Pleasure Seekers with inherited funds assuage this guilt by telling themselves one of two things: that their parents treated them so badly that they somehow earned the right to do whatever they want with the money by virtue of all they put up with, or that their parents would have wanted them to enjoy the money to the fullest. The vast majority of Pleasure Seekers, in fact, are not trust-fund kids but work hard for their money. However, the price of their pleasure-seeking is often that they must work at jobs they don't like or stay in uncomfortable relationships with people who provide for them. It's a vicious cycle: their purchases serve as rewards for the suffering they experience by staying in situations that fund these same purchases.

THE PAYOFF: DEATH-DEFYING BUYING

Most of us enjoy fine dining, massages, luxurious vacations, or shopping for things we know we'll love. In fact, everyone has a Pleasure Seeker in them. Humans are sensual animals; why shouldn't we satisfy our yearning for sensory stimulation and pleasure? It's part of being fully alive, and without these kinds of experiences we limit our growth as people. What could be worse than suffering a life of deprivation that is completely unnecessary?

As with all the archetypes, the real question is one of balance. Is your pleasure seeking creating financial harm? Is it satisfying you less than other possible uses of your money, such as knowing you've got some cash socked away in case your elderly mother needs to enter a nursing home someday or ensuring that your children's college fund is healthy? Is it, at base, motivated by fear—whether of a life of drudgery or some other anxiety?

A big payoff for Pleasure Seekers is that, in focusing on bringing themselves enjoyment above all, they don't have to look at the void—the painful feelings of emptiness that from time to time arise in all of us. By filling up this void with things that bring them pleasure, Pleasure Seekers don't have to ask themselves the difficult questions that might otherwise arise—about their life's purpose, whether they are living according to their values, or what their pleasure seeking is protecting them from feeling. Perhaps pleasure-seeking behaviors with money even mask a fear of dying without having fully lived. If this is the case, pleasure seeking is, ironically, far from life-affirming.

WHAT THE PLEASURE SEEKER FEARS

What drives Pleasure Seekers' spending behavior? For the most part, their surface-level fear is that one day there might not be enough to keep enjoying the good things in life. A friend of mine, Carol, once remarked that her income as a TV production assistant had declined over the past couple of years. I asked how she was responding to her situation. She said, "I feel I really ought to curtail my spending, possibly get a roommate or sell my house and move into an apartment, but I really don't want to. I get kind of nauseous when I imagine the places I'd have to live in order to meaningfully reduce my monthly nut."

Another Pleasure Seeker I know grew up as the youngest of nine children. In Vincent's childhood, Christmas gifts were recycled—the older kids would get new train sets, dolls, and other toys, while the younger kids were given their older siblings' rewrapped, repackaged gifts from earlier years. Vincent's disappointment was still palpable as he described to me the letdown of Christmas mornings, as he'd unwrap his gifts and discover—yet again—that he'd received his siblings' castoffs. As an adult, he spent 10 to 15 percent of his yearly income every Christmas—without ever budgeting for it in advance—to ensure that his wife and children were not deprived. He bought expensive gifts and gave elaborate parties not only for himself and his immediate family but for other family members and friends. Indeed, Pleasure Seekers, who are frequently perceived as generous, can be quite evangelical in their desire that others enjoy the fruits of money, too.

This passion stems from a deeper fear underneath their cravings. Vincent feared he was not good enough to deserve love, not as lovable or worthy as his older siblings, and he wanted to show that at least he could have—and give—new Christmas presents. Because this fear had remained mostly unconscious throughout his life, he hadn't been aware of using money to avoid these feelings of worthlessness or low self-esteem. Before he worked on these issues, Vincent could not stop his lavish holiday spending. He had to uncover the fears behind his financial behavior before he could make real changes in his behavior.

The nature of these underlying fears varies greatly by individual, but to be sure, if you feel a wave of resistance arise within you as you contemplate not buying something you want, chances are that your intended purchase is anesthetizing you to a deeper feeling. Initially, facing that underlying fear may seem daunting. If you resist the temptation to satiate your next craving with a purchase, you will likely experience a fair amount of resistance and even grief. The good news is that on the other side of this resistance, you will find that the anticipated anxiety is not nearly as terrible as you expected it to be. It might even open another doorway and be a path to fulfillment, intimacy, or love. Vincent told me that as a result of looking at and working with his underlying feelings, he was able to plan a gift-free Christmas with his family this year. Family members wrote on small cards what they loved about each other and what they wished for each other and decorated the tree with these cards. On Christmas morning, everyone opened the cards and read them aloud, making for a heartwarming holiday the family will never forget.

WHAT HAS MOTIVATED MY RECENT PURCHASES?

Whereas early hedonists believed that pleasure is the highest good, a later school headed by the Greek philosopher Epicurus, while accepting the importance of sensory pleasure, equated it with the absence of pain. The Epicureans taught that pleasure was best attained through the rational control of desire. To that end, make a list of the big-ticket items you've bought—and by big-ticket I don't only mean expensive, but also things you wanted badly:

1. _____

2. _____

3. _____

Then, for each item, answer the following questions:

- Why did I buy this item?

- How did I feel before I bought it?

- How did I feel after buying it?

- Do I still feel that way?

- If not, how long did this feeling last?

(continued on next page) ➤

WHAT HAS MOTIVATED MY RECENT PURCHASES? *(continued from previous page)*

What fears or other difficult feelings, if any, can I get in touch with that this purchase protected me from experiencing? The following list should get you started:

anger	joy	sadness	frustration
envy	rage	depression	hopelessness
confusion	worthlessness	greed	competitiveness
anxiety	shame	emptiness	inadequacy

If you can, write down a specific fear that each of these purchases protected you from feeling. These fears don't need to be rational or defensible. For example, perhaps you redecorated your house based on the fantasy that you'd be able to entertain more and not feel as lonely.

As you acknowledge these feelings, ask yourself this: How might you find real antidotes to the pain of these uncomfortable feelings, as opposed to sedating yourself with extra pleasure?

THE DARK SIDE OF PLEASURE-SEEKING: BUY NOW, PAY (BIG) LATER

Though many Pleasure Seekers blithely declare that they have a healthy relationship to money because they truly understand that life is not about the money, in its unhealthiest extremes it is fear that truly drives Pleasure Seekers: fear of deprivation, fear of facing uncomfortable feelings, or even fear of death. Until the creditors come knocking at your door, it is easy to ignore the dark side of this archetype.

Americans in general have been groomed by powerful marketing forces to cultivate and celebrate their inner Pleasure Seeker. Indeed, Sigmund Freud's American nephew Edward Bernays, considered by many to be the father of modern advertising and public relations, used his uncle's ideas about wish fulfillment to create a sophisticated industry devoted to catering to our Wanting Minds. Bernays envisioned a world in which people bought a new car not because the engine on their old one had given out but to increase their self-esteem or their sex appeal. They purchased a soft drink not because they were thirsty but because they wanted to join a group of people like themselves. The result? Unchecked spending and unconscious habits with money that often jeopardize the good life we so fervently seek. Many Americans, especially, are financially trapped in the Pleasure Seeker archetype. In fact, American consumer culture sets us all up to be Pleasure Seekers—so much so that we are even told we are doing our patriotic duty when we shop!

Those particularly pulled in by the Pleasure Seeker archetype need to be extremely compassionate and rigorously honest with themselves about what is driving their spending. The child in a Pleasure Seeker wants everyone to know "I deserve this!" How has developing this archetype protected them from greater pain? Anytime we are driven by fear and compensate with excessive desire, we create imbalance in our lives.

A CAUTIONARY TALE

I once had a client named Rose who was raised in a competitive family with a domineering father who controlled everything, including the family's money. Having grown up in the Great Depression, Dad was frugal to the point of deprivation. Though the family earned a middle-class income, they lived in a small house that was constantly in disrepair and ate day-old goods from the bakery and canned food.

Everyone in the family felt powerless, unable to forge their own way in the world of earning, spending, and saving money. Instead, Rose's father made all the decisions, shamed his children for their material desires, and never allowed them to make their own mistakes and gain their own sense of confidence in the world of personal finance.

By the time she was a young adult, Rose found herself rebelling against Dad's "tightwad" values, going out to dinner almost every night with girlfriends, buying the latest shoes, and indulging virtually all her material desires. Though her income as an account manager at a catering company was much higher than her parents had ever earned, it was no match for her expenses, so she found herself continually appealing to her father for loans and gifts, which he reluctantly agreed to, adding stern admonitions to change her behavior.

At twenty-seven, Rose married a successful sports agent whose income was well into six figures. Though his income was high, he was frugal, which created a

(continued on next page) ➤

A CAUTIONARY TALE *(continued from previous page)*

tension in their marriage similar to what she had experienced with her father. Nevertheless, the couple's income was high enough that she continued to spend as she wished. They had three children together, and as the children grew, so did the tensions about spending and how to raise happy kids. When the youngest was six years old, they separated and eventually divorced, primarily over their differences about money, especially his conviction that she was spoiling the children and her belief that he was depriving them.

She received a sizable divorce settlement, including $17,000 a month between alimony and child support and over $1.5 million of their joint assets. She bought an expensive house and continued to indulge the kids with the best clothes, parties, and family trips. Within five years, the alimony stopped. Through poor investments and spending, she had managed to decrease her assets to less than $300,000. Her spending was still at the same level it had been when she was married, and she had long since abandoned her career and had no meaningful ability to earn income. The child support would last for another five years, but it left her and her children well short of their monthly spending requirements.

Throughout the financial changes in her life, including the high income she earned, the upper-class lifestyle she and her husband enjoyed, and her sizable divorce settlement, Rose continued to experience the all-too-familiar feeling of deprivation and powerlessness she had known as a child and adolescent, even when she was spending freely. By embracing the philosophy that "you can't take it with you" in such an extreme manner, Rose couldn't really enjoy life, even though that's what her philosophy espoused so vehemently.

Pleasure Seekers tend to have a devil-may-care attitude about money. But when it comes to money, the devil is, unfortunately, often in the details! More than one Pleasure Seeker has been heard to say "I'm terrible with money." Still, burying your head in the sand when it comes to your finances puts extraordinary pressure not only on you but also on loved ones. Many Pleasure Seekers find themselves in conflict in their romantic relationships, relationships where the Pleasure Seeker is spending more than the couple can afford.

Debt is the natural result of unchecked pleasure seeking, and it is America's dirty little secret. In my work, I have seen firsthand that its costs are extremely high, not only in terms of dollars but emotionally as well.

Consider the following statistics:

- Total consumer credit: $2.5 trillion (Federal Reserve; June 2007).

- Thirty-six percent of those owing more than $10,000 on their cards have household incomes under $50,000 (VIP Forum).

- Average credit-card interest rate: 14.57 (BankRate.com; August 2007).

- Number of credit-card holders who declared bankruptcy in 2005: 1.3 million (Motley Fool).

Often, Pleasure Seekers imagine a retirement replete with trips to Europe and other luxuries, but because of their habits, these golden years remain illusory. Though the Pleasure Seeker is not the only archetype that has trouble saving for retirement, the reality of retirement is often a big wake-up call for Pleasure Seekers. Statistics show that many of us are going to be around for a long time. If you do not have enough saved for retirement, how pleasant will your later years really be?

A 2006 survey by the Employee Benefit Research Institute showed that Americans' confidence level about the amount they have saved for retirement is much higher than the data warrants:

- Most (68%) of those surveyed said they and their spouse had less than $50,000 in retirement savings.

- Many (58%) have failed to factor in rising health care costs and the need to supplement Medicare benefits by up to $210,000 if they live to age ninety.

- While 62 percent of current retirees say they spend more than 70 percent of their preretirement income, most preretirees surveyed anticipate needing less than 70 percent of current income after retirement.

- Most (59%) said that they hoped to have a standard of living in retirement that was equal to or higher than that they enjoyed in their working years. But when asked if they had calculated the amount they would need, 58 percent said no, and 8 percent said they'd arrived at the answer by guessing.

Clearly the dark side of pleasure seeking is bleak. Pleasure Seekers can face ruined credit, guilt, and dread when statements and bills come; they may have to face the hurt they've caused family members; and they may experience an impoverished retirement. I've seen an inheritor spend his entire lump-sum settlement to buy a trendy but unprofitable brewpub, leaving nothing to cover his and his children's ongoing living expenses. I know a couple who decided to remodel their house while telling their children they didn't have enough money to pay college tuition. I've observed people who have purchased an $80,000 car or a $250,000 boat on impulse, and who couldn't afford it.

> "You don't have to stop desiring something—you need to turn away from the object and look at what it feels like to be desiring."
>
> —GIL FRONSDAL,
> BUDDHIST TEACHER

Not only does pleasure seeking put you at risk of ultimately not being able to enjoy much at all, but at its unhealthiest extreme, it's a knee-jerk, Pavlovian response that robs us of personal choice and power.

A DIFFERENT KIND OF PLEASURE

Andy worked on commission in the commercial mortgage business and made an excellent six-figure income. Though hard-working, he did not enjoy his job but spent a lot of money impulsively on things like fine clothes, a watch, or his motorcycle collection. Although he didn't have much time to ride, when he looked in his garage and saw the gleaming machines, he felt that at least he had something spectacular to show for all his toil. "For years and years," he says, "I thought if I just made more, I'd be happy." But earn more and more he did, and he still didn't enjoy the work. So, just shy of forty, he left his position at Wells Fargo to start up his own business as a consultant for small companies and non-profits. He relocated to a beautiful rural town in the Southwest, thinking that by striking out on his own, he'd earn even more money and thus be happier. Andy's father had a "real Horatio Alger story," becoming a successful executive without any formal education. As a younger man, Andy believed the family myth that more money always makes things better. So it was a shock when he found that although his new consulting business did not bring him more money—in fact, he took a one-third drop in pay—it did bring him something he'd long been craving: joy. "I still seek pleasure; I just find it from different sources than I used to," Andy explains. Now it's the satisfaction he gains from helping other businesspeople realize their dreams. And he's recently fallen in love with a woman who has a young son. To his surprise, he delights in playing with the boy as much as he ever did in riding motorcycles. This new source of pleasure has allowed him to approach his financial life differently. Now he has begun to think about saving for his stepson's future, so saving doesn't seem so intangible. The prospect of providing for someone he loves gives him pleasure. It's quite a shift, one he's found to be "well worth it."

Like Andy, Pleasure Seekers can benefit from redefining the things that bring them pleasure. To allow new loves to surface, nothing is better than a little voluntary simplicity.

Remember, one of the mantras of the Pleasure Seeker is "I deserve it." One of the ways to break the pattern of satiating your every wish is to ask yourself whether what you are buying truly serves your values.

PLEASURE REDEFINED

Fill in this list. *For me, five of the most important things or ways of being in life are:*

1. _____
2. _____
3. _____
4. _____
5. _____

If you're like most people, some or all of the things you listed will not be things you own. You might have listed your family or free time. If you did list objects, they are probably items that serve a higher purpose, such as your house, or even your vehicle.

Five items that I spent money on in the last week are:

1. _____
2. _____
3. _____
4. _____
5. _____

Go back over your list and for each item, answer this question: When I spent money on this, how was I supporting or not supporting the five important things I listed first?

A DAY OF REST

Pleasure Seekers need to make a paradigm shift, finding different ways to experience pleasure in their daily lives. Rabbi Harold Kushner, author of many best-selling books, including *When All You've Ever Wanted Isn't Enough: The Search for a Life That Matters,* reminds us of the importance of taking a day of rest from wanting. Many religious traditions have a sabbath, which can also be a time to take a break from money. Try this: once this week, whatever day you choose, commit to twenty-four hours in which you will not handle money in any way. Buy groceries ahead of time; pay your bills another day. Avoid handing out cash or using credit. But this should not be a day when you become an ascetic. Find other ways to enjoy life. Why not play with a child, get out in nature, listen or dance to music you already own, or read a great book? Whatever it is, find sources of pleasure that don't require you to transact. There are many ways to feed your senses without ever spending a dime. Be creative!

MY HANDS ARE EMPTY

Plum Village is a lovely Buddhist community in the Bordeaux region of France. Founded by the Vietnamese monk Thich Nhat Hanh, it is set among lush forests and rolling green hills and provides a permanent home to about three hundred monks and lay practitioners. People come here for retreats and to learn to practice Buddhist principles. On one such retreat I had the opportunity to speak with Brother Phap Ang, a former engineer from Vietnam who had been educated at some of the top schools in the United States before giving up a successful career to become a monk. For over forty years, Ang has lived a simple life devoted to prayer and meditation. Like all Buddhist monks, he abstains from alcohol and remains celibate. He does not own anything. As I sat with this unassuming man, I couldn't help but ask him about how money worked at Plum Village.

He answered readily, explaining that the people who lived at Plum Village had no possessions but were given forty euros for spending money per month.

"And what do you spend that on?" I asked him, calculating that this amount was less than some American families dole out in allowance to their school-age children every week.

He paused to consider the question. "Oh," he said. "I might spend a few euros in town on this or that." But he usually has a lot left over each month, which he gives to orphanages and schools in Vietnam that Plum Village supports. His attitude toward money is simple: "I don't keep it. So most of the time, my hands are empty."

I sat, considering his words. I was struck by the fact that the inhabitants of Plum Village had little money, and yet what they received they gave away. They seemed to me to be the happiest people I'd ever seen. As they sat in silence, not doing anything in particular, they simply beamed from deep inside.

What was their secret?

The answer, Brother Ang explained, was that they had learned to "be with one thing." Although they don't drink alcohol or have sex, they are by no means sensorily deprived. They pay attention to one thing at a time. If they walk, they pay attention to the path in front of them, the trees they encounter along the way, or the flowers. I got a taste of this at Plum Village. When you walk there, you pay attention to one thing at a time, not a hundred things at once. Sitting down in the forest, you feel the wind on your face, smell the spring essences, the dampness of the soil, the oaky mustiness of the trees. Indeed, I experienced as much sensory pleasure in the week I was there as I had in years.

ONE THING AT A TIME

You don't need to go to a remote village in France to have this kind of epiphany. In your everyday life, learn to resist the mind's tendency to jump and shift, seeking a better experience through things you buy or do. When you eat a meal, chew your food a little bit longer, and don't talk. When you walk through your city or town, pay attention to your breathing, and notice how your senses respond to the people and things you encounter. When you talk with someone, listen deeply, noticing their expression, their words. When you do something, "be with it"—give it your full attention, putting aside for a time all thoughts of what's next on your agenda. Allow your senses to relish the world around you, just as it is. When your experience is pleasing to the senses and you give it your full, undivided attention, the joy you experience will be multiplied many times over. Full attentive presence enhances pleasure in a way that money never can.

For more practical recommendations on cash flow and budgeting, investing, insurance, taxes, gifting and estate planning, and philanthropy and generosity that are specifically tailored to the Pleasure Seeker, see the appendix, p. 267.

CHAPTER FIVE

THE IDEALIST

"Idealism is a setup for disillusionment. There's nothing wrong with idealism, but it can't really deliver the truth, because it's an idea about the truth. There's an ideal that no one can actually match and so then rather than questioning the ideal, the people who don't measure up are questioned or even disdained. If poverty is idealized, then there's actually a war against those who have money, or a feeling of being righteous or more pure, or more true, and that's a huge trap."

—GANGAJI, SPIRITUAL TEACHER

The first time Margaret spoke up in my workshop, I could see she was struggling with contradictory feelings. Another participant in the room, a man about twenty years her junior, had just talked about how wonderful the free market was for the world, and how with the fall of the Soviet bloc, every country was embracing a free-market economy. Margaret, a woman with white hair and piercing eyes who had earlier identified herself as a former peace worker, broke in.

"I'm questioning whether I belong in this workshop," she said abruptly.

"Okay," I responded. "Can you say more about why?"

"Well," she took a deep breath, "I want to have a healthier relationship to money. I really do. But isn't it pretty clear that the free market isn't free for everybody? Sweatshops are modern-day slavery. And even in the United States, not all of us start on a level playing field. Middle-class and rich people just don't see the extent of their own privilege. Not everyone inherits money from their parents or gets help with a down payment on a house. A lot of people struggle just to feed their families from week to week, through no fault of their own. I think capitalism is responsible for most of the suffering in the world. I don't know why people are so in love with it," she said vehemently. "I honestly think the whole system is corrupt! It doesn't value creativity or even guarantee every human being that their basic needs will be met. Poor people dying every day so that some rich CEO can have five mansions . . . that's wonderful? There is so much money in the world—if only it were shared more equally, we wouldn't see the kind of suffering we do."

I jumped in. "You seem to have some strong feelings. Would you be willing to share an example of how these beliefs affect your everyday relationship to money?"

She stopped and considered, then went on. "Well, I often get pretty angry about how unfair money is. I'm a guidance counselor at the local community college, and the salary they pay me isn't nearly enough to make ends meet, even though I'm responsible for guiding and shaping these young adults' lives."

"If your salary is insufficient, how *do* you make ends meet?" I asked.

"My husband earns a little as a freelance film editor, but not nearly enough to cover our monthly nut." Then she added softly, appearing embarrassed, "I'm lucky enough to have some family money that I inherited from my grandmother. But the truth is, I feel as though if my friends knew about it, they'd view me as a trust-fund brat. So I hide it, and I feel like a sham."

THE IDEALIST'S CORE STORY

More than any other archetype, Idealists are against money. They may also feel like outsiders in middle- or upper-class business and social circles, and feel shame and embarrassment regarding financial matters. When they think about money, they have a visceral negative reaction. Their thoughts may run something like, "Money is the root of all evil," "I'd be a sellout if I had more money," "Money isn't happiness. Money is what's in the way of happiness," "The system is corrupt. Corporations and government are immoral and are controlled by the wealthiest one percent of the country."

Those who are ashamed by money may feel, "How can I have so much when others have so little?" "If I were truly interested in a better world, I would share more of what I have." Even if it's not conscious, Idealists' aversion to money often contributes to an unbalanced and unsatisfying financial life.

The Idealist archetype includes many social activists, spiritual seekers, and artists.

Idealists bring intense focus to their vocation, the cause they fervently believe in, or the spiritual path they have chosen. They may, however, be confused about their financial needs and their true current financial condition. Even if they live frugally, managing their sparse income and few expenses, a lack of financial ease often forces them to take jobs they hate, and they spend time stressing about money instead of devoting time to their chosen field. Idealists may dream of a windfall that will somehow come when their work finds broad recognition. But though they are averse to money itself, they are often caught in a cycle of wanting just like anyone else, even if what they want does not involve their finances. The stress they feel when it comes to money only reinforces their strong aversion. Money itself, and not the way they relate to it, comes to seem like the problem, the thing that's keeping them from pursuing their true passion.

> "A friend was visiting me and he said, 'Why do you have such a sour face?' I said, 'Well, I'm thinking about money.'"
>
> —RAM DASS

One Idealist who is middle-class but comes from a working-class background explained that she just felt fortunate to no longer have to experience "the constant worry about food and heat that shrouded my parents' lives, as well as my own, all during my childhood and early adulthood." She went on to say, "To be relieved of that burden seemed reward enough for someone like me and basically all that could be expected."

Idealists don't always come from poor families. Sometimes, people caught in this archetype are financially dependent on money they didn't earn, be it the earnings of a spouse, a stipend from their parents, a divorce settlement, an inheritance, or credit-card advances. Because we live in a culture that values independence, those Idealists who are not financially self-sufficient usually experience a fair amount of guilt and a great deal of insecurity, even though most keep it well hidden. In today's world, money is synonymous with survival, and every being wants to survive.

You're probably an Idealist if:

- Your primary vocation is artist, musician, or entertainer, or you work for a nonprofit.

- You don't earn enough money to file a tax return, or you do earn enough but choose not to file.

- You rely on others (from your past or present) for much of your financial support.

- Your investments are primarily in small businesses, individual pieces of real estate, or an art or music collection, because you distrust big business.

- If you invest in stocks, they have been socially screened to eliminate some combination of tobacco companies, environmental polluters, weapons manufacturers, nuclear power, alcohol manufacturers, and companies deemed to have unfair labor practices (some percentage of people from the other archetypes also use screening, but virtually all Idealists do, or would if they owned stocks).

- You are more likely to give five dollars to a person on the street than to give to organized charity.

SEEDS OF THE IDEALIST—"THE EYE OF A NEEDLE"

Idealists are, as the name implies, highly idealistic. Often their views about money have an ideological justification, whether political or religious. They may identify themselves as socialists, communists, "true" Christians, or Buddhists. People operating under this archetype have often taken a vow of poverty, symbolically speaking, and it is very hard for them to break it.

As with any archetype, the views of Idealists do have a certain logic. The excesses of an unfettered free market have undeniably contributed to great human suffering, and many wealthy people do lose sight of anything beyond the bottom line. Recent scandals involving large companies that put profit before people or before environmental responsibility lend justification to the Idealist's natural distrust of "the system." Examples of people profiting from others' misfortune litter human history, and it is true that in many instances the desire for material gain has led to wars, destruction, and misery.

Some Idealists wish that they could return to a simpler time or some idealized culture in which money did not play the same role as it does in our society. They may feel a solidarity with the poor and, if they begin to earn money, experience a feeling of disloyalty or hypocrisy that leaves them unsettled.

But their views about money tend to put Idealists in a bind. Strategies for dealing with "the root of all evil" include these: "Just don't spend anything," "Pretend it doesn't exist," or "Don't hold on to it." These strategies are not always tenable in the world we live in, and the inability to resolve theory and practice often leaves Idealists feeling angry and frustrated.

"MONEY JUST SUCKS"

Just as Savers turn to saving and Pleasure Seekers to spending, Idealists use their convictions to protect them from feeling pain. When someone doesn't earn enough money to care for themselves, they become financially vulnerable because they must behave in "acceptable" ways toward the people supporting them or their very livelihood may be cut off. This is hard for Idealists, who are in many ways rebels. Often this vulnerability is too deep and scary to contemplate consciously, but it nevertheless creates great frustration.

When an Idealist is being financially supported by a spouse, a parent, the government, or a credit-card company, he often experiences deep ambivalence, which can manifest as a profound feeling of unfairness, of righteous indignation: "Why should I have to answer to you?" "What did you do to deserve the power you have over me?" "You're not perfect! Leave me alone and let me just be myself! I don't want to be part of your world!" Rightly or wrongly, this resentment about the unfairness of living in a world in which money is important is most often directed at the Idealist's benefactor because that is the person or institution that he mostly likely has to appease in order to survive. An artist relying on a government program or nonprofit foundation for a grant, for instance, may balk at any restrictions the grant imposes, while an activist whose parents support her but attach conditions to the money may rail against their materialistic values. Some Idealists are so averse to admitting their own vulnerability or culpability in being part of "the money game" that they turn a blind eye to the ways in which they depend on others to carry their financial weight. One man I know, a brilliant painter, is sincerely in love with a successful professional woman and has recently moved in with her. He justifies not paying half of his partner's housing costs because, he says, "She's chosen to live in a big house and would be paying her mortgage whether or not I were living with her. I'm more like a house guest, really, and I don't believe in owning property."

Though paying less if you have less can be perfectly workable in a relationship where both partners are clear and comfortable with the arrangement, such arrangements must be mutually nourishing. When the partner who is not as well off financially makes other kinds of contributions and matters are discussed openly, both people can feel that things are equitable and balanced. But when Idealists impose their views on partners who do not share the same vision, tensions ensue.

Whereas some Idealists are dependent on others for help, and often have mixed feelings about this dependency, others are not dependent on anyone else but would so much rather be dealing with their creative or spiritual or social endeavors than with money that they sabotage themselves financially. A musician I know recently admitted, "Why do I have to deal with this? It's my least favorite part of life. Money sucks, man. Dealing with money just sucks." All of us have had these sentiments at different times. Keeping on top of finances is hard work and not necessarily that interesting. But Idealists are generally so gifted in or attracted to another area of life that they'd much rather focus their intelligence and passion on their vocation than on money. They derive much more pleasure and fulfillment from their "real work" and often believe it represents their contribution to the world and, as such, inevitably calls for financial sacrifice.

HEADS IN THE SAND

Not all Idealists are poor, but most choose not to deal with money in some central way. A fair number of Idealists are not financially dependent on someone else. There is also a large class that actually has a substantial amount of money of their own, but like Margaret, generally feels guilty, ashamed, or otherwise burdened by it. One person I know, an inheritor in his fifties, admitted to me that he used to try to look poor at boarding school. "The spoiled brats there made me want to puke. I still kind of dress like a teenage punk," he said bashfully.

For some Idealists, the focus on doing what they love and believe in leads to an abundant livelihood (indeed, as mentioned above, some Idealists hope for fame or recognition for their work that might result in wealth, but see that possibility as a happy accident, not something to plan for). A sculptor I know who is clearly influenced by the Idealist archetype recently had a gallery opening in which his works sold for a total of over $1 million. However, he still finds it a real struggle to attend to the management of his very substantial income because he has been against money for so long. This avoidance behavior most often leads to Idealists at the end of ten years of professional success saying, "Where did it all go?" Or, if not as financially successful, "Why didn't it ever come?"

THE SKEPTIC'S LENS

Artists, activists, and spiritual seekers who operate under the Idealist archetype have a nose for hypocrisy and often see very clearly and accurately the limitations of "the system" or ideologies in general. If you have the kind of well-honed critical mind that is adept at debunking popular myths, I challenge you to take that same skeptic's lens and use it to look at the following:

- Leaving aside for just a moment the ways in which you believe "the system" to be corrupt, turn your attention to yourself. What is it that you might not be seeing about your relationship to money? In what way is your relationship to money contradictory or even hypocritical?

- If you're an Idealist with a substantial amount of money that you didn't earn, how would your life be different if you had earned the money yourself? Would your beliefs about money, or the way you treat it, be different? How so?

- Is your lack of attention to what it would take to be self-sufficient truly serving your art or cause?

- If you had more money, imagine for a moment all the good you might do with it. List the ways money could serve your ideals.

HIPPIES WITH MONEY

In the United States, tens of millions of people who came of age in the 1960s reacted against their parents' generation. They rejected "the system" and the war in Vietnam and adopted antiestablishment points of view and a countercultural lifestyle. Influenced by Marxism and other radical ideas, this segment of the population believed the world was on the brink of great change, old systems like "the money economy" would soon topple, and we would all return to a simpler way of life that relied on bartering and reciprocity. Many people collected unemployment or welfare, feeling it was almost noble to do so, a slap in the face of a corrupt government and a way to pursue their own important work. But the revolution many anticipated did not come. For scores of boomers, the passing of that idealistic era has been very difficult.

The generation that invented the motto "Don't trust anyone over thirty" is now between fifty and seventy years old. What's more, they are squarely in the peak years of wealth and earning power. In total, their parents are leaving them trillions of dollars in inheritances. Many have flourishing careers. Now, at the beginning of the twenty-first century, these former flower children collectively have a lot more money than they ever dreamed they would back at Woodstock. But they still hold strong to their progressive values.

These values, along with distrust of the establishment, are a hallmark of Idealists, whether they have millions or very little. In fact, Idealists are generally quite cynical about Wall Street, big business, and the established financial system. As a result, they tend to invest in real estate, art, or their own or friends' business ventures. However, now that this generation is facing retirement and, in some cases, inheriting vast sums of money, they are at a crossroads. They have to grapple with squaring their values and morals with the need to make concrete financial decisions, and the financial services industry is trying to figure out how to earn their trust.

Many Idealists, no matter when they came of age, have to take a harsh look at their values and attitudes about money once they begin raising children, and especially once they begin to think about their wills and estates. One man I know, an adjunct professor and environmental activist who has little saved for retirement (all of it in socially screened funds), owns almost nothing beyond his intellectual property. Before landing his current job, he made ends meet by working odd jobs and getting grants for the nonprofit he started. When he spoke about his two adult children, he said, "I never put much stock in money, but when the kids were growing up, I did feel bad not being able to afford to support their love of music with music lessons, or offer them a better education—which should be free but in our society isn't. I consoled myself with the idea that my work was making a difference in the world, and that I could help them that way, but I still felt—no, *feel*—guilty."

The convictions of Idealists, as intense and righteous as they may seem, can actually be a smokescreen, a defense against feeling the terrifying vulnerability that's lurking just behind them. Those who identify with this archetype may feel insecure about their own ability to succeed in the world or about their dependency on others. But there is no freedom in avoiding vulnerability. The more intense our beliefs and reactions are, the more we are unwilling to face what holds us back.

The good news, as we'll see, is that facing our deepest vulnerability is never as scary in reality as it is in anticipation. And as subsequent chapters will show, Idealists don't have to give up their most heartfelt values—compassion, equality, justice, environmental responsibility—in order to thrive financially.

THE PAYOFF

As with every archetype, there is a payoff to being an Idealist. Most Idealists believe they need to create a separation between themselves and the status quo in order to create great art, be effective activists, or be pure religious or spiritual students or teachers. Idealists often create this feeling of separation by not focusing on money—refusing to figure out how much they have, how much they spend, how much they make, or where they'd like to be financially. In the short term, this feels like a freer, easier way to go.

Instead of looking within, Idealists point to other people or money itself as the problem. It's obviously much easier to blame others or the system than to do the difficult inner work of unearthing our own assumptions, seeing how they serve or sabotage us, and then slowly cultivating new ways of being with money. Granted, there are many things that can and should be improved in our financial system. The myriad challenges faced by people born into poverty can hardly be fathomed by those who have had it easy financially, including me. No one can deny the gross abuses of power by some mega-wealthy individuals and corporations, and the playing field for those from different classes is far from even. But the people I've seen who are most effective at bringing about change have created balance within themselves, so that they're not living in opposition to what needs improvement in the world. An oppositional approach merely polarizes and repels the very forces

Idealists seek to influence, contributing more to the problem than the solution. How much more effective might these intelligent, passionate people be were they to focus on positive ways to change and improve things? When I meet someone with deep-seated negative beliefs about money, I'm often reminded of a saying I once heard: "Resentment is the act of stabbing yourself repeatedly in the heart with a knife and hoping the other person dies."

I know a woman who purposely limits her earnings to $7,000 a year so that she does not have to file a tax return. Other Idealists are so angry with the government's use of tax dollars that they don't pay their share of taxes even if they do make more than the limit. But these acts of defiance are only short-term fixes. Eventually, people tire of the financial life that an unexamined Core Story has created for them. For some Idealists, this point may come when they have children or can no longer look to governmental agencies to fund their work. At this juncture they are often motivated to make a change.

In Margaret's case, she had a great deal of anger not only toward society and toward her employers for undervaluing her profession but toward her husband as well. These feelings are common in the Idealist, in part because idealism often comes into conflict with reality. At one point in the workshop, she said, "I know it's wrong of me to think this way, but if only Bradley would get out there and hustle like our friend Steve, we'd have enough from his work to make ends meet." In truth, Margaret was projecting her yearning to be financially self-sufficient onto her husband (and she did recognize the irony in wishing her husband would earn money so she wouldn't have to sully her own hands with the nasty stuff). My guess is that if he were providing for all their financial needs, she would probably still feel resentful toward him, as well as have the unpleasant awareness that he was holding something over her. If not confronted, this would likely motivate her to gain power in some other part of their relationship, perhaps by usurping parental authority or withholding sex.

BREAKING FREE

Most people's beliefs are so strong they seem woven into the very fabric of their identity and changing them feels as remote a possibility as changing eye color. But I have seen Idealists change. I recall someone who was so caught up in his ideals and beliefs about how corrupt money was that he constantly sabotaged job opportunities. By looking deeply into the roots of his very strong beliefs and feelings, he saw that money wasn't the monster he had made it out to be and that he'd be a much more effective emissary for the social change he sought by getting his financial house in order first, which he then did over a three-year period.

Ask yourself this. Is your conviction worth the price you're paying in your financial life? Will you be more or less free to express your ideals if you're financially unshackled? If you're unhappy with your relationship to money, and you've identified yourself as being at least in part an Idealist, here are some inquiries and practical steps to help you break free.

SOME THINGS TO TRY

- **HOW DO YOU REACT TO MONEY?** Think about or write down three ways of completing this sentence: "Money is _____." What reaction do your answers produce in your body? In general, are you attracting or repelling money (as well as freedom, peace, compassion, and perhaps even creativity) with your beliefs? If you are always broke (or feeling trapped, anxious and unsettled, pissed off, and blocked), there is a good chance that you are repelling attraction, self-sufficiency, and abundance. Is your Core Story truly serving your ultimate creative, social, or spiritual ideals?

- **GET THE FACTS.** For almost every Idealist I've met, trying to track spending, figure out how to get out of debt, or set up an investment program without some help is bound to fail, or at least be unnecessarily frustrating. There's just too much aversion to dealing with money. But you don't have to manage your finances alone. If necessary, hire a bookkeeper or make a barter arrangement with a friend who is good with figures and tracking spending. Empower them to point out your blind spots, set up automatic debt repayment and savings programs, or dole out the cash you can spend each month.

- **INQUIRE.** Idealists often want others to be different. When you find yourself caught by strong feelings about other people and the way they're behaving with money, I highly recommend the following exercise, which comes from Byron Katie, who wrote a wonderful book about acceptance called *Loving What Is*. I've adapted her line of inquiry specifically to money.

(continued on next page) ➤

SOME THINGS TO TRY *(continued from previous page)*

First, write down all your judgments about money. Be as petty, non-spiritual, and unbalanced as you want in your statements. Do not take the high road here. In other words, don't write, "I prefer not to deal with money because it's distasteful." Instead write, "Money is evil. I hate money," if that is true for you. Then sincerely lead yourself through the following inquiry about each of your thoughts:

1. Is it true?
2. Can you be absolutely sure that it's true?
3. How does it cause you to react when you think that thought?
4. Who would you be without that thought?

For example, when Margaret began to follow this line of inquiry, she came up with the following:

I hate money and the pursuit of money.

1. Is it true?
Yes, it is true! Money and materialism disgust me.

2. Can you be absolutely sure that it's true?
Well, I guess I can't be absolutely sure that's true because not only do I hate money, I also want it—and I want my husband to make more.

3. How does it cause you to react when you think that thought?
When I think that I hate money and the pursuit of money, I feel angry, enraged. I feel powerless because it's so important to so many other people, to my students, and everyone else. My neck gets hot and my jaw feels tight. I'm barely breathing while I'm thinking that thought.

4. Who would you be without that thought?
Without that thought, I would be more peaceful, more comfortable with my own choices. I wouldn't feel these knots inside my own body, which would probably make me much more effective in my life, and I'd feel free to make different choices and accept my husband's choices. Sometimes I just get so angry at him, and it's confusing because I do love him and can't imagine being with anyone else. If I didn't hold on to the thought that I hate money, I might be free to love my husband and my life more fully.

For more practical recommendations on cash flow and budgeting, investing, insurance, taxes, gifting and estate planning, and philanthropy and generosity that are specifically tailored to the Idealist, see the appendix, p. 269.

CHAPTER SIX

THE SAVER

"Money is emptiness. When people who have money
are trying to get ultimate security from the money, it's
just impossible."

—TSOKNYI RINPOCHE,
TIBETAN MEDITATION TEACHER

Jeremy walked into my office dressed in simple green corduroy pants and
an old sweater. He smiled warmly as he greeted me and sat down at one
end of the sofa. Clasping his hands in his lap, he looked around the room
at the art, plants, and furniture. Jeremy had recently attended a workshop
of mine and had asked if he could see me privately, as there were some issues he felt he needed more help with. I told him I would be glad to see
him and gave him a questionnaire to fill out so our time would be more
helpful to him. I learned from Jeremy's completed paperwork that he had
grown up in a frugal family that valued education above monetary success. After earning a B.A. in psychology from Stanford, he went on to earn
a Ph.D. from UCLA and then taught undergraduate psychology classes
there. A few years later, he went into private practice in psychotherapy.
By the time he came to see me, he was earning $120,000 a year working
about twenty-five hours a week, which is considered full-time in the mental health field.

"So, Jeremy," I began, "tell me what the issues are that you wanted to discuss further."

"Well," he said, "I've always known that I'm really responsible with money. I've never really been in debt. I spend less than I earn. But as much as everyone says they wish they had my money habits, it's not all it's cracked up to be."

"What do you mean?" I inquired.

"Well, there are lots of times when I'm kind of distressed—where my money habits seem to get me into trouble."

I asked him if he could describe a situation where this issue came up. He shifted uncomfortably, obviously embarrassed about what he was about to say.

"Well," he said, "let's say I make plans to go out to dinner with a friend. I'd much rather eat at the simple Chinese place for $8.95, but my friends generally want to go to a more hip place, and I can't get out of there for less than $25."

He went on to tell me that he really wished this wasn't such a problem for him. He knew his resistance wasn't really about the money. He certainly could afford it, and he readily admitted that he enjoyed the $25 meal more than the $8.95 one. He had a successful practice, was making an excellent living, and had managed to save $50,000 in the past two years. But it still made him feel uneasy, as did virtually any spending that wasn't necessary to daily life. I asked him to tell me more about what he experienced when he went with friends to a restaurant they'd chosen.

"When I look at the menu, and when the check comes," he said, "I actually feel a momentary cold sweat come over me, and I get anxious that this is just a small part of a larger pattern of spending more than I'm comfortable with. But it's not only at times when my friends are spending that I'm anxious. Some days I just wake up feeling worried about nothing in particular, or I notice some stress when I sit down to pay my bills."

THE SAVER'S CORE STORY

"If you were to give voice to that anxiety, what do you think it would have to say to you?" I questioned Jeremy.

"I haven't really put it into words. But I guess it would say, 'You need to save more to be secure. You spend too much. You're being wasteful. What are you going to do if the economy turns for the worse and your practice dries up? Then where's the money going to come from for these fancy dinners? What can you do, right now, to increase your financial security?'"

"How do you feel as you hear yourself say those things out loud?" I asked.

"It feels true! The economy does ebb and flow, after all. It makes me want to work harder to save more money so that I don't have to be such a tightwad when I go out to dinner with friends, and so that I don't have to worry. I guess I feel kind of depressed because there's no end to what I can spend money on, and if I don't keep a tight rein on it, my spending will get out of control."

I knew that Jeremy had saved a high percentage of his after-tax income, relative to most people, in the past two years. I asked if his savings had alleviated his anxiety at all.

"Yes, I think it has. But it doesn't stop the worry from coming back on certain days or in certain situations. I do feel a bit more at ease knowing that I've got a safety cushion. And I really enjoy the times when I'm actually able to watch my account growing by a thousand here or a thousand there."

In a Saver's life, money represents security, stability, protection, and nourishment. In their most tense moments, Savers equate their savings with survival or, more accurately, equate a lack of savings with the potential for financial ruin. For these reasons, money takes on an inappropriate importance for Savers, often leading to a frequent and obsessive desire to count up their savings, excessive attention to the rate of return their investments are earning, difficulty in making purchases, or stress with a spouse, family members, or friends who are deemed to be "too loose" with money. At the extreme, Savers believe that if only they could accumulate enough money, they would feel safe and secure.

Savers have two possible orientations: (1) a focus on reducing spending, or frugality, and/or (2) a focus on increasing their savings. Jeremy belongs to the first type, as shown by his discomfort with spending, even on things that are enjoyable for him and that he can afford. Many frugal Savers have a "bag lady" syndrome. Like Guardians, their Core Story is that they are probably going to end up destitute or on the streets. Even if they don't literally believe this is true or likely, they relate to money in ways that are geared to avoid the inevitability of ruin. They have been told and shown all their lives that imprudent spending will precipitate a financial doomsday.

Other frugal Savers come from Depression-era ancestry. During the Great Depression, the stock market as a whole lost 83 percent of its value, about twice as much as the recent 2000–2003 bear market. But that was only the financial toll. Emotionally, the period from 1929 until the early 1940s literally was a nationwide depression, with an increase in suicides, clinical depression, and alcoholism. In this age of two- or three-car families and a cell phone for almost everyone, it is hard for us to conceive of how devastating this time was.

People who went through the Great Depression wanted to understand what had gone wrong and how they could prevent it from ever happening again. The following principles became hallmarks of Depression-era parents and their children, and affect all Savers to varying degrees:

THE SAVER'S MONEY MANTRAS

- Don't ever touch your principal (which means you can live off the interest that your investments earn, but you should never sell the investments themselves—known as the principal) to fund your spending.

- Live within your means. Never spend more than you earn.

- Don't ever sell your land or house, and if at all possible, have no debt on them.

- Frugality is the highest ideal. Don't spoil your children.

The second type of Saver isn't so much driven by fear or the threat of financial ruin, but instead is addicted to watching their savings grow. Sometimes this is because saving was reinforced and heavily praised when they were children or because they had a parent or another role model who saved a lot and whom they wanted to emulate. Or it might be because they saw someone in the past who didn't save and got into trouble, so they vowed not to duplicate that person's behaviors.

One dynamic that often occurs between Savers and their investment advisors is that the clients feel guilty for asking for some of their own money to spend. They feel as if they need to justify spending to appease their guilt or soothe their fear, much as they did to their parents when they were children. One client admitted, "I just hate calling your office to get money transferred. I have to talk myself into picking up the phone, as if I'm a teenager asking a girl out on a date. It's crazy!" Savers who don't have an outside financial advisor often experience this dynamic within themselves, feeling guilty, for example, for making a decision to spend a chunk of their savings on a long-awaited trip.

Sometimes, the Saver archetype is very active in people who have to struggle to make ends meet. In many Latino cultures, for example, there is an ideal of the *buen pobre*, or "good poor person." This term is used to describe someone living in an agricultural society, where there is less available money, who knows how to keep from wasting anything—perhaps making the clothes he wears, resoling his shoes, growing his own food, or walking instead of driving—someone who knows how to manage resources skillfully.

Not all Savers are as focused on frugality as Jeremy, and not all who like to see their savings grow are reluctant to spend. There are many Savers who spend or give away significant amounts each year and don't deprive themselves. However, what makes these people Savers is that they have already accumulated (or inherited) much more than they'll ever spend, or their income each year is much more than their spending and giving. This automatically puts them into accumulation mode. The Saver wants to see his or her financial net worth increasing each year. It is the accumulation and preservation, not the having, giving, or spending of money, that gratifies and appears to calm Savers most of all.

You're probably a Saver if:

- You save more than 20 percent of your earned income each year.

- You spend and give away less than 3 percent of your total financial net worth each year.

- Your net worth grows more than 5 percent from year to year (as you'll see, this metric can also be indicative of an Empire Builder).

THE DARK SIDE OF SAVING

Though our airwaves and newsstands are filled with images of materialism and consumer culture, Savers are the idealized personal finance archetype. A plethora of books have been written to help people become better Savers, including *Rich Dad, Poor Dad, The Automatic Millionaire,* and *The Millionaire*

Next Door. However, as with any archetype, there is a dark side to being a Saver that is rarely discussed by the personal finance experts or even among close friends.

Whether the fear is conscious or not, Savers are almost always afraid that their money might run out one day and leave them poor, alone, or dependent on others. They deal with this profound anxiety by saving, which serves to temporarily dull the intensity of their worry. Fear is by far their greatest motivator; often the people we look to as models of good financial behavior—self-made millionaires, frugal, hard-working families, and people who work and invest to bring themselves out of poverty—are having a difficult time of it on the inside, plagued by fears and anxieties that aren't rational given their significant assets. For these reasons, Savers often can't seem to enjoy the purchases they make for as long as most people, have a difficult time being generous, and don't consider themselves to be relaxed with money—unless they're saving.

As Jeremy and I talked further, I learned that his parents had been constantly worried about running out of money, admonishing him to finish all the food on his plate and to be happy with the clothes he had and not continually want new ones. They would judge other people's spending harshly in front of Jeremy, saying things like, "Look at that new car. What was wrong with their last one? It was only four years old!"

Because what they have in the bank represents so much more than numbers to them, Savers experience tremendous pain when they lose money, a house, or any financial asset that has been equated in their minds with inner security. By way of contrast, other archetypes, especially Pleasure Seekers, Caretakers, Stars, and Idealists, don't attach as much emotional well-being to financial assets. For Savers (and Empire Builders), what they've lost isn't just a financial asset that can be easily replaced; their experience of financial loss is more like facing their own death. When losses occur, most Savers redouble their tried-and-true method of protecting themselves from the pain of living: they commit to saving more, even if they still have more than enough. Savers who learn to pay attention to their inner experience during times like these are able to see that money is not the key to lasting stability. They realize that it can't really give them the deeper security they're yearning for. Though initially a startling revelation, this is ultimately very good news because it frees the Saver from unconsciously striving for more and more money year after year.

THE PAYOFF

Savers experience a rush of good feelings—happiness, relief, or optimism—right after they make a bank deposit, reduce their spending, or make a long-term investment. This is often when they feel most vital, most pleased with themselves, and most able to relax and enjoy the other aspects of their lives. They derive great relief from saving—it is the experience that most often hooks them and that their minds associate with security. However, as with every kind of archetype, this happiness is only temporary, albeit soothing. The Wanting Mind soon enough realizes that survival is still far from ensured, and it wants another pleasurable experience of more security, more abundance, more happiness, and so it looks for a way to save again. This is why there are so many people who from the outside seem to have more than enough money for their needs, but who continue to sock money away in ever-increasing amounts. I have worked with dozens of clients who are addicted to saving, even if they have enough money to sustain their lifestyle for the rest of their and their children's lives. It can be quite an unfortunate prison, and if it doesn't sound like much of a payoff, that's because it's not. The emotional costs of being an extreme Saver often outweigh the financial benefits.

THE NUMBER

What are you hoping your savings will bring you?

Complete the sentence "If only I had saved up $_____, I would be set!" Have there been financial goals like this in the past that you have reached? Did the number change after you reached that goal? Is there actually an amount in savings that will give you the peace you seek, or is your Wanting Mind keeping you in a perpetual state of "not enough"?

BREAKING THE SAVER'S DEATH GRIP

Saving, like many other behaviors discussed in these pages, is a form of futile self-protection that can only go so far. I have helped numerous Savers transform their addictive "save at all costs" habit into a more balanced approach to money. I recall one client whose substantial savings were primarily invested in real estate and stocks, and who insisted on living only off the cash flow generated by these assets, which was quite low. After showing her how much the value of her assets had grown in the past five years, and how much more they'd grow in the future, she was able to loosen up her purse strings and replace her fourteen-year-old car and contribute to her nephew's college education. If you have a strong dose of the Saver inside you but want to reduce its grip on your life, here are three suggestions:

BREAKING THE SAVER'S DEATH GRIP

- **CREATE A NOTICEABLE PAUSE** the next time you experience difficult feelings around money before you take action to alleviate those feelings. Usually, a Saver's response to any financial difficulty is to reflexively save more. Instead of committing to any external strategy, commit instead to a time period of self-reflection, no matter how short—five minutes, an hour, a day, or whatever you can handle. During this pause, be acutely aware of (or write down) the feelings that come up: how uncomfortable you're feeling by not saving, what you would normally do to alleviate your discomfort. It won't be easy because you'll be avoiding the unconscious habit that has served you so well for so many years, and especially because there is so much cultural support and approval of this particular behavior. But if you want a life of freedom instead of unconscious habit, this pause is essential. So the next time you are about to make a deposit in your account, for example, slow it down. What's behind this rush to the bank? It is natural to experience fear, anxiety, or even great panic when you pause. Appreciate the courage it takes to face your feelings. And ask yourself if you might use part of the money to do something else.

- **CALL IN THE PROS.** Visit a fee-only® Certified Financial Planner® (see p. 263) and have them analyze how much you need to save or whether your current savings are already more than ample to sustain your standard of living for the rest of your life. At Abacus, we call this analysis an Enough for Life report because it shows our clients that they will have enough for life even if the Great Depression were to hit tomorrow (a scenario that many Savers and Guardians consider altogether likely!). Being armed with real data that shows you are not going to run out of money even if a national calamity occurs can help calm the Saver's

➤

worries without having to resort to more saving. If in fact you do need to be saving, your financial advisor can help you set up an automatic bank account or payroll deduction program so that you can relax, knowing that the necessary saving is already happening without you having to deliberate over every spending decision.

- **TURN OVER THE MOST TROUBLING TASKS.** Some Savers I've worked with have found the most relief by turning over bill-paying to a trusted spouse or bookkeeper. Sometimes not seeing each and every expense allows you to create the breathing space you need. Similarly, if you find yourself making too many changes to your investments or constantly second-guessing yourself, I recommend empowering a trusted financial advisor or family member to handle the investment decision-making process for you.

- **AUTOMATICALLY SET ASIDE SOME MONEY FOR SPENDING AND GENEROSITY.** Would you be more fulfilled over the long haul if you used less of your money for future accumulation and more for spending on pleasurable purchases, like buying yourself time to do more of the things you love in life? How would it feel to give more generously, whether to charities, neighbors, friends, or family members in need? Set aside some amount of money—$1 a day or $100 a month, whatever feels right to you given your financial and emotional situation—and spend half of it on material objects or experiences that bring you pleasure and fulfillment right now, in this moment (remember, the Saver loves to delay gratification). With the other half, be generous, whatever that means to you. Expect that you're going to have some conflicts; you're going to feel nervous as you spend on yourself or practice generosity. But allow yourself to be nervous, and do it anyway without overthinking. Set this up automatically so you have less of an emotional battle each month as you work to change your savings habit. For example, have your bank or employer automatically transfer your chosen dollar amount into a separate "play" account each month, or do it one time and don't allow yourself to use that account for anything other than generosity or spending that brings you immediate pleasure. Does it feel uncomfortable as you try on these ground-breaking behaviors? Do it anyway!

For more practical recommendations on cash flow and budgeting, investing, insurance, taxes, gifting and estate planning, and philanthropy and generosity that are specifically tailored to the Saver, see the appendix, p. 271.

CHAPTER SEVEN

THE STAR

"No amount of money can make others speak well of
you behind your back."

—CHINESE PROVERB

Isabella is a working actress who lives in Los Angeles and has played supporting roles in four feature films and dozens of commercials. For the last
several years, she's earned a mid-six-figure income, which enables her to rent
a gorgeous four-bedroom house in the Hollywood hills, where she lives with
her husband and her six Persian cats. You can tell at a glance that Isabella
cares a great deal about her image. It's not that she's vain, but she is the first
to admit that in her profession the reality is that how one looks can translate
into being hired or not. As a result, Isabella has had three expensive plastic
surgeries that were not covered by her medical insurance. She often visits a
spa for everything from microdermabrasion to pricey hair coloring. She is a
regular customer at the best clothing stores and spends a significant part of
her income on her appearance. Even on a Saturday morning walk down to
Sunset Boulevard to get a cappuccino, her hair is pulled back in a tight bun
held by a Gucci clip, her sweatsuit is wrinkle-free and fits perfectly, and her
nails are impeccable. "You never know who you might meet," she explains.
She's also active in fundraising for several nonprofit organizations, where
her leadership is instrumental in raising hundreds of thousands of dollars.
Recently, she co-chaired a black-tie charity ball for a local food bank; during the program, the emcee announced that Isabella had pledged a $20,000

gift to the charity. When I saw her the next day, she mentioned with obvious delight that there had been nice coverage of the event, and her gift in particular, in that morning's local paper. Laughing, she admitted, "A little good press never hurt anyone."

On the other end of the spectrum is the boyfriend of a friend of ours. Marc, a smart, gregarious young man, lives and works as a cable installer in Culver City, a middle-class neighborhood of Los Angeles. Marc and his two brothers were raised by a single mother who worked for the Veteran's Administration. Marc is a handsome man, always sharply dressed and clean-shaven. He has a wide circle of friends and admirers. When he's not at work, he's usually decked out in low-riding Tommy Hilfigers, a brand-new pair of Adidas sneakers, and Ray-Bans. When more formal attire is called for, he pulls out one of his five designer suits. He receives a lot of positive recognition for his appearance and seems to believe in the old adage "Clothes make the man." He cruises around town in a new German performance coupe and carries himself with obvious pride. Though his income is not as high as Isabella's, the bulk of it goes to maintaining his appearance. In addition to attending to his image, Marc studied media in college and has aspirations of starting his own media consulting firm. Because of his magnetic personality, several backers have promised him support when he is ready to launch his business.

THE STAR'S CORE STORY

What do Marc and Isabella have in common? Though these two people move in very different social circles, they are both perceived by the outside world as elegant, natural leaders, and have very similar motivations. Whether literally famous or (more often) not, Stars want attention, recognition, significance, respect, or prestige. This craving affects most of their financial decisions, including how much to spend and what to spend it on, what kind of career to have, where to live, and even whom to marry. To put it simply, for Stars, money buys love. This may mean they spend an excessive amount on clothes and beauty, prioritizing their physical attractiveness. Or their financial resources might be directed toward the trappings of success as seen by others: the right address, a fast German sports sedan, making sure their kids are enrolled in the right schools, or having an exclusive club membership. Still other Stars may use their charitable giving, their choice of career, or the neighborhood they live in to impress people and garner social attention.

Things that are not literally necessities *feel* like necessities to Stars. They believe that money is a means to ensure others' respect and admiration, and it is from others that they gain their own sense of identity. Indeed, ours is a celebrity-obsessed culture, and no matter how much we might pay lip service to the idea that what others think of us doesn't matter, most of us are caught up to varying degrees in spending to increase our status, buying ever thinner and more versatile cell phones, the hottest handbag, or the latest model car. Sometimes the image we project does translate into financial gain in the form of being hired for jobs, attracting backers, or drawing other forms of support. But even though we may spend as if we were celebrities, not all of us can actually be celebrities. For those in whom this archetype is dominant, a cycle of spending to be recognized can lead not only to debt but also to a terrible feeling of emptiness.

> **"I don't want to make money. I just want to be wonderful."**
>
> —MARILYN MONROE

You're probably a Star if:

- More than 25 percent of your overall spending goes toward clothing, hair, beauty, jewelry, entertaining, body image enhancement, and other items bought primarily to enhance your image (these could but don't necessarily include cars, furniture, artwork, an elaborate home theater system).

- You seek to be acknowledged for your generosity most of the time.

- You frequently alter your investments to keep up with the latest trends.

SEEDS OF THE STAR—BRING ON THE BLING

Those of us with children know what sophisticated marketing can do. Our children often demand the latest brands of designer clothes, toys, and computers, and aren't satisfied with knockoffs or substitutes. This is because in the hierarchy of childhood society what you own often signals who you are. In many ways, the Star is caught in this childlike state. Effective marketing targets the Star in all of us.

Far from being naïve, however, Stars are in many ways realists. Though it's easy to dismiss the coping strategies of the Star archetype as superficial, the reality of life in the twenty-first century is that people *are* often judged on appearances and rewarded accordingly. Studies have shown that beauty boosts wages. An employee's height and weight also factor in. According to studies conducted by Malcolm Gladwell for his book *Blink,* a poll of half the companies on the Fortune 500 revealed that, on average, male CEOs were just under six feet tall—three inches taller than the average man. Though one would have to go to extraordinary lengths to change one's height, millions of people resort to everything from liposuction to expensive dental procedures to hair replacement surgery to enhance their looks.

What is the root of the Star's focus on external markers of wealth and beauty? Why do Stars continue to be caught in a cycle of hoping money can buy them love or acceptance? The causes are myriad and each person's situation is unique, but the following themes have emerged from the work I've done with my clients. Though these storylines might seem rather obvious, it's amazing how the human mind works to mask the sources of pain.

Many Stars may have suffered very real discrimination in their early lives, based on race, class, or sexual orientation. As a result, they have vowed never to put themselves into situations where others make assumptions about them based on outward appearance. Though the money they accumulate in their adult lives doesn't always protect them, it does offer very real padding in a world where those with wealth call more of the shots.

Still other Stars have some form of the Ugly Duckling syndrome: an experience of feeling unattractive based on a physical condition in childhood, either real or invented. One woman I worked with, the wife of a well-known architect, freely admitted, "I always have to be the most beautiful person in the room!" She goes to great lengths, and great expense, to ensure that she is. Very astute about the origins of her desire, she shared that as a child she was injured in an accident and had to undergo painful reconstructive surgeries, leaving her very insecure about her appearance. Though not everyone's story is this extreme, very often something in the Star's past taught him how painful it is to be judged on appearances.

Finally, the desire for attention from others is usually strongest in people whose childhoods were marked by a strong lack of parental approval, encouragement, or unconditional love. For example, Isabella still winces when she describes how her mother would compare her to the other kids in her class. From the time this attractive, perfectly groomed woman was a young girl, her mother was constantly harping on her looks and her grades, focusing on how Isabella's achievements never measured up to those of the others.

Like all of us, Isabella just wanted to be loved, and when she couldn't get the love or attention she wanted at home, she looked for it from other people in her social circle and career. It is often during painful experiences like these that we make promises to ourselves: "If I can't get attention for being smart, I'll get attention for being cute or beautiful." Isabella did get a lot of positive attention for how beautiful she was, not just from other members of her family but from outsiders as well, who often stopped her mother in the street to remark on how cute she was. She was also extremely talented artistically, having won several awards for her painting. Less secure about her intelligence, she developed a coping strategy to "maximize her assets" by going into a profession where a lot depends on appearance.

Stars were often raised by parents who themselves had a notable lack of self-esteem or who were Stars in their own right and had succeeded in garnering the attention of those around them. These parents were frequently overly concerned with the opinions of other people. They admonished their children to take particular care with their hair or clothes, saying, "You're not going out looking like that, are you?" "What will the neighbors think?" Sometimes parents of Stars, lacking wealth themselves, envy the success of others, instilling in their children a yearning for outer signs of worth.

Stars differ from Pleasure Seekers in that the primary motivator of each financial decision they make is the response of others and not their own sensory enjoyment. Of course, many people are affected by both archetypes at different times. And sometimes our financial decisions may have dual purposes, satisfying two masters, if you will. A new living room set will likely bring us sensory enjoyment in addition to attracting the admiration of others. But those primarily affected by the Star archetype will often endure discomfort for the sake of spending on something that brings them recognition. For example, if Antarctica is the trendy new vacation spot, they will endure hours of uncomfortable travel and subzero temperatures to be able to say they have gone. If painful, expensive plastic surgery will bring them the appearance they crave, they view it as the necessary price to pay.

THE PAYOFF

None of us likes to admit that we enjoy or yearn for the admiration of others; but it's actually quite an innocent human trait. Children crave attention from infancy, and the impulse doesn't change a whole lot—we just get better at disguising it in a grownup package.

Stars have found that receiving this attention is important enough to their sense of self that many of their major life decisions, including their financial decisions, are dictated by it. This attention is the high that gives the Star satisfaction and enjoyment, and so the mind latches onto behaviors with money that impress other people. We all want to repeat the behaviors that get us the payoff we want. For Savers, it's accumulating more and more money. For Pleasure Seekers, it's enjoying something with their senses. And for Stars, it's feeling classy, elegant, cool, or hip among their peers.

Of course, we all enjoy and value the attention of others. The key question is to what extent this yearning affects your financial choices and priorities, and whether you're paying too high a price for it, given the other things that are important to you.

A PAINFUL CHASM

Isabella admitted, "There is a huge rift between what I think of myself and what others think of me. My husband tells me I am beautiful inside and out, but I don't believe him. I sometimes feel trapped in this way of life, but I've always been this way. It's important that I look a certain way because of my career, and yet none of those surgeries really made a difference . . ." Her voice trailed off. It was clear that on some level she felt trapped in this focus on the external. Isabella seems clear on what drives her. So why isn't it easier for her to make a change?

Remember, Core Stories run deep. When we're caught in the Star's grip, there is a chasm that separates our self-image from the public image we project. We want others to see us differently than the way we actually see ourselves. This often applies to money as well. Though some may have ample financial resources, almost all Stars want others to believe they have more money than they do, or that they handle it better than they do. By buying the right clothes, appearing at the right parties, giving to the right charities, and driving the right cars, Stars are often able to get others to believe they are wealthier than they are—which, at least temporarily, helps them feel good.

By the way, being a Star doesn't always mean going with the herd. There are Stars who enjoy the attention they get for rebelling against the establishment, seeming to live on the edge of society. But the counterculture or social underground is still a social circle, and these alternative Stars are still seeking notoriety. They use money, or sometimes a lack of money, to enhance their visibility. I recently learned of a young woman who lives in a small RV—a veritable green home on wheels. She uses the vehicle to travel to peace gatherings and music festivals, with the aim of getting as much press as possible for her dramatic act of voluntary simplicity.

INQUIRE

At the core, most Stars feel a sense of emptiness and worthlessness they're afraid to examine. When you're feeling unhappy, do you look to others to cheer you up, maybe by getting dressed up and going out to a place to see and be seen? Think of the last time you felt a rush of pleasure when someone else paid attention to something about you—perhaps telling you that your outfit looked really good, or that your new flat-panel television was cool, or even that they admired you for a large charitable donation you'd made. Did the experience cause you to crave more of that kind of attention? Did you make any declarations to yourself that might eventually affect your finances? Isabella recently suffered an undermining offhand comment on a set for a movie shot in New York in which she was proposed to with a diamond ring. The casting director loved her work in the engagement scene but commented when she saw the outtakes, "You'll never be a hand model, that's for sure." It was only when I inquired whether the comment had stung that Isabella realized that her subsequent purchase of a sapphire ring had been an attempt to stave off that kind of hurtful criticism.

FREEING THE STAR

Most everyone wants to be loved and accepted just as they are. But when we are caught up in using our money to try to increase the attention, recognition, or admiration that others give us, we are not loving and accepting ourselves. In addition to teaching the importance of honoring one's self, most profound spiritual traditions teach that we are all one at the core. Allowing the Star to run your financial life is a shell game, a way of underscoring your separateness from other people, which is only an illusion. This behavior will not increase either your ability to offer love or your inherent lovability. Neither will it ultimately support your self-esteem.

But change is possible. I have a client, a visual effects producer in Hollywood, who was obsessed with what everyone else thought of her. When the high-pressure L.A. lifestyle became unbearable, she took off for a month to Vietnam to work in a children's orphanage. Through this experience she came to define her contribution as something much broader than before and replaced much of the love and approval she had been seeking from others with a sense of value and self-esteem that emanated from inside herself.

Loving yourself, one of the most important tenets of Eastern spiritual practices, is also one of the hardest things for us humans to do. Yet the love you seek is your birthright, not something that any financial decision can truly give you. If you feel caught or influenced by the Star archetype, I recommend these practices:

FREEING THE STAR

- **BECOME AWARE.** Notice one time in the next few days when you want to buy something or give money away primarily to make others think more highly of you. Be as honest as you can because the real motives of this archetype are usually well masked. Try to figure out what payoff your mind is promising. If you buy that overpriced pair of sunglasses, for example, will you feel more sophisticated, and if so, what feeling lies behind that? Will the latest piece of audio equipment make you feel more techno-savvy? You come up with the examples that fit best, but try to dig a bit deeper to see what's really motivating your actions. As I've said, for most Stars, it's usually an attempt to buy approval or a sense of belonging. Assuming it's not a purchase that is completely self-sabotaging, go ahead and buy the item but keep on examining your motives.

  Pay attention to how your mind reacts in the ensuing twenty-four hours. Are you invested in how people react to you or your new purchase? How long does your interest in the item last? If the purchase doesn't get the desired reaction, do you up the ante by wanting to buy an item that will draw even more attention? Or if you do get the desired reaction, is the payoff as good or as long-lasting as you thought it would be? Continue to do this practice each time you feel that a purchase might be primarily motivated by the Star archetype inside you.

  Once you've identified the deeper motives behind these financial behaviors, they will begin to shift and change. Is there a way for you to receive an even better payoff that doesn't involve money? For example,

  ➤

could you elicit genuine appreciation by showing an older relative how to download music onto his iPod?

- **RESIST THE IMPULSE.** With this greater awareness of what is motivating you, try just once in the next week to resist the impulse to buy an item or give money away in order to improve your image. This may be quite difficult because such behavior has been your protection, your way of feeling good about yourself in the world. Take the perspective of a witness to your own thoughts and feelings. Don't try to respond to the thoughts that come up; just let them wash through you, no matter how urgently they compel you to do something. How long do the thoughts and feelings stay focused on that purchase or gift you were considering? Does another item or action intended to fill the same need quickly replace it?

- **GIVE UP YOUR SHTICK.** *Shtick* is a Yiddish word that literally means an "entertainer's routine." Where is your shtick most powerful when it comes to money? Be brutally honest about this. What's something financial that's been hard to admit to other people? It might be something about how you spend, an investment failure, a hidden secret in your family business, your income or savings level, or how much debt you have. For Isabella, it was realizing that she still felt ugly on the inside, despite the many thousands she invested each month in her outer appearance. For Marc, it was the realization that his car payment was eating up half his monthly income and making him rather less than the success he wanted to project. There is no need to change anything about your own shtick right now. Just be aware of this truth you've been hiding. Write it down and post it somewhere you can see it so you can't keep pushing it under the rug.

- **STEP OUT OF YOUR COMFORT ZONE.** When you feel that the time is right, and you are not just following what you "should do," find a way to behave differently in regards to your charitable giving. For example, you might choose to go to a place where you are unlikely to meet anyone you know, where no one will judge you on appearances, and spend some time volunteering and giving of yourself. As author and teacher David Deida says, "When you want more, give more." Perhaps you will choose to visit a retirement home, an animal shelter, or the burn unit at a children's hospital. Give not money but just a little bit of your time, and don't tell a soul about it.

(continued on next page) ➤

FREEING THE STAR *(continued from previous page)*

• **SEEK THE TRUTH.** What do you know about yourself when it comes to money that you actually don't want to know? Maybe you know that you are giving more money to charity than you can really afford but wouldn't be giving anything if no one knew about it. Maybe you are addicted to designer labels because you want others to see you as hip and prosperous. Or perhaps you live in a house that's way beyond your means because you want to be able to throw the most talked about dinner parties in town. If you're really courageous, pick one person to share this truth with. For most Stars, being honest about their hidden agenda defuses the need to act that agenda out. This is especially true if they are able to find other ways to nurture their self-esteem. It's as if just speaking about their motivations robs the behavior of its power. This truth-telling allows them to then channel their resources toward things that will create more balance and lasting fulfillment in their lives—toward retirement, for example, instead of purchasing a bigger house. When Marc began looking into his Core Story, he realized that all the money he was spending to try to appear successful in his neighborhood and social circle was actually sabotaging his efforts to launch his media consulting firm. When he began to gradually redirect his spending, it only took six months before he was able to leave his job installing cable and go into business for himself.

For more practical recommendations on cash flow and budgeting, investing, insurance, taxes, gifting and estate planning, and philanthropy and generosity that are specifically tailored to the Star, see the appendix, p. 273.

CHAPTER EIGHT

THE INNOCENT

"Procrastination and instant gratification are the two biggest reasons people don't save. There is a very real issue with lack of knowledge in our country. Money is very mysterious and complex to people, and when something is that complex, they tune it out."

—Carrie Schwab-Pomerantz,
chief strategist, Consumer Education,
Charles Schwab & Co., Inc., and president,
Charles Schwab Foundation

Mary was a massage therapist who worked out of a chiropractor's office two days a week and saw as many private clients as she could on her days off. One weekend she attended my Yoga of Money workshop. After the workshop, the thirty-six-year-old came up to me and said, "When you were talking about the unconscious Core Story and how it can get its own way and keep us stuck in the same pattern with money forever, I knew you were talking about me. But I also felt really hopeless. Doing bodywork is my third job in four years. Before that I was a receptionist and, before that, a personal trainer, but no matter which profession I go into or how much I make, I can't seem to get out of debt or afford many of the things I really want."

I studied her worried face and said, "That must be incredibly frustrating." Then I inquired, "Why do *you* think you're in this position?"

"I don't know," she said quietly. "Money has always been a struggle for me. Even when I have a good month, it just seems to disappear so quickly. Last year, when I was working two jobs, my car's transmission went out, and there went what little savings I had."

THE INNOCENT'S CORE STORY

Mary is just one example of the Innocent. There are Innocents who have eked out a living in the same job for thirty years and others who have had over a million dollars in savings at one time or another. But it's not about how much money they do or don't have. The common thread is that all Innocents have been unable to master money to the extent necessary to create long-term financial self-sufficiency.

For many people in our culture, the focus, attention, and linear thinking required to make and manage money aren't as developed as other important traits, like intuition, artistic creativity, social activism, the ability to do academic research, pursue religious and spiritual studies, or simply to relax and have fun. There are millions of people who feel stranded in our present-day economic system because the areas in which they're naturally gifted are not financially rewarding.

Unlike Idealists, Innocents aren't necessarily against money or the financial system, but they have an ongoing experience of "not enough" and are confused by money. Those who have had money can't seem to hold on to it. Those who haven't had it feel like they never will.

The Wanting Mind is especially active in Innocents. They want more money to make ends meet, but they often have different passions and skills than those valued by the financial system. Innocents often avoid money because it's not a strength of theirs. "I'm just not good with money," they'll say, or "I can't hold on to it." Those who identify with most of the other archetypes have created a Core Story as a response to their frustration, fear, or anger. For example, Savers rely on their habits to feel secure and safe, and Guardians turn to compulsive behaviors, constantly analyzing their financial affairs in the hope of finding some reassurance. The Innocent has no such financial coping strategy, and so he or she experiences difficult feelings about money more often and more acutely than other people. Innocents' suffering can be quite close to the surface and even visible to others.

You're probably an Innocent if:

- You've had personal debt (not counting a mortgage or car loan) for more than a year and have less than three months of living expenses in savings.

- Life circumstances such as illness or disability, or lack of education or training, have you in a position where you can't make ends meet.

- You're in a never-ending struggle for survival, spending everything you make—even if you make a lot—on your lifestyle.

- You received a lump-sum payment from an inheritance, lottery winnings, a divorce, a job, or another one-time event in the past ten years, and now have little or nothing to show for it.

- You'd rather get a root canal without anesthesia than balance your checkbook, pay your bills, and write down your expenses.

- You pay the bank more in monthly charges and overdraft fees than they pay you in interest.

WHAT THE INNOCENT BELIEVES

Innocents aren't necessarily penniless or on government assistance, although some may be. However, Innocents either cannot attract money or, if they do attract it, cannot keep it. Many are living paycheck to paycheck, are in chronic debt, or live at a much lower standard of living than they would like to. They unconsciously believe that they aren't going to have an abundant financial life, whether due to messages and ideas about themselves they adopted as children, or just because they do not possess economically valued skills. They have little or no surplus with which to make enjoyable purchases, give generously, or save.

I recall asking one client, a middle-aged general contractor, to imagine himself earning more than enough money for his family's needs and actually having $10,000 saved up. He said, "I can't picture it. I feel like I'd have to be someone I'm not in order to make enough money for that—either a phony or incredibly lucky." Innocents don't feel competent or capable when it comes to managing money, and for many, this feeling of ineptitude extends to earning enough money as well.

THE INNOCENT'S MONEY MANTRAS

If you are an Innocent, changing your relationship to money may seem like a tall order. Money mystifies Innocents. This group has not been trained at all to earn, save, or understand money. Their unconscious mind has internalized messages like "I don't have enough financial smarts to get my money situation together" or "Life's too short to worry about money" or "I'm hanging in there" or "There is never enough" or "Let someone else worry about it." These thoughts often don't register consciously, but they act as powerful barriers to financial success.

Most Innocents don't feel like they have the ability to change their situation. They often feel they should have the ability, but unconsciously they feel they just don't have the power to change things for themselves. Many wish that good luck or grace would bring them a financial windfall or raise so they could get out of debt and have a nice nest egg saved up. But underneath the fantasy is a deep-seated belief that they're simply not going to be able to build a stable financial foundation for themselves.

Because of this, Innocents are the most likely group to participate in lotteries and multilevel marketing. Their frustration with their situation is often so desperate that these get-rich quick schemes offer an attractive quick fix. Unfortunately, most of these endeavors only serve to deepen Innocents' lack of confidence in themselves, as well as exacerbating their sense of financial failure. Occasionally, there are Innocents who do win the lottery, sign professional sports and entertainment contracts, inherit, or even make a lot of money from their profession. But the lucky few who manage to do well financially end up back in exactly the same sparse financial predicament they were in before their windfall, nine times out of ten, because that's where their unconscious mind feels they belong. This is unfortunate, but the good news is that with just a few of the right tools, no matter what your history with money has been, you can earn and keep money, and even grow wealthy if that's what you want. This book will share these tools with you.

SEEDS OF THE INNOCENT

What distinguishes Innocents is that they have a really hard time either attracting or keeping money. They tend not to value their own positive attributes—such as the ability to care for children or the elderly, or their compassion and empathetic qualities—as highly as they might. Given that earning money is such a high priority in our culture, this is not surprising.

Mary, the massage therapist, told me, "Well, we never really had any money. We didn't spend that much, but there still wasn't enough coming in. One of my first memories of money was when I was about six years old. We were driving home from my grandmother's house, and when we pulled up to our building, there were two men standing at the front door. They were sent by the bank to repossess our car. They took it away that day, and for the next six months, my Dad had to get a ride to work with someone else, or take the bus."

"Do you remember how you reacted to that?" I asked.

"I felt that people like us would just never have money, like the odds were against us no matter what we tried or how hard we worked. It made me feel hopeless, I guess, and kind of scared. A couple of my friends went on to have successful careers and financially stable lives—they were always told by their parents and teachers that they could do it. I just never felt that way about myself, and still don't. I want to have money, but it feels out of my reach."

Some Innocents can attract money just fine but can't keep it. I had a client who earned over a million dollars a year as a personal injury lawyer, but couldn't figure out how to hold on to any significant portion of it. When we discussed the main lessons he had been taught about money when growing up, he said, "In my family, a great education and career were valued above all else. No one ever taught me how to manage my money. So now I earn enough, but I don't save or invest any of it." Even though this attorney received an excellent education, not having learned the basics of money management came back to haunt him.

Parents who feel stuck with whatever financial hand they've been dealt are often unable to teach their children and adolescents these basics. One client told me that no one had ever taught her to balance her checkbook. When she was younger, she went through a long period when her finances were a mess. Her bank account would get overdrawn, and since she couldn't sort through the tangle of checks, bills, and overdrafts, she would just close the account and open another one elsewhere. Eventually, after a few closed accounts, she realized that this behavior wasn't helping her get what she really wanted: clarity about how much she made, how much she had in her account, and how much she could afford to spend. With help, she began to focus her attention on answering these questions in a practical way and in time was able to create much more financial stability for herself.

Innocents, remember, are not always poor. Some clients I've worked with have inherited substantial amounts of money or are still being supported by their parents. In either case (and especially if they're female), they are often given messages of financial inadequacy: "Don't worry about money, sweetheart. We'll make sure you're always taken care of." Even if nothing is said overtly, the fact that the heads of the family are so gifted with money often leads the children and grandchildren, both male and female, to avoid financial matters. This is why almost all inherited wealth disappears within two generations. In other situations, children of parents who were successful but abusive or unloving often unwittingly become Innocents as a form of rebellion.

THE PAYOFF

As I said earlier, people who identify with this archetype suffer a great deal when it comes to money, so it's hard to imagine there being any payoff at all for them. But on closer examination, there are a few.

Many Innocents receive a lot of attention for their suffering and for the difficult plight the world has thrust upon them. Innocents are often victims, whether of abusive spouses, addictions, a string of really bad luck, discrimination, or lack of education. Because these situations are often so horrific, being in the role of the victim who is pitied is the only positive (if perverse) payoff. Other Innocents become financially dependent on another person, without any overt agreement as to the terms of this arrangement. One woman I know, Miriam, lived in the guest cottage of a wealthy friend for years in exchange for some gardening work that was never clearly defined. Miriam knew her friend was becoming anxious about the situation, and she was too, but neither knew how to broach the subject. This kind of ambiguity can offer a short-term payoff in the form of the Innocent not having to face the underlying beliefs and choices that have led to his or her current situation. On some level, it's nice to be taken care of, to avoid having to do the difficult work of taking care of ourselves. Being in dependent relationships in which there is no clear and equitable arrangement, though, can lead to Innocents being further hurt. In Miriam's case, her friend lashed out at her one day, accusing her of being a "freeloader" when all along she had thought she was cultivating a wonderful garden as informally agreed.

Last, there's the payoff of avoiding dealing with money: avoiding facing how much one spends and how much one earns and what changes one would need to make to be free. Staying in the dark, Innocents don't have to face their fears of inadequacy, confusion, or incompetence. To Savers, Guardians, and Empire Builders, for whom looking at this data is a necessity or even enjoyable, the Innocent's avoidance behavior seems insane. I can't emphasize enough how much courage, support, and self-love it takes to be willing to look at the truth of our financial situation, whatever it is. This truth-seeking requires that we be willing to question our beliefs about money and face the feelings these beliefs protect us from. That's when change and healing can begin.

GET COMFORTABLE WITH MONEY

The fact that you have acted like an Innocent in the past doesn't mean you have to be stuck doing so in the future. Think about it this way: if you had experienced different conditioning in your life—if your parents had given you different messages about money, if you had received some kind of financial education, and if, instead of failing when you tried your hand at making and managing money, you had succeeded—might you have adopted an entirely different self-image from the one you have? If so, how would your relationship to money look today?

Transforming an archetype that's had a hold on you is hard work. You may even feel a bit sick to your stomach as you do the exercises that follow. But I'm asking you to face your demons squarely and not be distracted. As many a meditation teacher has said, "Whatsoever we resist, persists." But if you look truthfully at the beliefs running your financial life, you can transform them. There are a number of ways to integrate other, more rewarding approaches to money.

FREEING THE INNOCENT

• **INQUIRE.** Are your beliefs about money true? I'm going to ask you to begin by thinking about the ideas, concepts, or thoughts you have about yourself and money.

Here are a few examples of beliefs that Innocents sometimes hold:

I'll be in my current financial situation forever.

I'll never earn more than I'm earning now.

I'll never be able to retire because of the hand that life has dealt me.

I'm never going to have enough money to support myself or my family.

I'm stuck in this marriage/job/town because of money.

Now write your own list without passing judgment. For at least sixty seconds just keep writing whatever comes to mind. Don't censor anything, even if you think "That's not really my belief" after you write it down. Just make a nice, long list. Don't feel you have to be spiritual, smart, respectable, or mature as you write. Just free-associate and let it rip.

Now look at what you've written. I invite you to use each of the four questions author Byron Katie gives us (first presented on p. 87) to question your beliefs one at a time:

Is the belief true? Is it any more true than its opposite? For example is "I will never be successful" any more true than "I will be successful"?

Can you be absolutely certain that your belief is true?

What reaction do you have when you think that thought? What happens in your body?

Who might you be without that concept or belief about money?

For example, when Mary the massage therapist did this exercise, she came up with the following thought: "I will never get ahead when it comes to money." When she examined this belief, she came to these conclusions:

➤

Yes, it seems true because I haven't ever in the past. But I guess there's really no telling the future.

I can't be certain this is true.

When I think this thought, I feel very sad and tired. I have very little energy, and my limbs feel weak. I have a sense of heaviness.

Without that thought, I feel happier. Less tired. I have more energy to take on more clients! I feel lighter and might even make a better living.

- **HONOR YOUR CURRENCY, WHATEVER IT IS.** For many Innocents, it really is not about the money. Their currency might be creativity, compassion, activism, scholarship, or service. What is it that you love to do? Don't sacrifice your natural gift to fit into an economic mold. You can create a plan that allows you to feel peace and abundance at your current level of income, whatever that is. Here are some options:

  Create an overt understanding with your spouse or partner (or perhaps other relationships) that acknowledges that your gifts are not financially remunerative. Agree on other ways in which you can contribute to the marriage or relationship that feel balanced to you both.

  Learn the truth of your financial situation. Then, to the extent that you can, make the changes necessary to live within your means. These changes may seem radical at first, but so will the feeling of being financially free! For one couple, this meant trading their $500,000 home in Los Angeles for a $150,000 home in Silver City, New Mexico so that she could keep teaching tai chi and he could do hospice work with terminally ill patients. Or it might mean a willingness on your part to live within a budget so you can take a job or switch to a career that may not pay as well but leaves you with ample time to pursue your noneconomic passions. Begin by writing down at least five radical steps you could take after which you would be living within your means. If you don't yet know what your means are or what type of lifestyle change would keep you within them, then engage an hourly Certified Financial Planner® or a credit counselor from the nonprofit organization Consumer Credit Counseling Services (see p. 264) to help with the analysis.

  Follow the steps outlined in the section on the Pleasure Seeker archetype to reduce your spending and set up an automatic

(continued on next page) ➤

FREEING THE INNOCENT *(continued from previous page)*

investment plan (see p. 246). Remember, you can live an abundant financial life on any income or assets, even $10,000 per year. (Read *Your Money or Your Life*, by Joe Dominguez and Vicki Robin, for a radical but no-nonsense approach to living within your means, no matter how small.)

- **WHAT COMES IN STAYS IN.** The next time you have a surplus, even if you're still in debt, leave a period of at least three days between receiving the money and sending it back out. Most Innocents actually feel discomfort having a surplus around, so just as soon as it comes in they send it off to pay their bills or reimburse family members who lent them money recently, or they make a new purchase they've been putting off. Of course, if you're literally about to be evicted or some other drastic consequence will ensue, do what you need to do. But barring that, hold on to the money for at least three days, preferably a week. Imagine having an entire year's worth of your expenses in savings and no debt. Think or write about the good feelings: the relief, the confidence, the freedom. What about the difficult issues: do you feel unworthiness, discomfort, confusion, or unfamiliarity?

- **MAKE IT UNTOUCHABLE.** Pick an amount to save each month, no matter how small (yes, even five dollars a month), and invest your savings in a completely separate account from the one you use for your usual income and expenses. Do this by having your bank set up an automatic transfer. This will lower the temptation to see an excess and spend it down. If that doesn't work, have a trusted family member or investment advisor act as a barrier between you and the money so that you don't think of it as yours. Don't even look at the statements. If you still find yourself spending more than you earn by using credit cards, resort to using only cash for all your expenses and make the cuts that will allow you to have a real surplus. This is not a sacrifice. This is saying no to a lifestyle that is in direct conflict with your soul's deepest yearning or just your own common sense. Your aim is to express your gifts with ease and without financial pressure.

For more practical recommendations on cash flow and budgeting, investing, insurance, taxes, gifting and estate planning, and philanthropy and generosity that are specifically tailored to the Innocent, see the appendix, p. 275.

CHAPTER NINE

THE CARETAKER

"It doesn't matter how much you have or haven't, just the burden of having to hand out money all the time can be hard on the psyche."

—DAVID WHYTE,
POET AND ORGANIZATIONAL CONSULTANT

Brenda is a middle-aged, down-to-earth mother of five who has a toughness about her born of hardship. A self-proclaimed survivor, she retained me to help her manage her financial affairs several years after going through a difficult divorce. She had a higher tax refund than she'd expected, and instead of spending it on her family, she decided to treat herself to some professional advice. Brenda prided herself on keeping up with the latest trends in business. But when she came to her first appointment, her financial paperwork was noticeably disorganized, although she made it clear that she had always managed to make ends meet. She was doing so now, despite the fact that two of her grown children, along with their four children, were living with her in her three-bedroom house. Brenda went on to tell me about her ex-husband and his financial indiscretions. He was a gambler, an avid bettor on professional football and basketball games; as a result, during their marriage he had racked up tens of thousands of dollars in debt to his bookies, which was one reason she had sought the divorce.

As Brenda spoke, it became clear that she had a long-standing pattern of being the financially responsible partner. Whether it was with her ex-husband, her grown-up children, or her friends, Brenda always came through for others financially.

Later on, after we'd been working together for a while, I asked whether she found it problematic to be the financial caretaker for the people in her life.

"Are you joking?" she blurted out. "All my life I've been helping people out. I resent it, but what can I do? They're family." I asked her if she'd be willing to tell me a little about how she'd been raised when it came to money. "For as long as I can remember," she said, "my parents fought about money. My mother used to yell at my dad that he was wasting our money at the track. He was always betting on the horses when the gas bill was overdue. My dad would yell back that what he did with his money wasn't any of her business. And my mother? She spent on stuff we didn't really need." Brenda paused, and shifted her normally direct gaze to a spot on the ceiling. "By the time I was ten years old, I was taking any cash I could find in their wallets or stashed around the house and going to the post office to get money orders to pay the bills. This way, my parents couldn't spend it or gamble it away." The irony of having married a man just like her father wasn't lost on her. She thought it would be different for her, but was in her words, "blinded by love." Brenda expressed to me how badly she now wanted to get her kids out of her house. She was extremely tired of all the responsibility, but didn't know who would help support her children and grandchildren if she didn't.

THE CARETAKER'S CORE STORY

Caretakers use their money, time, and energy to assist their immediate family members and often extend that help to friends. In fact, some sacrifice themselves financially for the success of others, even if those people aren't financially dependent on them. One Caretaker I know quite well is always coming to the aid of various family members, paying for one to go on a much-needed vacation, helping another buy a car, and working a dead-end corporate job she hates so that her lover can pursue his entrepreneurial dreams. Caretakers put the needs of others before their own and occasionally believe that the people who rely on them financially would be destitute without their help. Often the circumstances of those they take care of are dire indeed, and Caretakers can end up paying for everything from grocery bills and rent to electric bills.

Not all Caretakers direct their energies to caring for family members or friends. Those with a more broadly humanitarian perspective sacrifice their own financial stability to help the underprivileged in general. They devote their time and money to support causes they feel will benefit mankind. They're employed in fields such as health care or social work, putting in extremely long hours, for which they aren't highly compensated. Or they may give a disproportionate amount of their money to the poor in developing countries, to AIDS research, or to the environmental movement, perhaps believing that the importance of contributing to their own Roth IRA, for example, pales in comparison to saving the rainforests.

Often, Caretakers have incredible gifts. For one, they usually have their financial lives much more in order than those around them. Caretakers are not only self-sufficient, but they are "other sufficient," meaning that others can depend on them financially. Regardless of how painful or destructive some of their relationships might seem, especially to outside observers, at their core Caretakers are likely to exhibit more than their fair share of compassion, empathy, and generosity. We have all needed to be taken care of at one time or another. And without Caretakers, the world would be an uglier, harsher place.

WHAT THE CARETAKER BELIEVES

Like Idealists, Caretakers are not interested in money for its own sake, believing that its best use is sharing with and caring for other people. At times, as in the case of a client of mine who will continue to provide for his special-needs child for decades to come, Caretakers indeed do not have a choice in the matter. The people who rely on you financially may really need you and have very few if any other options. Their very lives may depend on you, and this is a profound responsibility that no amount of meditation or positive thinking can (or should) erase. If you fall into this category, your thoughts run something like this: "If I don't hold it together, no one will." "They need me." "Lean on me." "What would they do without me?" Your beliefs, you feel, are less beliefs than facts.

Whether or not those you help truly don't have other options, you tend, as a Caretaker, to view your own financial well-being as secondary to the well-being of others. This chapter will help both voluntary and involuntary Caretakers experience more freedom when it comes to money, as well as better relationships with those they are helping.

Caretakers tend to see themselves as generous, and very often they do give away more than other archetypes would consider prudent to help people in need. Sometimes, though, their behavior arises not out of a generous impulse, but rather out of a feeling of necessity or obligation or a deep desire to be needed. Caretakers have a hard time spending money on themselves, and when they do, they may feel disproportionately guilty about it because others need it more.

You're probably a Caretaker if:

• You spend more than 20 percent of your income on others in need, either family members, friends, or charities, but you're not financially generous with yourself and don't feel a sense of ease about your generosity.

• Other people in aggregate are more financially dependent on you than you are on them, and there isn't some other exchange that's reciprocal (e.g., child-rearing, homemaking, engagement in a humanitarian or creative profession).

• Your total savings amount to less than six times your monthly spending because you're always using money to take care of others.

• If you have investments, you keep them liquid because you are thinking that you will likely have to rescue someone.

SEEDS OF THE CARETAKER: "HE'S NOT HEAVY ..."

Those living out the Caretaker archetype were often put in the role of caring for others early in life, like Brenda. They may have been the eldest in their families, the "responsible one," or the child of parents who were irresponsible with money. They may be the only ones in their families to have succeeded financially, whether rising out of difficult circumstances or, in a well-to-do family, being the one chosen to receive the best education or training in the family business. As such, they carry a form of survivor's guilt and, to appease that guilt, take on the role of savior in their families. Many Caretakers have a fear of not being needed. Growing up, they were much more likely to be told "Thanks, you saved the day" than "I can see you had a hard day—what can I do for you?"

Remember, we all develop behavior patterns because they are the most intelligent responses to key events or conditions in our upbringing. Far from being fools duped into caring more for others than they do for themselves, Caretakers have made the most intelligent choice they could. Early on, they recognized the necessity of taking care of others as a way to thrive themselves. In extreme cases, their life circumstances forced them to take care of people who, without this care, might have otherwise perished: the handicapped child, the chronically depressed parent, the abused friend.

In some situations, others may be financially dependent on Caretakers simply because they don't have skills that are rewarded financially in the world. Or they may have their own gifts to give but the Caretaker, because of love or a familial relationship, doesn't feel resentful about what he is providing. If the caretaking given these people is not a repetitive pattern in the Caretaker's life and the giving feels reciprocal, this is a healthy relationship, and the Caretaker will naturally feel good about it.

THE PAYOFF

Being a Caretaker can be a beautiful thing, especially when it comes to using money to help others. Caretakers' empathy, caring, and sharing of themselves and their resources are traits that many of the other archetypes would do well to emulate. If you are a Caretaker, you should indeed be proud of the loving attention you devote to your fellow human beings.

Many spiritual traditions teach the importance of giving:

- Like many other Native American traditions, the Lakota tradition teaches generosity as one of seven important virtues. *Wopila* is the ceremonial act of giving away things that are precious to the giver, especially when much has been given to us, such as at the birth of a child or a wedding.

- The Talmud compels us to tithe at least 10 percent of our annual income.

- Hinduism teaches a spiritual path of selfless service, or karma yoga, in which we give of ourselves (whether through work service or financial contributions) without expecting anything in return.

- The Bible says, "It is better to give than to receive."

- Islam places a strong emphasis on charity as a means of balancing injustice in society, both formally, in the form of *zakat* (tithing) and informally, in the practice of *sadaqat* (spontaneously giving to those in need).

- In Buddhism, *dana,* which means generosity, is understood as the natural condition of the human heart, which manifests spontaneously when misunderstanding is cleared away.

WE ARE ALL ENTITLED

Ram Dass, popular Hindu teacher and author of *Be Here Now*, was born Richard Alpert, the son of a prominent Boston family. Ram Dass's father had made his fortune in the railroad industry and was instrumental in founding Brandeis University. Like other holy people throughout the ages, Ram Dass left his family's wealth behind in favor of a life of service to others. He gave most of his wealth to the poor, worked on many humanitarian projects, including restoring sight to many people in rural Asia, Africa, and Latin America, and encouraged his father to give generously as well. Interestingly, even Ram Dass freely admits that it isn't always easy to extend the same kindness to yourself. After suffering a stroke in 1997, he found himself on the receiving end of the charity he had mostly given in his life. His friend, author Wayne Dyer, sent a letter to millions of people requesting help for Ram Dass, and he received an outpouring of money to help with his expenses. Ram Dass shared with me that despite his years of spiritual study and practice, receiving this generosity made him feel ashamed. In striving to understand this archetype, we might ask, "Why would this gentle, generous man, after all his years of service, consider himself less entitled than the poor people to whom he had given so much?"

"I had always identified myself with the rich," he told me. That kind of conditioning, those divisions between those who are supposed to give help and those who receive help are hard to erase.

Many of us deal with a feeling of shame about our relative affluence by giving money away to worthy causes. But we can also give out of a sense of compassion and interconnectedness with other people. For Caretakers to truly make a difference in the world, care must begin at home, in their own treatment of themselves. As the Buddhists say, do not take that which is not given freely, but *do* accept with grace that which is freely given.

The payoff of healthy giving can be enormous, even in terms of material gain for the giver. Many who give generously of their time and resources report that they have received back tenfold or more what they've given. Many highly evolved spiritual people grew up in wealthy families but chose to give all they own to the needy to pursue a life without possessions. Famous examples from history include Saint Francis, the Buddha, and Mahatma Gandhi, each of whom renounced a privileged upbringing and affluence to devote himself to a spiritual life that included helping the poor.

But most of us are far from being saints, and striving for sainthood can be quite a trap. If you haven't given sufficient attention to uncovering the source of the emptiness or longing that motivates unhealthy martyrdom, your caretaking may not be helping to create balance or lasting fulfillment for you.

If their giving isn't rife with guilt or other codependencies, Caretakers derive a tremendous sense of self-worth from the vital role they play in others' well-being. Hearing someone say, "I couldn't have done it without you"— whether "it" is getting through college, buying a house, or surviving a difficult divorce—is often a Caretaker's greatest reward. Caretakers do provide invaluable help without which their loved ones and other dependents would have to make drastic changes, and knowing this is a significant payoff.

THE DARK SIDE OF CARETAKING

At its most extreme, caretaking depletes the Caretaker to the point of no return. They unconsciously seek out situations where they are needed, where they can take care of people who are not as financially able as they are. Eventually, feeling depleted or just unthanked, they often begin to feel entitled to the devotion and caretaking of others. But because they have not created reciprocal relationships, they rarely receive the nurturing or caretaking they yearn for.

Caretakers tend to think that those they support are not as competent or generous when it comes to handling money. They think that by providing a loan or money to help pay expenses, they are helping their children, family, or friends, but this help doesn't really serve the other. It enables others to be dependent on them, whether by paying an adult child's rent or loaning money to a sibling who never pays it back but asks for more the next time a crisis rolls around. Because of their "selfless" generosity and all they've sacrificed, Caretakers get to play the martyr. They may stock up on points that they later cash in on with the loved ones they helped. This quid pro quo may take the form of verbal or emotional abuse, sexual demands, or an expectation of financial payback. Or it can be as quiet and masked as a sense of moral superiority and purity.

If you suspect that you are going overboard with caretaking, ask yourself this: Who are you really helping? Why are you giving of yourself and your money, and what exactly do you expect in return? Enabling behavior creates dependencies that are very hard to break. You may think you're helping your children, family, and friends when you give or loan them money or pay their expenses, but are you really? If the people you assist financially always know they can turn to you to bail them out in times of need, it will be much harder for them to learn to care for themselves and create healthy financial lives. Think about the old saying "Give a man a fish, and he eats for a day. Teach a man to fish, and he eats for life." In what ways can you gradually help your dependents begin to care for themselves? In what ways are you conditioning them to be dependent, just as you were conditioned to become a Caretaker?

In my experience, the vast majority of Caretakers are women. Globally, women have many more dependents than men, especially in developing countries where, on average, a mother has financial and caregiving responsibility for a family of five. In my practice, I've seen a wide variety of female caretaking, including encouraging or allowing adult children to live at home without contributing to expenses, supporting but resenting a spouse who gives up paid employment to pursue an unpaid vocational dream, allowing friends of the family to move in for many years at no cost, buying a house out of guilt for an old college roommate, volunteering more time than they have to give for the school or other causes, or impulsively gifting or loaning large sums of money to causes or family members in need.

Though Caretakers are frequently women, men also take on this role. Male Caretakers are often the sole breadwinners in their families, shouldering the financial burden along with the power that being the financial provider often brings. Too often in my business, I have seen male patriarchs disempower their children, particularly their female children, creating dependence for decades to come. I once worked with the daughter of such a Caretaker, an extremely wealthy entrepreneur who provided for all his children's financial needs and then wondered why they seemed to have little ambition or drive. His daughter was forty-seven years old when she came to me. Her father, who had passed away many years before, had released her younger brother's trust when he was twenty-one, but the provisions of her trust ensured that she would never have control of it and would have to justify her requests for money to a corporate trustee after her father's death. She bitterly complained, "He never thought I'd be able to handle the responsibility without being overwhelmed, taken advantage of, or blowing the money."

TRUTHFULNESS

In the yoga sutras, *Asteya* means truthfulness, a practice of inquiring deeply into the truth of any situation. Get yourself to a place where you can be very, very still, away from others and without distractions. Breathing deeply in and out, reflect on all the ways you exhibit caretaking in your expenditures of time and money. Choose three people or organizations that are the focus of your care-taking and, for each, ask yourself these questions:

1. What is the truth of this situation?

2. Did I feel a little resentful of or underappreciated for my giving?

3. What, if anything, did I overtly or covertly expect in return?

4. In the process of giving, did I put myself in a precarious position financially?

5. Did I use my giving to cover over painful feelings or self-images?

Sometimes Caretakers are trying to make amends for something they feel guilty about, whether appropriately or not. For example, a Caretaker who is financially dependent on her spouse may in turn give excessively to people she sees as less fortunate. The only sibling in a family to have been put through college may feel obligated to help his less financially successful brothers and sisters. But until we learn to truly care for ourselves, we cannot meaningfully care for others. Until we derive a sense of identity that is not primarily dependent on our relationships with others, we cannot really take care of anyone.

Whenever we derive too much of our self-worth and identity from the others we help, we are trying to stave off the feelings of worthlessness or fear that are an inevitable part of being human. We fill our lives with the demanding (and seemingly important) work of making sure our family and those we love are well provided for and safe. But what happens when they move on, either through death or simply a change in life direction? It is essential that Caretakers learn to treat themselves at least as well as they treat everyone else.

The exercises in this chapter are extremely simple, take very little time, and yet can be more profoundly helpful to Caretakers than a week on a Caribbean cruise! In the spirit of self-care, please try them.

NOT DOING

Caretakers are so accustomed to being with others that they often don't allow themselves time alone—time when they are not needed by anyone else. Make a habit of carving out some time for yourself each day to enjoy the pleasure of your own company, even if only for five minutes at first. You may decide to take a solitary walk or go for a drive and listen to music. If you're at someone else's party or house, try to not be one of the more helpful people there—doing the dishes, refreshing drinks, tidying up, or whatever form your care usually takes. Allow yourself to be in relationship without being needed. Regardless of the activity, allow and notice your feelings, whatever they are. You may experience the fear of loneliness or isolation, or you may experience simple joy. When fears or anxieties do arise, focus on your breathing and try to notice what's on the other side of the fear. Or, if you are feeling good, bask in that and carry it into the rest of your day.

A DIFFERENT KIND OF CARETAKING

The way out of unhealthy caretaking is not to become a cold, callous person who cares for no one else, which is what many Caretakers fear they must do. I am by no means asking you to just stop caring for the people and causes in your life that are so important to you. But I am suggesting that you can help them much more effectively if there is a balance between your care of them and your care of yourself.

One of the first things I ask Caretakers to do is to recognize that, however real the situation that created their responses, they have been conditioned to behave as they do. When Caretakers fully realize that they are products of their conditioning, they can begin to explore different ways of showing concern for their loved ones. Simply imagining a different set of past experiences allows us to see how different our choices might be today. For example, what if you had been cared for in a stable financial environment, where no one was dependent on you and there was no guilt? What if you'd felt more cherished and given to? Stepping back and asking yourself "How did I get here?" can help to move you out of a rut.

IT CAN BE DONE

I once worked with an inheritor whose money had come to her late in life, and who tended not to regard it as her own. When she discovered that her best friend was being verbally and physically abused by her husband, my client invited her friend and her young child to stay rent-free in a condo she owned. Although my client had intended it as a temporary arrangement because she relied on the rental income from the property, the arrangement dragged on and on.

I helped my client set up transitional benchmarks. Giving her friend plenty of notice, she first asked for half-rent, then full rent after six months. Her friend was able to adjust to the new arrangement, and though it was difficult and she eventually moved to a less expensive place, they remained friends. The hardest part was helping my client to see how generous she had really been in offering her friend free shelter for so long, and to allow for the possibility that she might not be needed or valued by her friend after her financial support was withdrawn.

People caught in an unhealthy manifestation of the Caretaker archetype are stuck in a negative pattern of caring for others before they care for themselves, neglecting their own financial security or well-being while ensuring others are being taken care of. They do not have healthy, well-defined boundaries, and this creates a vicious cycle of dependence and resentment ("They don't even appreciate what I'm doing for them." "They couldn't last a day on their own.")

The truth is that our loved ones can change on their own, but only if they want to change and if you gradually help them transition from dependence to self-sufficiency. Of course there are some situations where individuals don't have the capacity to change because they are disabled, infirm, or just never developed economically valuable skills. It is critical to discern what is true about their situation. If necessary, seek others' assessments of how capable these people really are.

Even if you're an involuntary Caretaker—caring for people who truly need your help because life circumstances have thrust that role upon you— you can still find relief in clarifying the financial aspects of your relationship with them. I once had a client, a sweet older man named David, whose spouse of three years, Lila, was dying of a terminal disease. He was entirely focused on providing her physical and emotional care. A schoolteacher for many years, she had just started drawing on her state teachers' retirement pension two months before her illness worsened, and it was evident that she wouldn't live much longer. With all the anger and grief surrounding this turn of events, there had understandably been little attention paid to how David (who had no pension and had given up his own job to care for her) would make it financially after Lila died. I brought this to his attention, and with my encouragement, he asked her what she wanted to have happen with her pension, given that she had other heirs who had previously been named as beneficiaries. She said, "Well, of course I want it to take care of you." I literally saw a weight drop off my client's shoulders. It took an enormous amount of courage for David to ask Lila if he was going to be taken care of. Her answer freed him to spend their last days together unencumbered by resentment or financial worries.

LOVING KINDNESS

Loving kindness is a practice from Buddhism in which we are encouraged to foster an expansive compassion within our hearts and direct it first toward ourselves, then toward those in our immediate families, then people in our wider communities, then everyone in our country (including those we don't like), and finally to every living being on the planet. Practicing loving kindness does not mean you give everyone everything they demand. It may mean that you say no sometimes. The most loving act may mean that you have to wean those who depend on you, allowing them—in stages and over time—to become independent. You may say to your dependent children, for example, "I'm going to put a lump sum into an account so you will have a fixed amount of money coming in on a regular basis, but you are not to come to me for loans when you come up short." Your happiness is a critical component of others' well-being. That is being kind and loving, redefined. (See p. 234 for a guided loving-kindness meditation.)

CARING FOR THE CARETAKER

The following activities will lead you toward more joyful giving and a rich, safe, and secure life for you and those people and causes dear to you.

- **RIGOROUS INQUIRY.** Ask yourself:

    Am I abandoning myself to care for others? How so?

    Am I actually being of help, or do I seek to control others, elicit a certain response, or further a self-image that has been working for me?

    Could I be exaggerating the dependency of those I am helping?

    Alternatively, are there other people in need whom I could actually be helping more, or more effectively, than I am?

    How do I imagine my relationship with this individual will change if I withdraw my financial support? If I am not needed, will I still be loved or welcome? Am I willing to find out?

    Is my approach really empowering those who depend on me, or is it fostering more dependency? Do I have a choice in the situation or not?

    If my dependents are capable of more independence, what is the first small step *I* could take to help empower someone to be more independent?

    If my dependents aren't capable of more independence, what are the ways I could create more personal space so as to have more balance in my life? (Examples include less or only written communication, better boundaries, sharing the burden with others.)

(continued on next page) ➤

CARING FOR THE CARETAKER *(continued from previous page)*

- **HAVE THE CONVERSATION.** One mistake Caretakers make is to assume that they know best what their dependents need. It can be uncomfortable to discuss these matters openly with the people who have been relying on your help for years, if not forever. Whether the parties are a parent and adult child, members of a couple, or two friends, there may be shame on both sides and a tendency to deny the truth of the situation. But questioning those assumptions can sometimes lead to valuable information that will help to break old patterns. Ask those who rely on your help the following questions, or if it's too difficult, ask someone who is more neutral to do this for you and share the answers with you. Tough as this may be at first, you won't regret getting the answers!

    What do you really want in your life?

    Am I serving you?

    How can I better help you achieve your goals?

    What would our relationship look like if I lessened or withdrew my financial support?

- **ACTION PLAN.** In order to break out of the Caretaker's role, try the following action plan. Put your promises to yourself in writing and keep them:

    Think of three simple ways you might express compassion for yourself before leaping to express compassion for others. This might be as simple as starting your day with a meal you love, ending it with a warm bath, or doing anything that makes you feel healthy and happy. None of these things need involve money, though they might. *To express compassion for myself, I will _____ , _____ , and _____ .*

    Ask for help from someone, for some part of your life. Lean on someone else for a change. *I will ask _____ for help with _____ .*

    ➤

Experiment with saving for your future (by having more than six times your monthly expenses in investments). *I commit to saving $_____ this month, and $_____ the next, and $_____ the next, no matter whose needs arise.*

Buy yourself something (and it could be time) that will feed your greatest joy in life. *I plan to buy myself _____ by this date:_____ For this, I will need $_____ and I plan to get it from/by _____.*

Put energy into relationships that feel mutual and reciprocal. Ask those people what they value about you and the relationship.

In what ways are you just as deserving of care and support as the people or causes you give to? List the many ways in which you are worthy of the same benefits you work so hard to provide to those you love, and post this list in a place where you will see it every day.

For more practical recommendations on cash flow and budgeting, investing, insurance, taxes, gifting and estate planning, and philanthropy and generosity that are specifically tailored to the Caretaker, see the appendix, p. 277.

CHAPTER TEN

THE EMPIRE BUILDER

"I propose three steps for a businessman who is caught, who does not have the time to live his life and to love and to take care of his beloved ones. The first step is to go back to himself and practice, so that he is able to relax, to enjoy the here and now. Then he brings this joy back to his wife, his children, and helps them so they become joyful as well. And then, as a family, they can do the third step and bring compassion and under-standing to the people in your business. And you don't have to separate business and spirituality any more."

—THICH NHAT HANH

At a swanky Santa Monica hotel, three entrepreneurs and I were sitting in plush lounge chairs, staring out at the ocean as we discussed our businesses and their growth prospects. One of the men, Alan, a portly thirty-seven-year-old from Sacramento who ran his own software development business, chimed in, "If you had told me ten years ago that I would have what I have today, I never would have believed it. I would have said 'Of course I'll be satiated. I won't need to earn any more than that.'"

"How much do you have today?" I inquired.

"About five," he answered, referring to a financial net worth of $5 million.

In turn, each of the other businesspeople shared his situation and perspective. A few minutes later, Alan spoke again: "When I get to twenty million, which I'm hoping to do by age forty, then I'll definitely be done."

I smiled. Based on my clients' and my own experience, I doubted Alan would stop at twenty million. After all, he did not seem to recognize that he was doing exactly what he had done ten years prior—setting a goal for his business and his net worth that he believed would bring him satiation. I knew the cycle all too well. He was ignoring the fact that he had already achieved his old number but that it hadn't made a significant difference in his inner experience of sufficiency or wealth. He was a classic Empire Builder.

To clarify, I am not using the word *empire* to refer only to business ventures. Empires include all types of activities where someone can make a large-scale impact on society or a local community, exert power and control over a vast pool of people, or leave a legacy after death. The most common examples of Empire Builders are people who have created successful business ventures, be they worldwide companies like Microsoft and Wal-Mart or a multistate distribution company that you've never heard of. But Empire Builders who fit the above definition can also include artists and musicians with large and well-known bodies of work, art collectors, social activists, inventors, politicians, and large-scale philanthropists.

As an example, two women I know are children's book authors, and both hope to inspire confidence, imagination, and hope in their respective audiences, in one case girls between the ages of nine and thirteen, and in the other, children with chronic illnesses such as leukemia and diabetes. Another client is an inventor looking to patent truly innovative products for golfers. Yet another client has started an elementary school focused on nature-based alternative education. While none of these clients would use the word *empire* to refer to their endeavors, the vision, innovation, and fortitude required to create their legacies is little different from that of Empire Builders who are primarily focused on their for-profit businesses.

A cautionary note: this archetype can elicit strong reactions from readers who are predominantly Idealists, Innocents, and Caretakers, in part because Empire Builders are so driven to succeed, especially financially, and can appear (and often are) self-involved. If you suspect or notice this type of reaction in yourself, I invite you to look for the positive aspects of the Empire Builder that you may have disowned in your own life. Often it is the archetype we reject that we most need in order to create balance and freedom in our lives.

You're probably an Empire Builder if:

- Your number—the amount you've told yourself would be enough to never have to work again and enjoy life to the fullest—has increased more than the rate of inflation over the past five years. If your empire isn't financial, then perhaps the scope and scale of your artistic or philanthropic legacy keeps increasing.

- Your business or career occupies more than 75 percent of your attention during waking hours.

- You won't pull money out of your empire, be it a business, a real estate portfolio, or a single asset, other than what's necessary for ongoing spending.

- Your empire represents more than 75 percent of your financial net worth.

WHAT THE EMPIRE BUILDER BELIEVES

Most Empire Builders do not simply crave a large amount of money or a legacy, even though, like Alan, the money may be what they talk about or focus on. In fact, Empire Builders are visionaries who believe that they will be happy when they've made a significant and lasting contribution to the world. Deep inside, many Empire Builders feel that they will be somebody when they achieve their vision. And indeed, they often do make significant, lasting contributions. Almost all of the comforts and conveniences we take for granted today, from prescription drugs and computer technology to safe air travel and cell phones, were brought into our lives by Empire Builders. These innovative and tireless visionaries have also endowed universities and charities and preserved important art throughout the ages, having saved or improved countless lives. Sometimes, their ambition even leads them to pursue careers in politics, an arena in which they further impact human lives on a large scale.

Throughout the ages, many Empire Builders have been motivated in part by a larger vision for humanity. Often having experienced personal hardship in their early lives, these Empire Builders may feel for the poor and seek to alleviate difficult conditions in others' lives through philanthropy. One immediately thinks of the likes of the steel baron Andrew Carnegie, who not only made a fortune but used it, among other things, to establish the now-famous public library system that gave working people access to education.

Clearly, society can reap tremendous benefits from Empire Builders, and they themselves often enjoy very comfortable lives. Depending on the level of grandiosity of an Empire Builder's dreams, however, there can be a tremendous personal cost for the societal benefits they create. Empire Builders are often workaholics although few would label themselves as such. The bigger the perceived future payoff for their dreams, the more imbalances those dreams justify today. At the extreme, they may sacrifice almost anything for their vision, including marriages, close family relationships, business partnerships, and in several recent notable cases, even their own morals and values.

I've met many Empire Builders over the years who keep their family's financial details obscure from their spouse as a way of holding on to power in the relationship. But it's not only spouses that the ambitions of the Empire Builder can affect. Even Andrew Carnegie, with all of the good works his money ultimately supported, is said to have paid his employees extremely low wages and at times extended their hours without extra pay.

THE WANTING MIND AND THE EMPIRE BUILDER

Perhaps more than any other archetype, the Empire Builder can never have enough. The Empire Builder's Wanting Mind is fully in control, believing that the creation of the empire will truly bring significantly more happiness, fulfillment, life balance, and relaxation later on down the line. This causes Empire Builders to spend a disproportionate amount of time focusing on the future. After all, it's then that the empire will be bigger and better, and they will be happy.

Ask almost any entrepreneur if he's satisfied with his progress over the past year and he'll immediately focus on what didn't get done, what can still be accomplished, how much potential remains untapped. This is the classic Wanting Mind at work, focusing on the empty part of the glass instead of the full, creating a problem of "not-enough" that then requires the Empire Builder's innovation, decisiveness, strategic thinking, and effort to overcome. But Empire Builders don't just want to solve the problem at hand, they want to create something so significant that it will solve almost all problems, both now and in the future.

THE PAYOFF

There are many payoffs to being an Empire Builder. Society respects and even idolizes this archetype, which of course feels good. Empire Builders are often powerful, charismatic leaders who command attention and can influence their businesses, their families, and the many others with whom they interact. Empire Builders get a great thrill from achieving their grand and impressive goals, and their egos are fed tremendously both from their accomplishment and from the recognition it garners.

> "Making money is not a reason for being in business. It's a by-product. When it becomes a reason for being in business, then everyone treats you as a transaction. The people who have the best perspective on money know that their money is on loan. People get in trouble when they think they own things."
>
> —KEN BLANCHARD,
> ORGANIZATIONAL CONSULTANT
> AND AUTHOR

But dig deeper and underneath this facade you'll likely find a fear that is driving these individuals, even if that fear isn't known to them. Perhaps it is a fear of being out of control, of being abandoned, powerless, helpless, or abused, or a fear of financial loss. Almost every Empire Builder has come close to loss or had a painful experience along these lines. If you go back far enough, many Empire Builders experienced feeling like they were nobody, or were worthless, or would never amount to anything great. But because they have talent and ambition, Empire Builders have been able to compensate for these painful feelings by building an identity that shows the world, every day, that they're valuable and important. For them this is a phenomenally positive payoff.

One of my clients is the daughter of a very successful businessman. Growing up in circles of influence and affluence, she felt that the only way she would amount to anything was if she were able, without her father's help, to make it even bigger than he had. She has driven herself for the past thirty years and has had some incredible successes in two successive technology businesses, including more financial wealth (but not more fame) than her father ever had. But she does not feel fulfilled. She has taken antidepressants for years and can't seem to figure out why her wealth hasn't cushioned her from the sense of competitiveness she feels.

The reason Empire Builders don't feel satiated when they reach a temporary external goal is that they're not satisfying the right need. To the extent that their empire building is compensating for something else—unworthiness, shame, vulnerability, or fear of abandonment, to name a few possibilities—they have an ongoing fear that there's something dangerous lurking out there and if they take their eye off their growth and expansion, they might regress. They use their ambition to avoid looking directly into the nature of their fear, but in so doing, Empire Builders continually experience a hunger that is truly insatiable, a hunger for more, bigger, better. That is why it's so difficult for Empire Builders to stop building, even when they have far surpassed their stated (or unstated) goals.

In our interview, Rabbi Harold Kushner addressed this problem the following way. In his matter-of-fact style, he said, "The danger in letting your money or your work define you is that, should you lose your money or your job or retire, is there a 'you' left?"

TREAT YOURSELF LIKE YOU TREAT YOUR BUSINESS

Though I've included creative people and philanthropists under this umbrella as well, Empire Builders are predominantly involved in business. While the most successful businesspeople are financially astute when it comes to their business, they just as often lack sophistication or prudence when it comes to their personal financial affairs. For example, they often insist on a very cautious investment strategy, believing that their business will provide the growing nest egg they'll need one day.

Those who try to figure out the number for themselves—the amount of capital necessary to never have to work for pay again—generally do an overly simplistic job of it. One very sophisticated businessman said, "I'm going to want to spend $250,000 per year, so I need $10 million at today's bank interest rates of around 2–3 percent." Unfortunately, this man ignored the fact that his plan had not accounted for the cost of living increases that are sure to occur over the three to five decades of his retirement. To make ends meet in his later years, he would either have to set aside more money now, spend less, or invest more aggressively to earn a higher rate of return.

And while he built his empire, he had over 95 percent of his money invested in one small company—his own. This is an extremely risky strategy. He knew he needed balance in some way, but planning to go from his present hyper-risky behavior to a hyperconservative investment strategy in a later phase wasn't balanced—it was bipolar.

The financial pattern Empire Builders are most comfortable with is the building, not the having. When Empire Builders receive a windfall by selling a business that represents the majority of their net worth, for example, they can go through a major identity crisis. Their whole sense of self has been about growing their empire, and they have never really had the experience of enough. That is why Empire Builders can never stop. I have known many entrepreneurs over the years who have built well-known and successful businesses, creating tens of millions of dollars for themselves. However, in allowing their net worth to remain concentrated in just one asset, they lost it all when the next bad business cycle hit their company or industry. Some Empire Builders thrive so much on the challenge of growing a new empire that when they do succeed, they lose interest and unconsciously allow themselves to lose what they've earned, ensuring that they will have to build another empire.

Empire builders want to feel free, powerful, and significant. They want to leave a legacy that they will be remembered for, be it a business, a major family foundation, or an art collection. And though such a legacy can be wonderful for others, the hidden costs of structuring one's life to leave that legacy too often become astronomical.

REMOVING THE BLINDERS

If you are an Empire Builder, you probably have a lot to be proud of. But acknowledging the ways in which you may be too single-minded—holding a little too tightly to your pride and relating to work and money in unhealthy ways—requires that you look at your situation from a different perspective. I recall a client who began his career as a teller at a community bank and, in relatively short order, rose to become the president of a major California bank holding company. Over a two-year period, I worked with him to uncover his most important aspirations, after which he decided to resign from the holding company so that he could stay closer to home and work less than his customary sixty-hour weeks.

REMOVING THE BLINDERS

The following exercises will help you break free of old patterns.

- **MOVING TARGETS**. Pick a time, five or ten years ago, when you set a financial or other ambitious goal for your future empire. What was it? Have you now reached or surpassed your goal? Which of the nonfinancial benefits that you had hoped for back then (such as more time to relax and enjoy your family, more peace of mind, or the ability to be more generous with your resources, financial and otherwise) have you actually received as a result of surpassing your old goal, presuming you have? Which of the benefits you promised yourself have you not yet received? What is your goal today? How confident are you that you will receive the nonfinancial benefits you're promising yourself today when you reach your new goal?

  ☐ Very confident

  ☐ Somewhat confident

  ☐ Undecided

  ☐ Not so sure

  ☐ Not at all confident

- **WHAT IF**. Imagine that you have reached your most lofty, expansive, visionary goals. You have everything you've ever dreamed of, and your empire is no longer your responsibility. (If it was a company, it has been sold; if something else, you are no longer expanding it.) How will you spend the next week, beginning tomorrow morning? Focus on what brings you joy, gives life meaning, and include activities and states of being your heart and soul yearn to experience before you die.

- **WHAT ARE YOU MOST AFRAID OF?** Write down at least one, but preferably several, experiences you remember from your past that were either traumatic or powerful and that bear some re-

➤

lationship to your motivations around your empire. For example, one client of mine had a father who was a famous architect. People would travel great distances to admire his buildings. My client vividly remembers the feeling of being excluded from grand openings and fancy parties at which his father was being honored. Now as an adult he works very hard to build his reputation as a screenwriter, and even though he has had some significant financial and creative success and is even exploring the possibility of starting his own independent film company, he still feels like he lives in his father's shadow. When you think of your own experiences, ask yourself what emotions you are attempting to shield yourself from by building an empire. One way to get to your unconscious motivations is to handwrite answers, changing your writing hand, to the following questions as if you were now living through a formative traumatic experience from the past. If you are right-handed, use your left hand to record the answers of your younger self. If you are left-handed, use your right hand. Don't worry about your handwriting or the speed with which you can get words down. The underused hand will naturally be slower and more awkward, but using it may unleash feelings and memories you were unaware of.

Here are the questions, with examples of answers:

What do you want to do when you grow up?
I want to be rich and famous.

Why? What will you feel?
I'll be safe.

Did you ever feel the opposite of the feeling you just listed above? Put yourself back into that moment and describe it.
I am sitting in my room on Oak Avenue and my mom and dad are fighting. Dad just lost his job.

What are you afraid of?
I am afraid he is going to leave us.

(continued on next page) ➤

REMOVING THE BLINDERS *(continued from previous page)*

Whatever events you come up with, look closely at each feared scenario, one by one, and imagine the events happening again today. What would your experience actually feel like? How would you respond? Imagining different outcomes can be a powerful way to heal past wounds.

- **BE FREE NOW.** Experiment and live just one day or, if you can, one week or one month, as if you had already arrived. Do what it takes to get rid of any and all things in your life that are not going to exist once you've reached your goal(s) (for example, business interruptions, crammed scheduling, thinking about business while doing something unrelated). If you had your ultimate empire today, what would be different, really? Is it possible for you to stop striving during this experiment? If not, how will you stop striving in the future? If you tend to tell yourself it will be different when X has happened, explore whether that's really true before dedicating all your time and energy to getting there. As the Buddhists like to say, there is no "there" there. Ask yourself, "What is the optimum way I can prepare for relaxing, for enjoying peace of mind right here, right now?"

- **CREATE AN "ENOUGH FOR LIFE" BUCKET FOR YOUR ASSETS.** This is an idea that my business partner, Spencer Sherman, came up with to help wealthy clients who have been in accumulation mode their whole lives to break that cycle. Most people will need to engage a well-trained Certified Financial Planner® professional for this calculation (see p. 263 for ways to locate one). A detailed explanation of how to do this is beyond the scope of this book. The quick explanation is that our planners first calculate, using the most conservative but realistic assumptions they can, how much financial net worth will be needed to cover a particular client's chosen standard of living until at least age one hundred. They factor in increasing costs of medical care, children's educations, and all future living expenses for the client and their loved ones. They assume a conservative rate of

➤

return on all assets, including real estate, privately held businesses, stocks, bonds, and cash, using figures that are several percentage points below the actual returns of the past thirty years. Once we know the amount of capital needed to cover the client's chosen standard of living for life, we place the assets that will fund these needs in an account titled "Enough for Life." If the client has a strong Guardian archetype in addition to their Empire Builder (saying things like "But you never know what's going to happen" or focusing on the next global crisis), we might increase their Enough for Life bucket by 50 percent, or show them that even if the Great Depression were to strike again, they'd still have enough, just to give them additional peace of mind.

- **AUTOMATICALLY SET ASIDE SOME MONEY FOR SPENDING AND GENEROSITY.** Whether you have substantial assets that you can parse into an Enough for Life bucket or not, Empire Builders need to put money toward their own pleasure or their desire to be generous. (See p. 144 for details on this exercise.) If you have enough to create the Enough for Life bucket, then the balance of the client's assets are then placed in a Loving Life bucket. This money is only to be used to enhance their fulfillment in life, whatever that means to them. Some Empire Builders have been so consumed with accumulating for themselves that they have lost connection with the outside world, with their compassion for other people's suffering or with enjoying their closest relationships fully. The Loving Life bucket is for these purposes. Some people might use it to buy the second home they've always dreamed of, to travel to parts of the world they've always wanted to see, to fund their most heartfelt philanthropic causes, or to help extended family members with education expenses or business start-up costs.

For more practical recommendations on cash flow and budgeting, investing, insurance, taxes, gifting and estate planning and philanthropy and generosity that are specifically tailored to the Empire Builder, see the appendix, p. 279.

FINDING YOUR FINANCIAL ARCHETYPES

Now that you've read through the individual financial archetype chapters, you likely have a good idea of which ones are dominant in you. Take the following multiple-choice quiz to confirm your intuitions. More than one answer may apply, in which case, please choose up to three answers that best describe your relationship to money. For my most up-to-date quiz that automatically calculates your financial archetypes, please visit www.BrentKessel.com.

QUESTIONS	ARCHETYPES

1. Money *primarily* allows (or would allow) me to:

☐ not worry — Guardian

☐ buy things and experiences that I enjoy — Pleasure Seeker

☒ create freedom for other pursuits (i.e. creative, spiritual, political, philanthropic) — Idealist

☒ have an ever-growing sense of security and abundance — Saver

☐ have a sense of importance and recognition from family, friends, and society at large — Star

☐ have faith that things will always work out for the best in the end — Innocent

☐ take care of others, sometimes at my own expense — Caretaker

☒ put time and money into something that makes a lasting impact (e.g., my business) — Empire Builder

2. When it comes to money, at my most extreme, I'm:

☐ avoidant and sometimes confused — Innocent

☒ generous, perhaps to the point of being enabling or self-abandoning — Caretaker

☒ impulsive and pleasure-seeking — Pleasure Seeker

☐ frugal and disciplined — Saver

☐ worried and anxious much of the time — Guardian

☐ distrustful or mystified — Idealist

☐ grandiose and ambitious much of the time — Empire Builder

☐ hungry for attention and praise — Star

➤

3. Over the last five years, my financial net worth has:

☐ grown, primarily due to good
saving and investing habits   Saver

☒ declined, primarily due to lack of   Innocent,
focus or gifts to family/friends   Caretaker

☐ grown, primarily due to job-related promotions,
bonuses, or stock options, or growth in the value   Empire Builder,
of home(s), a business, or investment portfolio   Star

☐ declined, primarily due to overspending   Pleasure Seeker,
                                                     Star

☐ not kept me from feeling nervous   Guardian

☐ I have no idea or don't think it's important   Innocent,
                                                     Idealist

4. Which of the following "rules" do you seem to mostly live by?

☐ You can't take it with you, so you might   Pleasure Seeker,
as well enjoy it now.   Star, Innocent

☒ It is better to give than to receive.   Caretaker,
                                                     Idealist

☐ A penny saved is a penny earned.   Saver,
                                                     Empire Builder

☐ Big corporations and/or government   Idealist,
can't be trusted.   Empire Builder

☐ If I'm not vigilant, it could all fall apart.   Guardian

**5. Which of the following has been most true of me over the past
three years?**

☐ I have been financially dependent on others   Pleasure Seeker,
(including credit cards or other debts).   Idealist, Star,
                                                     Innocent

☒ Others have been financially dependent on me   Caretaker, Saver,
(including employees).   Empire Builder

☐ There are no dependencies either way.   Guardian, Saver

(continued on next page) ➤

FINDING YOUR FINANCIAL ARCHETYPES *(continued from previous page)*

6. What I have to show (financially) is:

☐ a lot of "stuff" that I've bought over the years — Pleasure Seeker

☒ I don't have investments (other than
possibly a home) — Innocent

☐ ownership in a closely held business or real estate — Empire Builder

☐ financial investments like stocks, income
property, or mutual funds — Saver

☐ socially screened stocks, collectibles,
or my creative or academic work — Idealist

☐ a showpiece home, nice cars, a restaurant
or retail business, wine, jewelry, or art — Star

☒ parents, adult children, charities, or friends
who wouldn't have made it without my help — Caretaker

☐ mostly fixed income investments such as
bank savings accounts, CDs, bonds, or T-bills — Guardian

Now, for each box that you checked above, place a tally mark next to the archetype name(s) that correspond to your answer. For example, if for question 4 you selected the first answer, you should put a tally mark next to Pleasure Seeker, Star, and Innocent. If you selected the last answer, you should only put a tally mark next to Guardian.

_____ Guardian |_____ Pleasure Seeker

||_____ Idealist ||_____ Saver

||_____ Innocent   _____ Star

||_____ Empire Builder ||||_____ Caretaker

Now add up your tally marks for each archetype, and list the top three in order from the most dominant to the least:

CARETAKER

IDEALIST / INNOCENT / EMPIRE BUILDER / SAVER

PART 3

In the World and of It

CHAPTER ELEVEN

THE MIDDLE WAY WITH MONEY

"For the Buddha, freedom from craving is the essential point, not one's outer circumstances. One could be living in a cave filled with desire or living in a palace free of desire. There's no inherent problem with wealth. What is more important is one's relationship to it. Of course, for monastics, renunciation of worldly possessions is part of the path; but for laypeople living in the world, the practice is about skillful mindstates in whatever circumstances we find ourselves."

—JOSEPH GOLDSTEIN, CO-FOUNDER, INSIGHT MEDITATION SOCIETY

I have discussed how our Core Stories regarding money can create imbalance, constriction, and downright painful financial circumstances in our lives. When we are caught in extreme thoughts, beliefs, and conditioning, we sow the seeds of financial discontent. The preceding chapters have explored the eight financial archetypes to provide a framework through which we can understand our beliefs regarding money. There is, of course, no way to completely escape the influence of our Core Stories, nor would it be desirable to do so.

With so many ways of behaving in relation to money, some of them healthy and some of them extreme, how do we approach this important aspect of our lives? The answer is the Middle Way. A philosophy originally espoused by the Buddha, the Middle Way teaches that the path to true freedom lies neither in self-indulgence nor in austere asceticism. In the second century CE, the Indian philosopher Nagarjuna developed respected teachings on this simple but profound practice, becoming known as the master of the Middle Way. Nagarjuna expanded the concept in one of his texts by saying that there are two legitimate human goals. The Dalai Lama explains Nargajuna's teachings in *The Art of Happiness at Work:* "One goal is material fulfillment, and the means for that is the creation of wealth, which today would include the accumulation of the most powerful U.S. dollars. The second goal is the attainment of liberation, and the means for that is spiritual practice."

> "The strength of a man is in the extremity of the opposites he can hold."
>
> —ROBERT FROST

The good news for people who want "healthy wealth" is that these goals—the pursuit of material fulfillment and the pursuit of liberation through spiritual practice—are by no means mutually exclusive. None of the spiritual teachers I interviewed for this book said that money is an inherent obstacle to spiritual attainment, whether one defines such attainment as getting into heaven or becoming enlightened. These teachers have instead pointed to our *attachment* to money as the primary obstacle.

Someone walking the Middle Way is influenced most of the time by positive aspects of the archetypes. For example, if we were living the Middle Way, the Pleasure Seeker might invite us to relax and enjoy life while the Guardian makes sure that we're not spending to an irresponsible degree. The Caretaker might feel empathy with a friend and inspire us to pick up groceries for her family, and the Saver might make sure that we are not jeopardizing our own self-sufficiency in the process. The Star might plan a fabulous party for charity at which the Innocent's optimism is contagious. The Empire Builder might be working on our grand vision while the Idealist is making sure that our efforts will truly help other people and society as a whole.

YOUR DOMINANT ARCHETYPES

What do you suspect your dominant archetypes are? Using your results from the quiz you just took as well as the following chart, think about the role that each archetype plays in your current life, then express it as a percentage of the whole you.

ARCHETYPE	FINANCIAL FOCUS	YOUR PERCENTAGE
The Guardian	is always alert and careful.	
The Pleasure Seeker	prioritizes pleasure and enjoyment in the here and now.	10%
The Idealist	places the greatest value on creativity, compassion, social justice, or spiritual growth.	10%
The Saver	seeks security and abundance by accumulating more financial assets.	10%
The Star	spends, invests, or gives money away to be recognized, feel hip or classy, and increase self-esteem.	
The Innocent	avoids putting significant attention on money and believes or hopes that life will work out for the best.	20%
The Caretaker	gives and lends money to express compassion and generosity.	40%
The Empire Builder	thrives on power and innovation to create something of enduring value.	10%

(continued on next page) ➤

YOUR DOMINANT ARCHETYPES (continued from previous page)

The following chart represents all eight archetypes and two words that capture the most common gifts of each one, all equally weighted. Admittedly, this ultra-balanced person exists only in theory, but how do your weightings compare?

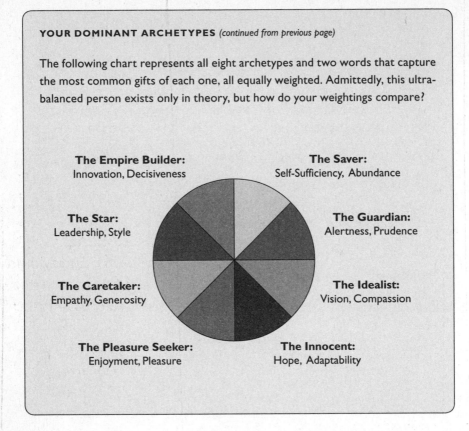

The Empire Builder:
Innovation, Decisiveness

The Saver:
Self-Sufficiency, Abundance

The Star:
Leadership, Style

The Guardian:
Alertness, Prudence

The Caretaker:
Empathy, Generosity

The Idealist:
Vision, Compassion

The Pleasure Seeker:
Enjoyment, Pleasure

The Innocent:
Hope, Adaptability

THINK MORE

Most of us are caught in one, or maybe two, of these archetypes almost all the time. And we stay stuck in our present situation because we believe without question its story about how to survive and be happy. Our Core Stories are invariably focused on money or objects that are external to us: the Saver wants to save more; the Pleasure Seeker wants to buy enjoyable new things; the Caretaker wants to help others. If we're unhappy with our situation, we tend to focus on the symptoms of our Core Story, not the cause: "My boss is too demanding"; "My car keeps breaking down"; "My spouse spends too much." But this focus on the external can blind us to what needs to change within.

It can be hard to keep our focus inward when we live in a world of alluring external objects. But instead of "turning off our brains," it is in fact the opposite that will allow us to turn inward.

In the summer of 2006, on a trip through North America, the Dalai Lama was giving a talk at the Gibson Amphitheater at Universal Studios in Hollywood. How ironic, I thought, to be visiting one of the world's living saints in a place that is a nucleus of commerce and savvy marketing. The juxtaposition was most pronounced as I watched late-model V-8 pickups and SUVs jostle with a disproportionate number of hybrids to get into the valet parking lot, everybody quite anxious not to miss His Holiness's speech, "Compassion: the Source of Happiness." Most of us, I noted, seemed to be missing the opportunity to practice compassion in the parking lot.

As the throng moved slowly across a footbridge toward the security screening area outside the amphitheater, a massive green figure with googly eyes and horns of sorts emerged from a backstage door below. A dozen people began jumping up and down around me, waving and yelling, "Shrek! Shrek!" Obligingly, he turned and waved back.

During the discussion that followed the speech, I asked the Dalai Lama whether he could describe a method for Americans—rich and poor alike—to be happy. The bespectacled wise man, sitting serenely in bright robes before a crowd of thousands, leaned in closer and raised his eyebrows. With his gruff but kind voice he responded, "When there's too much stress or too much worry, look inward! Read more. Think. Trying to find the answer from outside yourself is nonsense! Think more."

> "If your strategy is just an idea that's on top of an abyss of emotional need, then ultimately it won't satisfy, and so finally, we have to return to that pit, that void, that abyss, that nothing can satisfy. If you have become disillusioned enough with everything you have tried to do to avoid that edge, then there's a willingness to face that which has not been faced, and the recognition that running from that in one direction or another hasn't been ultimately satisfying."
>
> —GANGAJI, MEDITATION TEACHER

To borrow His Holiness's phrase, you will have to "think more" to live the Middle Way in your monetary dealings. You have probably made resolutions about spending less, saving more, eating better, paying your bills on time, or getting out of debt. And most of the time, I'm guessing that your resolutions haven't worked. This is because resolutions are made in the conscious mind, but most of the power resides in the unconscious. For this reason, the Middle Way is not about abandoning our unconscious Core Story or attempting to force it to let go through willpower. If we try to dismiss our Core Story out of hand, it will just find new, sneaky ways to manifest and keep us stuck in the rut we say we want out of. If you want to walk the Middle Way, you have to fully face both components of the self: the unconscious with its self-concern and powerful beliefs and your mature, adult wisdom with its priorities and visions. The Middle Way as we apply it to money is a challenging but incredibly powerful practice of including in our plans both the unconscious Core Story and our conscious wisdom as we move forward.

A FOUR-YEAR-OLD RUNS YOUR FINANCIAL LIFE

As I've said earlier, the unconscious Core Story was formed very early in life as a strategy to survive and avoid pain, and as our primary hope for happiness. Many psychologists have postulated that by the age of four, the unconscious identity is fully formed. This product of childhood holds 90 percent of the power to control our adult decisions. In explaining this phenomenon, spiritual teacher Jeru Kabbal likens our mind to an iceberg. In his book *Finding Clarity,* he says:

> An iceberg floats with about nine-tenths of itself beneath the surface of the water, while only one-tenth shows above the water. If we compare this to the mind, we could say that the nine-tenths of the mind below the surface is the subconscious, and the part above the surface is the conscious mind.... [S]uppose that our "iceberg" is somewhere in the North Atlantic. The part that is below the water is considering floating up to the North Pole for a vacation. At the same time, the part that is above the water is thinking of floating down to Sicily for a vacation there. Where do you think the iceberg will actually go for its vacation? Obviously, it's going to go where the bigger part—the unknown part, the unseen part—wants to go. That's where the power lies.

But how to see the unseen? The first step is to admit, with as much honesty and courage as we can muster, who in fact is running our money show right now. To do that, we're going to dig a little deeper to get to the nitty-gritty of how our unconscious is operating.

LET THE FOUR-YEAR-OLD SPEAK

What does the young child inside you believe about money? Not the adult. Not the cool, spiritual, balanced, or mature part of you, but rather the little boy or girl who throws a tantrum when things go badly. Whatever your dominant archetype, remember that each Core Story wants more. No Empire Builder thinks his or her business or legacy is big enough, no Pleasure Seeker thinks he or she is getting enough pleasure. No Saver has saved enough. So take a moment to tap into the most self-indulgent, self-absorbed, and primitive part of you. Try to answer the following questions about money using simple four-year-old language and absolutely no censorship:

1. I will feel safe if _____.

2. If only I could have _____, then I'd be happy.

3. What I want more than anything is _____.

One of my clients, Sally, answered the first question "I will feel safe if I'm out of debt." Sally is a highly successful, sought-after public relations professional who borrowed quite a lot from investors to launch her firm.

I responded, "Does the young part of you, the four-year-old, even know what debt is?"

She answered, "No, I guess not."

"So, try again. Your little four-year-old girl inside will feel safe if . . ."

"I am totally taken care of by someone else financially."

She blushed. Sally is an independent woman, the president of her own firm, and hearing herself virtually asking to be financially dependent gave her the creeps.

"I can see it's hard for you to admit that. But stay with me. That was an incredibly honest response. Let's move on to the second question." I said.

Sally read it through, pondered, and then said, "If only I could have no need to work for money, then I'd be happy."

(continued on next page) ➤

LET THE FOUR-YEAR-OLD SPEAK *(continued from previous page)*

"What would you do with your time if you had no need to work for money?"

"I'd travel the world. I've always wanted to explore other cultures, but I've never had the money."

"Great. And now number three."

"What I want more than anything is to be carefree!"

"Wonderful!" I responded.

As you do this exercise, I encourage you to exaggerate this very young place inside you. Your four-year-old has very clear ideas about what will make you safe and happy and what won't. Don't censor at all. Most of us have spent a lifetime managing, controlling, and spinning our most primal needs and wants rather than really listening to them. I'm now asking you to go to the other extreme. Don't try to accurately present what you think your four-year-old wants. Instead, exaggerate it, amplify it, blow it way out of proportion, let it go completely nuts and express itself, even if it seems extreme. What does the four-year-old self-indulgent kid in you want in order to feel safe, secure, and happy? This takes great courage because it is not the way we usually like to see ourselves. By actually seeing who is running the show, we have an extraordinary chance to really "think" about what is affecting our lives.

_____

_____

_____

_____

_____

_____

I recently asked this question of a business acquaintance of mine who is mostly an Empire Builder. James is a software wizard whose famous products have been the cornerstone for a twenty-year-old business that is very successful. After some additional encouragement, here is the answer he gave me:

"I want to have so much money that nothing can hurt me. The stock market can crash. The real estate market can crash. And it won't matter to me. I'll be sitting pretty on a beach somewhere. I want to be the best, the fastest, the strongest company in my field. Gobs and gobs of money so that nothing can hurt me. I want to be safe even if the world falls apart."

YOUR MONEY MASK

If you really took the above exercise to heart, I imagine that you're a little bit embarrassed right now. Most of us don't want to acknowledge that young child inside of us. And we certainly resist showing him to the world.

As the next step on our journey toward the Middle Way, I want you to examine this young and vulnerable part of you and how you want to be seen by the world—what I call your money mask. As discussed in chapter 7, we all have a shtick, a way we want to be seen with money.

A friend of mine, I'll call her Ana, was living on very little money, essentially a tiny stream of royalties from a screenplay she had sold years earlier and some state disability income that she had been awarded because she developed chronic fatigue syndrome while working as an accountant. Her friends, however, all had well-paid jobs, money to burn, and nice cars. When she accompanied them to fancy restaurants, she would pretend to have already eaten dinner, ordering a small dessert to save money. Ana's shtick

> "There is a huge part of you that will do anything to survive. You're never going to eliminate it— you must just be able to understand that it's actually trying to have you survive to the next generation. But you also have an immortal soul, which has more freedom than that too. And so I would say that money has become the ultimate physical shield."
>
> —David Whyte

was that she wanted to appear like them, just a talented professional between jobs. Her four-year-old self was terrified to have her friends see her true financial condition, which had declined so much. It was only after she nearly collapsed from sheer physical exhaustion that she finally began to look in earnest at her Core Story and its requirements for safety and happiness. When we respond to our Core Story in a reflexive, conditioned way, we only reinforce that story. My Core Story is that life is unpredictable and money will give me the security and freedom to have all my needs and desires met. So each time I embellish that Core Story by saving a bit more or building my business a bit more, I'm telling myself that I'm not enough without that outer action. It's the same when the Pleasure Seeker spends money, the Caretaker takes care of others, and the Innocent puts his head in the sand. These actions allow us to avoid looking at the root vulnerability that our actions are designed to protect us from. But when we look at that vulnerability squarely, we realize that it's not nearly as scary as our four-year-old self thinks it is. Just in looking, we develop more flexibility and greater options.

UNCOVERING YOUR MASK

Think, write down, or speak to someone with whom you feel safe about the answers to these questions.

1. What is your shtick with money (how you present yourself to the world)?

2. What do you know about yourself regarding money that you would rather not know?

3. How do you want other people to think of you when it comes to money?

4. What is the most shameful thing for you about your relationship to money?

5. In what areas of your life are you most unrealistic and dreamlike with money?

6. What thoughts do you have about money that are most distorted? Be specific.

7. What feelings do you have about money that you find most uncomfortable?

8. What behavior patterns with money have you most relied on to avoid facing difficult feelings?

After writing your first round of answers, you may want to go back and take a second pass, being even more extreme as you give voice to the youngest part of yourself.

YOUR INNATE FINANCIAL WISDOM

No matter who you are or what your present financial situation is, you have an innate wisdom about money that is profound and unique to you. It is not your money mask, which is looking for external validation. And it is not your conditioned Core Story, your young place with money. It is rather the financial life you would live if you were wholly unfettered by your habits, tendencies, and perceived limitations.

If the young place and the mask are the unconscious, reactive sides of your path with money, this innate wisdom is the conscious, visionary side of that same path. The Middle Way is the art of understanding both sides of the path so we know where to find the middle. We have spent some time excavating the hopes and desires of your young place. Now let's unearth your most profound vision for your future and the role money will play in it.

It is often very difficult to separate your innate financial wisdom from your conditioned Core Story. Arguably, everything is conditioned. Every thought we can possibly have, including the most profound insight and wisdom, is based on our prior experiences and influences. So, what's the telltale sign that you've tapped into your innate wisdom?

The key is found in your body's response. When you are listening to your innate wisdom, you can feel a very deep part of you relax and let go. It will feel pleasing, calming, and wholehearted. There will be an absence of pressure. This goes beyond the sense that something is a good idea; it is not above the neck but below it. Some of the words that may come to mind in describing this state are: naturally strong, connected, peaceful, trusting, generous, receptive, grateful, and present. You will experience an absence of anxiety, a feeling of well-being that permeates your body.

If you are not yet having this kind of response, don't worry. One of two things may be happening: either you haven't yet found a truly liberating voice that expresses your innate wisdom, or you have, but your internal four-year-old is so scared at the prospect of you following that voice that it has rejected it outright. Either way, don't force anything. Understand that your conditioning still has a pretty firm grip on the steering wheel and continue to turn your attention to this soul-searching question. For a guided meditation on tapping into your innate financial wisdom, you can also visit my Web site at www.BrentKessel.com.

YOUR INNATE FINANCIAL WISDOM

When have you experienced the most joy in your life? What were you doing? Was it when you all piled into the car and took a family trip? When you played hooky from work one day and went hiking with your best friend? What was your state of being (e.g., relaxed, peaceful)? Elaborate. _____

_____

_____

If you could write the blueprint for the most enriching life you could have, with no financial or psychological constraints, what would that life look like? Remember that "enriching" could mean a very simple kind of joy, peace, and fulfillment—it doesn't have to contain grandiose dreams. Focus on as many areas as you want, from family, travel, creativity, social action, or volunteering, to religious/spiritual practice, health, recreation, work, career, or philanthropy. Do your best to separate out your adult voice from your conditioned Core Story. Leave out any shoulds dictated by society in general. The heartfelt goals you uncovered on p. 15 may well be repeated here. This blueprint is just between you and you, no one else. Though this may seem hard at first, once you get going you'll see that your thoughts will flow. How would you live your most complete, fulfilling life?

_____

_____

_____

_____

_____

_____

_____

_____

_____

_____

HOLD BOTH

What is the way to a happier life in relation to money? You can probably tell that the answers that your young place gave and the answers that your adult innate wisdom gave are rather different. In fact, they're often, on the surface, in opposition to each other. A couple who participated in one of my workshops went through this exercise, and by the end of it, both were clear that what they most wanted in their life was to feel unpressured and relaxed. For them, this meant pursuing their dream of getting out of the hustle and bustle of Los Angeles and opening a small café in Washington state.

When they did the innate financial wisdom exercise, they both had a visceral response to their vision of moving to Washington and slowing down professionally. Their mutual Core Story was "If I could only have enough income to just follow my dream, I'd be in bliss." Interestingly, they did have enough money to follow their dream, but only if they were willing to sell their $400,000 house and rent instead of buying a new house after moving. The idea of selling the house, though, brought up a strong negative response. "I'll feel like an idiot if I don't own a home. Everyone knows that over thirty years it's better to own than to rent." The insight, no matter how visceral, was not strong enough to convince their unconscious conditioning to let go of this belief.

Our discussion continued. "How old will you be in thirty years?" I asked the husband. He paused to calculate.

"Eighty-two."

"And what will the quality-of-life have been during those thirty years, or even just the first five years, if you pursue what your Core Story wants you to?"

"Well, I guess my Core Story thinks we have to buy a replacement house in Washington, which will mean having to continue to work more hours as an urban planner to pay for it. That feels like quite a burden compared to the feeling I had a few minutes ago."

We continued to speak about the comparative quality of life of their two possible scenarios, weighing pros and cons. Near the end of our conversation, the woman chimed in. "I think what you're telling us is we *should* own the house." In fact, I had been saying nothing of the kind. But her conditioning was still so much at odds with her yearning that she wouldn't allow herself to entertain the notion that renting might be the best decision for their situation.

HOLDING BOTH

Think back to what your Core Story believes will make you safe, secure, and happy. You might look back at the "Let the Four-Year-Old Speak" exercise on p. 157, or at your answers to the exercises in chapter 2.

Then, shift your attention to the path that your innate financial wisdom wants you to follow. Without making any decisions about when or how you're going to make changes, just recall the primary message of your innate wisdom.

Shift your attention back to your Core Story, to your four-year-old. But please do so gently, in such a way that you're not rejecting what the four-year-old has to say or what your wisdom has to say. Your Core Story was created to protect you, and at the time, it was the most intelligent response you could muster toward a life that was unpredictable and uncertain. Be willing to listen to its fears, objections, even its tantrums for as long as it takes.

Then shift your attention back to your innate wisdom, appreciating its un-bounded nature, its ability to dramatically increase your quality of life.

Now here's the trick. See if you can make the shifts between the two per-spectives more and more frequently. Express your conditioning and your wisdom together in the same breath. Say, for instance, "I want to be taken care of financially and every other way and be an independent career person who blazes my own path to wealth." Know that both perspectives want what's best for you, even if they appear contradictory or mutually exclusive.

I can't emphasize enough that *this is not a quick process*—it's an ongoing prac-tice. I'm here to tell you that the conditioning will keep coming back for years, or even decades. This practice will, however, lessen its hold on you. The more you do the Hold Both practice, the more you'll start to believe and embody what your innate wisdom is telling you, and the more compassion and relaxation you'll experience when your conditioning does arise. With dedication and sincerity, this practice of Holding Both can be the start of living a life that is not unconsciously driven by your financial conditioning—a life of turning your iceberg southward toward a warmer climate. This is the heart of the Middle Way.

No matter how profound your wise insights seem, you can't believe or fully trust what you know until you blend it with your primitive condition-ing. The key is to live with both perspectives—the unconscious Core Story *and* your innate financial wisdom—for some time. Again, this is not easy and requires great intentionality. Keep reminding yourself of this. As you repeatedly practice allowing your innate wisdom and primitive conditioning to exist together, true change will occur.

THIS IS DEPRESSING!

As your Core Story begins to lose some of its power, you're very likely going to feel a bit depressed. It does not feel good to abandon strategies that are so deeply habitual. This discomfort is usually what causes us to go back to the tried-and-true, the old familiar behaviors with money. The unconscious thrives on, well, *unconsciousness*. Once we become aware of our Core Story, our four-year-old's agenda, and we hold it in our wakeful awareness, it invariably begins to shift. If the attention we put on it is negative, it will just shift underground and show up again in a slightly different form, still trying to protect us from the same fears by following the same behavior patterns and beliefs. By contrast, if we hold our Core Story in our attention compassionately and patiently, it lets go, but this still doesn't feel very good at first. This is a lifelong path. In fact, we might as well assume that we will always have our Core Story with us—until we die. The goal isn't to get rid of it; it is to create a closer relationship between the extremes of our innately wise and our four-year-old selves.

This practice of the Middle Way requires a commitment to surrender to what is most wise and divine within, a sort of inner elder. In addition, it requires that you accept and remain aware of that part that is very young. If you're a Christian, then you might call this process surrendering to God's will or finding answers through prayer. If you're an atheist, you will need to surrender to what you might call your highest intelligence. If you're a Buddhist, you might surrender to your Buddha nature. However you begin, if you start to examine and to release your old beliefs and strategies, you will feel more and more free to craft the financial life you want.

THE MIDDLE WAY FOR EACH ARCHETYPE

In the preceding chapters, which archetypes bugged you the most? Did you skip past any of them, or feel impatience or incredulity as you read a particular story? If so, chances are good that the archetype you were looking at is the one you most need to incorporate into your life to create balance. The extreme Saver is repulsed at the thought of using her precious savings to make frivolous purchases or help others in need. The Innocent is disgusted that an Empire Builder who already has enough money ten times over would go out and build another business—how incredibly egotistical! And the Star might be repulsed by the lack of class and self-respect that she believes an Idealist exhibits through her unkempt appearance and lack of material possessions.

These strong reactions all stem from the fear that we could end up behaving in that same way and, more primitively, the fear of what that behavior would mean to our survival or happiness. Ironically, though, if we can make gradual moves in the direction of the archetypes we are most avoiding, we will create a more balanced and fulfilling life. The natural movement toward balance occurs when we are not caught in the mind's strategies to be secure or happy. Remember, there is nothing more wrong nor right with any of these archetypes; it's just a question of balance.

In addition to creating or refining several of the concepts and exercises in this chapter, Robert Strock, a psychotherapist and spiritual counselor with over thirty years of experience who has been the most significant mentor in my life over the past twenty years, assisted me in creating the following profiles. These list, type by type, four areas of focus to help you identify which archetypes are dominant in you and how best to counterbalance them:

1. Painful emotional states commonly felt by people with each archetype.

2. Thoughts commonly held by people with each archetype, which can be healthy if cultivated in moderation but more often run the show in a distorted way.

3. Liberating wisdom on which to focus.

4. Balancing archetypes you ought to try to emphasize more in your life. As mentioned, the ones that most repel you are likely the ones you most need, but go slowly.

In many ways, the Holding Both exercise above is asking you to hold both the second and third sections (Common Thoughts and Liberating Wisdom) in your awareness simultaneously. For example, if you're a Pleasure Seeker, your Core Story might include the thought "I want to live for today"; I'm asking you to simultaneously hold the thought "Living within my means and taking care of my future creates a very real, albeit different kind of pleasure for me and those I love." Or if you're a Caretaker who naturally feels, "My needs are secondary to those of others," I'm asking you to also put your focus on the more challenging truth "I cannot effectively help others unless I'm first taking good care of myself."

THE GUARDIAN

Painful Emotional States

Anxious

Fearful

Worried

Common Distorted Thoughts (Conditioned Beliefs from the Past)

If I'm not hypervigilant, it's all going to fall apart.

My worry helps me hold it together.

There is an impending catastrophe.

Liberating Wisdom or Ways to Focus

Today I am going to pursue a calming activity that I love (for example, music, taking a nap, playing tennis or golf, watching a movie, being in nature, reading a book, doing a spiritual practice).

I am most moved to be of service to others by_____.

I most want to spend time with _____ in the next hour.

Making concrete changes that will simplify my life and financial needs is a high priority.

Archetypes You Most Need to Emphasize to Create Balance

Pleasure Seeker: enjoyment, pleasure

Empire Builder: innovation, decisiveness

Innocent: hope, adaptability

THE PLEASURE SEEKER

Painful Emotional States

Hungry
Greedy
Impatient
Self-Absorbed

Common Distorted Thoughts (Conditioned Beliefs from the Past)

What I want and will enjoy is more important than what I might need.

I want to live for today.

Liberating Wisdom or Ways to Focus

Living within my means and taking care of my future creates a very real albeit different kind of pleasure for me and those I love.

Archetypes You Most Need to Emphasize to Create Balance

Guardian: alertness, prudence

Saver: self-sufficiency, abundance

THE IDEALIST

Painful Emotional States

Weary
Skeptical
Distrustful
Rebellious
Angry

Common Distorted Thoughts (Conditioned Beliefs from the Past)

A lot of suffering and sacrifice is necessary to be creative or spiritual.

It's better to feel pain than to be financially free.

Liberating Wisdom or Ways to Focus

Self-sufficiency is empowering and will support my ideals. ✶

Money is good if it's used to create balance.

I love not having to rely on other people or the system. ✶

Compassion comes more easily when I'm not in a state of financial need or dependence. ✶

Archetypes You Most Need to Emphasize to Create Balance

Saver: self-sufficiency, abundance

Innocent: hope, adaptability

Star: leadership, style

THE SAVER

Painful Emotional States

Fearful

Obsessive

Tense

Hyperanalytical

Futuristic

Common Distorted Thoughts (Conditioned Beliefs from the Past)

If I save enough, I'll be happy, safe, secure.

I'm worried that I won't have enough.

I have to keep a close watch on my nest egg.

What am I worth now? How much has that grown/shrunk?

Liberating Wisdom or Ways to Focus

Relaxing and enjoying my life is a high priority in this next hour.

I will find a way to connect to the world through a relationship or one of my passions right now.

My fulfillment is my highest priority today.

Relaxing is a much more important part of my life than I realize.

Archetypes You Most Need to Emphasize to Create Balance

Pleasure Seeker: enjoyment, pleasure

Idealist: vision, compassion

Caretaker: empathy, generosity

THE STAR

Painful Emotional States

Sensitive to criticism
Anxious
Insignificant
Worthless
Lonely
Phony

Common Distorted Thoughts (Conditioned Beliefs from the Past)

Using money to feel classy, elegant, cool, and hip will make me happy.

Liberating Wisdom or Ways to Focus

Making sure my use of money is truly nourishing all parts of me is very important.

Giving to others brings me joy and happiness.

Resisting the temptation to buy something for attention is very self-loving.

Archetypes You Most Need to Emphasize to Create Balance

Guardian: alertness, prudence
Innocent: hope, adaptability
Caretaker: empathy, generosity
Idealist: vision, compassion

THE INNOCENT

Painful Emotional States

Frustrated

Overwhelmed

Desperate

Inadequate

Helpless

Victimized

Common Distorted Thoughts (Conditioned Beliefs from the Past)

Money doesn't come easily—in fact, it's a constant struggle for me.

I'm never going to have as much money as I need to live the life I want.

If I don't look at my financial situation, I won't feel the pain, and somehow my situation will get better.

Liberating Wisdom or Ways to Focus

I can simplify my lifestyle needs to create self-sufficiency.

I can find a vocation that I enjoy and am passionate about that will bring me enough income.

Archetypes You Most Need to Emphasize to Create Balance

Empire Builder: innovation, decisiveness

Guardian: alertness, prudence

Saver: self-sufficiency, abundance

THE CARETAKER

Painful Emotional States

Guilty
Martyred
Overburdened
Angry
Selfless
Superior

Common Distorted Thoughts (Conditioned Beliefs from the Past)

They couldn't make it without me.

My needs are less important than theirs.

Liberating Wisdom or Ways to Focus

I cannot effectively help others unless I'm taking good care of myself.

Archetypes You Most Need to Emphasize to Create Balance

Innocent: hope, adaptability

Pleasure Seeker: enjoyment, pleasure

Saver: self-sufficiency, abundance

THE EMPIRE BUILDER

Painful Emotional States

Driven
Insatiable
Insecure
Stressed
Lonely
Grandiose

Common Distorted Thoughts (Conditioned Beliefs from the Past)

Once I have _____, I'll be happy.

Power will make me safe and fulfilled.

Liberating Wisdom or Ways to Focus

I have enough today to enjoy my life fully.

Achieving my goals is not going to make any real difference to my inner quality of life.

The only place I can be truly happy is in the present moment.

Archetypes You Most Need to Emphasize to Create Balance

Pleasure Seeker: enjoyment, pleasure

Idealist: vision, compassion

HEART RACING?

Don't be surprised if you feel strong resistance or have a response like, "They're totally contradictory—which one am I supposed to follow?!" Don't worry about picking your course of action just yet. Just being aware of both your conditioned beliefs and liberating wisdom is a huge step.

Once you feel ready to take some concrete steps forward, your heart may be racing as you move toward the middle. If you're uncomfortable and you're directly addressing the source of your suffering ("I'm suffering because I believe _____ and it's just not 100 percent true"), you deserve huge congratulations. At first, every move toward balance creates inner conflict. Savers who start to be generous experience nervousness. Pleasure Seekers who begin to put money away for the future feel oppressed. At first you might be very frightened and anxious. Your new behavior might make you feel worse. It will very likely take a period of just tolerating these feelings before you get to a place of freedom. This is why most people never change—they can't get through the initial period of resistance.

Ninety-nine percent of people will die having not examined their conditioning and beliefs in any meaningful way. The liberating thoughts above are meant to guide you, not to eliminate your Core Story; it will be with you until you die. The only variable is how much power it has to run your financial life.

OPPOSITES ATTRACT

Money can be one of the most divisive, stress-inducing forces in modern human relationships. Be they romantic, business, or familial, where money is concerned, our relationships too often falter. Many psychological surveys count money as the number one cause of separation and divorce.

Much of the reason for this lies in the fact that the Wanting Mind, as a result of its "not-enough" perspective, is always making the outer world a problem to be solved. So when we find ourselves in a financial relationship with a spouse, business partner, parent, boss, child, or employee, we relate to that person as a problem to be solved, the cause of our insecurity and pain around money. We believe that if only they would behave differently around money our problems would cease, and of course, they rarely do.

THE MASCULINE-FEMININE DANCE WITH MONEY

Author David Deida, renowned for his insights into men's and women's relationships and his books on spirituality and sexuality, shared with me his ideas about masculine and feminine roles regarding money. "When a man and a woman dance together, or masculine-feminine partners dance together, it's not as fun if they both just do exactly the same steps," he said. "As humans, we actually thrive on this dynamic of opposites. So that tension between 'Should we save money for future disasters or do we help now, with as much as we can?'—that's a creative tension that never gets resolved."

Our Core Story also has a significant effect on our relationships, because so often we are merely relating unconscious-to-unconscious. We attract romantic partners who play their part in helping us create the financial life our unconscious Core Story is most comfortable with. But it is our own Core Story, not the actions of others, that creates this life and its attendant suffering.

The Middle Way is the antidote to an imbalanced Core Story. But instead of cultivating the opposite Core Story inside themselves, many people instead choose a romantic partner or spouse who exemplifies an archetype that balances them. Find your own archetype or archetypes on pp. 167–174, and then look at the archetypes in the bottom section—are any of them dominant in your life partner?

It is rare that I encounter a couple where both parties ascribe to the same archetype. Instead, Guardians tend to attract Innocents or some other archetype that is mostly oblivious to things financial. Idealists often attract Empire Builders, and Pleasure Seekers attract Savers. And on and on.

In this way, people perpetuate the idea that the solution to their money problems lies outside of themselves—in this case, with their partner or spouse. This, of course, only complicates the dynamics of a relationship. Even though we might unconsciously seek out our opposite, we then spend a huge amount of energy consciously resisting and fighting with our partner, when the real change we seek is within ourselves.

GO SLOWLY

Changing the unconscious Core Story is slow work. As discussed, it may help to think of this process of shifting our archetypal identification as being analogous to yoga. There we trans-form the body one millimeter at a time. So often when a student (or teacher) ad-justs a pose with a visual destination in mind (i.e., lifting the leg a little higher so it will look like that star student's pose), injury occurs and it takes that much lon-ger for real flexibility or strength to be cultivated. It's the same with building in-ner and outer wealth. The news is filled with stories of overnight sensations who made their fortunes in sudden and sur-prising ways. What we don't hear about is the overwhelming number of self-made millionaires who got to be that way quite slowly, over decades, not months or years. Transformation, be it physical or finan-cial, takes time, a lot of time. The con-solation is that you will reap rewards all along the way, so the destination ought not be the focus.

People living the Middle Way do not look sensational from the outside. Their lives are not the glamour-filled, stress-free idylls that we so often naïvely ascribe to the rich and famous. However, people living the Middle Way are much more adaptable to the myriad financial situations life throws at them. A person who identifies with more than just one archetype has, by definition, a much broader worldview than someone who has only lived from one archetype. A di-verse, flexible approach to finances may be reflected in a myriad of ways, from a healthy, diversified investment portfolio to a willingness to switch careers, to something much less tangible and visible, such as maintaining a balanced checkbook and enjoying simple pleasures like dining out and family vacations.

> "The majority of people are too involved with [money], with making a living and having a comfortable life. But it doesn't have to be this way. You can live in this culture and not be overcome by this materialism. Our culture doesn't really value the spiritual side, that's the important part. If it valued money and valued the spiritual side, then it would be balanced."
>
> —A. H. ALMAAS,
> AUTHOR AND TEACHER

PLAY!

I have a client, I'll call her Ariel, who was a Saver, and I mean a hard-core Saver. The ultrafrugal millionaire next door. One restaurant meal a month. Two new pairs of pants and shirts a year. A new car every ten years, no less. Then this Saver became more of an Empire Builder as her graphic design and marketing business took off. She had a few Fortune 1000 clients. But then the Internet came along and put a huge crimp in the traditional advertising budgets of large corporations, and her revenues plummeted. Her Guardian took over, with its prudence and awareness, causing her to scale back her lifestyle and business overhead. In the last three years, however, her business has adapted to the digital age, and she has higher revenues than ever before. But she isn't dreaming of the massive-scale enterprise she envisaged during her Empire Builder days. She's discovered the Pleasure Seeker, Caretaker, and Idealist within her. Ariel now has an enviable life, traveling to Vancouver and Maine every other year, supporting a local shelter for abused women and children, working twenty to thirty hours a week in her business, and deepening her commitment to religious study. If I could use one word to sum up the difference in her approach to money, it's *playfulness*. She doesn't take herself too seriously, no matter what her mind is telling her to do in a given moment. She's held extreme points of view in the past and realized the impermanence of all of them in her own experience, so she doesn't buy into her own Core Story's extreme positions. She is also able to cultivate other points of view—which are lying mostly dormant now—by referring back to other times in her life when they were dominant.

YOUR DIVINE NATURE
AND YOUR HUMAN NATURE

At first glance, the Middle Way can mistakenly appear sort of boring, like the color beige. But is it a characterless, bland compromise that leaves us devoid of passion and inspiration? No. It is the exact opposite.

By freeing up all the energy your Core Story has been spending in its fight to survive, you will be inspired to create whatever financial life you want. You will create the life that most deeply satisfies you and not be stuck with the one that was programmed by your past experience. This liberation is wonderful, but make no mistake, this is an ongoing process. The old thoughts don't completely disappear. Ever. The unconscious patterns still circulate in your brain. The difference is that you're no longer bound by them. This is true freedom.

If you can get to a place where you simply experience your own divided, contradictory experience, congratulations! You've done what very few people are able to do.

How honorable, noble, and dignified it is to go through the struggle, holding both your distorted thoughts and your liberating focus. Yet the mind's tendency is to want the final solution so badly that it goes into denial. We put our heads in the sand so as not to feel the division, the conflict. The Middle Way is pulling our head out of the sand, looking at our conditioned beliefs and often distorted thoughts, at the same time as our innate financial wisdom, holding both in our awareness as often as possible. Walking the Middle Way, we are aware of distorted thoughts and are not delusional in our optimism about the voice of our innate financial wisdom. We remember that without our inner four-year-old, we would not have grown to be the adults we are. We don't deny our unconscious or try to repress it. We emphasize equally the spiritual and the worldly. We emphasize equally the archetypes into which we were indoctrinated through decades of searing life experience and the completely visionary and transcendent wisdom that is at the core of every human being.

If Shrek and the Dalai Lama can co-exist at the Gibson Amphitheater in Hollywood, then we mere mortals can surely learn to walk the Middle Way!

CHAPTER TWELVE

THE CONSCIOUS INVESTOR

"Your future and your fortune depend on your neighbor. This is more evident today than ever before."

—THE DALAI LAMA

Thus far in these pages, I have been encouraging you to focus within so that you can start to build true wealth from the inside out. Now, having begun that process, I want you to keep that information in mind as I lead you to focus on the outer world. Whether your financial goals are primarily geared to increasing your enjoyment, your savings, or the effectiveness of your generosity in the world, one of the surest ways to build a solid financial life is through smart investing. What you're about to read is not some Pollyanna New Age theory. In fact, I have seen it grow money faster and with fewer ups and downs than virtually any other investment program, and it is espoused by some of the world's most successful investors, as you'll soon see. The style of investing I'm going to share with you is grounded in the principles of yoga and the world's great spiritual traditions, as well as in the top Western academic research into how financial markets work. Best of all, it is absolutely in line with the kind of internal focus I have been talking about throughout this book.

This way of investing:

- Directs the investor's attention inward rather than outward because the key to successful investing, as with all other money matters, is to know ourselves. Knowing ourselves means we are steadfast, not letting emotional reactivity make our investment decisions for us.

- Rests firmly on the premise that we are all interconnected and interdependent. Instead of the all-too-common emphasis on making investments in one's own city or country, this approach is global, empowering the best minds no matter where they live. This system of investing includes many more companies and, by extension, human beings than almost any other.

- Requires one to listen to what the markets are telling us about where to invest rather than to speak our opinions, as so many investors, advisors, and money managers are prone to do. In many spiritual traditions, we are encouraged to listen to the wisdom of our own bodies, our deepest inner truths, or the word of God, rather than our ego's cravings and judgments.

- Employs a receptive, collaborative perspective rather than approaching investing as a competition to be won or an aggressive activity in which only the best can thrive. In the process, this methodology improves on the returns of the majority of competitive-minded investors.

- Comes with costs and fees that are well below industry averages, leaving more to fund our goals instead of the investment industry's profits. Similarly, in yoga, we are meant to expend as little extra energy as possible. "No unnecessary effort" is one of my teacher's favorite expressions. In investing, this translates as "No unnecessary fees, costs, expenses, and taxes."

It has been said that the most successful investment strategy is the one you'll stick with for twenty-five years. However, as mentioned, most people who invest allow their emotions to unconsciously guide their investment decisions—such as which stocks or mutual funds to buy, when to sell, and how aggressive or conservative a portfolio to build—and thus change strategies much too often. As you'll soon see, studies of typical investors have shown that most earn drastically lower returns than they ought to for the risk they're undertaking. There is a better way.

HOLY INVESTING!

Sound and successful investing is actually quite simple. Many of the most successful investors in the world employ the principles of receptivity and steadfastness in their investment approach, often without knowing it. In short, they behave very much like people who have achieved a high level of spiritual equilibrium do—holy men and women, if you will.

> "Everybody wants to think that they can get rich out of their investing experience. That leads them to do silly things. People tend to overreact to recent data because they don't understand the randomness of returns and they don't appreciate the risks of being undiversified. All the marketing and all the press goes the other way."
>
> —Dr. Eugene Fama, professor of finance, University of Chicago Graduate School of Business

This chapter unearths the basic truths about investing—truths mostly drowned out by the noise of the investment industry's self-promotional hype and touchy-feely but hollow advertising campaigns. These truths allow us to build an investment program that is free of much of the stress and uncertainty investors feel, and it grows wealth faster and with less of a roller-coaster ride. As a wonderful by-product, this style of investing is also much more interconnected with the rest of humanity. This chapter is not meant to convince you to throw your entire investment strategy and your current advisor (if you have one) out the proverbial window. But by moving your investing in the direction I suggest, or starting to invest using these principles for the very first time, you will receive tremendous inner and outer benefits. For those who don't have a well thought-out investment program or who are interested in a complete overhaul, see the appendix (p. 246) for ready-to-go Conscious Investor strategies based on the amount of assets you have to invest.

WHAT INVESTING IS

When we think of the word *invest*, we might conjure up images of painful self-discipline as we sock away our hard-earned dollars for retirement, or the thousands of tiny, meaningless numbers in the business section of the newspaper, or perhaps power-hungry titans of Wall Street taking advantage of the less fortunate. Though all these things exist in modern society, investing is, at its core, much more simple and straightforward.

The word *invest* comes from the Latin *investire,* meaning "to clothe in." The meaning, "to use money to produce profit," expresses the notion of giving one's capital new form, or "clothing." If we think of the money we have earned as representing our life energy (a theme explored by Joe Dominguez and Vicki Robin in *Your Money or Your Life*), the question becomes, "What form do we want our life energy to take?"

At its best, investing is about being an active, contributing member of the human race. It is about providing our capital to other human beings so that they can live more productive lives. When we buy stock in a company, we, along with all the other owners (shareholders), are providing capital so that, for example, the company can build a new factory, which employs workers to build a product, which, if all goes well, makes the lives of its customers better. When we invest in an apartment or office building, we are effectively using our capital to give other people a place to live or work.

Our financial capital is the amount of resources we have that exceeds our present needs. It is our "extra," and with it we forge relationships with others. The level of interconnectedness available to today's investors was not possible among human beings until quite recently. Think of a time before money, when there was no abstract way to represent surplus. A person who figured out a faster way to weave clothing had no personal financial incentive to teach others to use her technique and no means with which to accumulate the fruits of her productivity—or capital—and provide it to others, so she just wove what her family could use. This was a huge waste of productive capacity, which lowered the quality of life for both our uber-weaver and the other people in her clan. (There were, of course, collective societies that used barter and storing of commodities and products to benefit the wider community, and such systems really were the basis for money as a means of exchange among people.) We can think of today's global economy like a human body, where money is the life force that travels, ideally, to wherever it can do the most good.

INTERCONNECTED VERSUS ISOLATED WEALTH

Say what you will about a market economy, but one of the bonuses of such a system is that it gives us the opportunity to benefit both other human beings and ourselves. Most people, though, whether individual investors or professional money managers, are much too narrowly focused on how they share their capital with others. The most isolated investors don't provide their capital to others at all. Instead, they keep their money in cash, or invest it in their own home or business. This is akin to saying, "No one can make more productive use of my capital than me." A second type of investor might buy a single piece of investment real estate, or perhaps invest in a friend's business, thus widening the circle a little bit and using their capital to be a bit more interconnected. Still, they're also effectively saying, "This piece of real estate or my friend's company will be the most efficient use of my extra resources," when it rarely is. Yet a third group is willing to invest in a more diversified group of stocks or mutual funds, meaning that they become owners of twenty to a few hundred companies. But invariably their strategy relies on selecting a relatively small group of companies to invest in, which they think will yield better results than investing in all companies. In investment lingo, this all-too-common behavior is called stock-picking, or active management, and is employed knowingly or unknowingly by more than 90 percent of individual investors. Stock-pickers' hopes for superior returns are not borne out, though, in the academic literature. As the following graph from academic researcher Mark Carhart shows, the returns among all active managers engaged in picking large stocks is no better than if they were flipping coins to help them make their selections.

For those of you who may get the heebie-jeebies just looking at this graph, allow me to be your tour guide. As we travel along the horizontal (X) axis to the right, we see higher and higher returns, known as "outperformance." So, 0.0 represents the funds that don't outperform or underperform, the negative numbers to the left represent those that

> "We are geared by nature to look for patterns.... And what is most confusing to people is the case when there is no pattern, when it really is governed by luck. The stock market is a perfect example of that. Today you have Abbott and Costello on CNBC. One says the market will go up, and one says the market will go down. You have nobody who says, 'I simply don't know, and there is no way of knowing.'"
>
> —Dr. Meir Statman, professor of finance, Santa Clara University

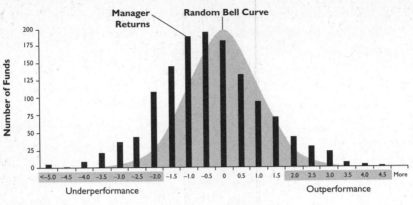

Performance Distribution

underperform, and the positive numbers to the right represent those that outperform.

But the really interesting lesson of this graph comes by comparing the gray bell-shaped curve to the vertical dark gray bars. The shaded gray bell-shaped curve is the distribution of investment returns that would occur if you were essentially flipping coins or throwing darts to help you pick stocks. The highest point on the curve is where the funds added no value. As you move right, you can get a sense of how many funds (coin-flippers) should randomly be doing better than the average, and as you move left, you can see how many should be doing worse. Remember that this is random—in other words, there is no presumption of extra skill or effort on the part of the fund manager.

In contrast, the vertical bars represent the actual returns of actual fund managers, with all their fast computers, business-class flights around the country to interview corporate managers, and teams of freshly minted and experienced MBAs. As you can see, there is a distribution of actual managers similar in shape to what we're seeing in the random (coin-flipping) distribution. As you move out toward the tails, fewer managers do much better than the average, and fewer do worse. Most managers earn close to the market's average returns.

Bottom line? *The distribution of actual managers is significantly to the left (worse) than the average returns that ought to be generated through random coin-flipping. This means that, overall, the actual fund managers do worse than coin-flipping or dart-throwing would have done.*

The information on this chart might also cause us to hope that we are picking the best managers ahead of time, because some do earn better results. But this is mostly a matter of luck—just like one can flip a coin and get heads ten times in a row. As David Booth, the chairman and CEO of Dimensional, a $150 billion passive investment firm (more on this type of investing in a minute), told me, "It's like the lottery. Everyone knows that lottery tickets have a negative expected return"—meaning that in aggregate, all players will walk away with less than they put in—"but people will keep playing on the hope that they're one of the lucky ones."

Bottom line? *In trying to pick winners in the investment game, most individual investors experience substantially lower performance than they would if they just bought and held a broadly diversified index of stocks.*

INVESTING AS THOUGH WE'RE ALL ONE

So what does any of this have to do with fulfillment on the spiritual plane? Every major spiritual tradition states that we are all one. And the style of investing this chapter describes is a very practical application of that lesson, as you'll soon learn.

The way to own the stock market is through passive investing, more commonly known as indexing (I will use these terms interchangeably from here on out). In its simplest form, passive investing involves buying a broadly diversified basket of stocks that is defined by a set of financial screens, not any investor's subjective preferences. The most familiar examples of passive investing are the index funds based on the S&P 500 index (a well-known investment benchmark that includes roughly the five hundred largest U.S. corporations). These funds must buy all five hundred of the companies in the Standard and Poor's Index in direct proportion to their weight in the index. In other words, if General Electric is 2 percent of the index, an S&P 500 index fund must put 2 percent of its assets into GE. By buying and holding this fund, investors provide their capital to the largest companies in the United States proportionally, with no subjective bets on which companies might do better than others.

> "The reality is you don't need to understand any of the complex aspects of the stock market. You don't need to own stocks. You need to own the stock market."
>
> —JOHN BOGLE, FOUNDER OF VANGUARD FUNDS

These five hundred companies employ tens of millions of people and make products that are used by billions around the world. Compared to a typical portfolio of perhaps twenty to thirty stocks, or even the typical mutual fund portfolio of two hundred stocks, even just this common index strategy is much more interconnected. But the five hundred largest companies in the United States are a small minority of what can be indexed. The strategies we employ at my investment firm actually invest in over 11,500 companies—and thus affect all their employees and customers. Bottom line? *The more companies you invest in, the wider an impact your money will have.*

> **"Those following [the path of indexing] are sure to beat the net results (after fees and expenses) delivered by the great majority of investment professionals."**
>
> —WARREN BUFFETT

DOES IT REALLY WORK?

"We're all one" might be a nice, touchy-feely spiritual saying, but who would want to employ it in their investment strategy if it might mean lower returns and having to work harder or longer to reach our goals? You'll remember from the Wanting Mind chapter that most investors pour cash into mutual funds as those funds rise and sell out as funds' performance declines. The following chart from Dalbar's QAIB® study (previously cited in chapter 1) displays the difference in the rate of growth between the typical investor in mutual funds and one who buys and holds the S&P 500 index.

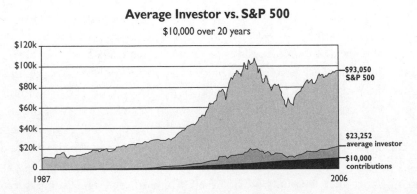

Average Investor vs. S&P 500
$10,000 over 20 years

As you can see, there are tremendous financial benefits to removing human subjectivity from the investment equation: in this case, the potential to end the twenty-year period with over four times the capital you would have had. If you can't remove this subjectivity on your own, a professional advisor might be just what the doctor ordered. For some, trying to follow their own financial and investment plan is as difficult as trying to perform psychotherapy on oneself—there's just too little objectivity.

Bottom line? *Use a pro or some other objective third party to temper your emotional impulses.*

WHEN THE PAST DOES NOT EQUAL THE FUTURE

As we saw in the coin-flipping example above, there are always better-performing stock-pickers and worse-performing stock-pickers, whether we're looking at actual money managers with their computers and MBAs or coin-flipping monkeys. As the following chart shows, even if you employed a strategy of buying the top thirty performing funds over a historical five-year period, the likelihood is that none of them would be among the stellar performers in the subsequent period.

Subsequent Performance of the Top Thirty Mutual Funds

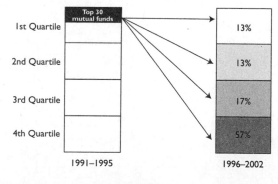

Source: Micropal™ (excludes international, balanced, and specialty funds).

This chart shows us that of the thirty top-performing funds in the period from 1991 to 1995, a full seventeen (57%) dropped into the bottom quartile (the quarter of all funds with the worst performance) between 1996 and 2002. Only 13 percent, or four funds, were even in the top quartile, even after their stellar performance in the first time period.

> "To buy when others are despondently selling and to sell when others are greedily buying requires the greatest fortitude and pays the greatest reward."
>
> —SIR JOHN TEMPLETON

(Just in case you're wondering, looking at ten years of historical performance rather than five doesn't provide better results. In fact, the winning managers tend to drop even further.)

Bottom line? *Great past performance is not predictive of better-than-average future performance.*

DOING GOOD AND DOING WELL

Some of you may be cringing at the thought that a book on conscious investing would suggest that you buy the S&P 500, given that it includes several companies that social activists deem to have dismal environmental or workers' rights records, or whom our court system has forced to pay huge damages for intentionally trying to get our kids addicted to nicotine. There are indeed too many examples of companies that build products that many people believe are useless or even harmful, as well as wealthy investors who enhance their fortunes at the expense of others. In the mid-1980s, socially responsible investing (SRI) began to become a large-scale movement in the investment markets, with major players like California Public Employees Retirement System (Cal-PERS) and large university endowments deciding to withdraw their investments from companies that still did business in South Africa, which at the time was led by the Nationalist government and its racist system of apartheid. Mutual funds began to spring up with a variety of social screens, including funds that avoided investing in South Africa, tobacco companies, and environmental polluters, to name but a few. Though these mutual funds broke new ground by incorporating their shareholders' values into the investment management process, they unfortunately exhibited the typical behaviors that have hurt investors' performance for decades, including subjective stock-picking, high expenses, and tax-inefficiency. In other words, doing good came at the cost of doing well financially.

In 1991, Amy Domini, a former stockbroker who was one of the earliest proponents of SRI, combined passive indexing and social screening and created the first socially screened index fund, the Domini Social Equity Fund. Then, in mid-2000, Vanguard teamed up with Calvert to offer the

Vanguard Calvert Social Index Fund (now called the Vanguard FTSE Social Index Fund) with an expense ratio (the amount per year that the fund management company takes out of the fund's return to pay its operating expenses) of only 0.25 percent, about one-sixth of the industry average. In an ideal world, there would be socially screened index funds for all asset classes, including large, small, international, domestic, and value stocks. But these do not exist as of this writing, and so some complain that the few index funds that employ SRI, including the two funds cited above, screen and invest in only large U.S. stocks and ignore small and foreign companies, both of which are very important building blocks of a well-diversified investment strategy, as you'll soon read. The social investment industry's defense is that it's quite a bit more difficult to convince teenagers to smoke, build a massive carbon-dioxide emitting plant, or wreak havoc on an ecosystem if you're a very small company, and most of the biggest "sinners" are based in the United States. For this reason, most of the companies that SRI index funds exclude are large, U.S.-based blue-chip companies. At the time of this writing, the Vanguard fund, in my opinion, represents the best way to index U.S. large stocks on a passive, socially screened basis. Other index strategies, which focus on small and foreign companies, are under development but are not yet available to the retail investor.

Another approach that some SRI investors take is called shareholder activism, in which one intentionally buys shares in companies whose policies one would like to change. Being an owner allows one to vote for board members who might steer the company in a better direction, voice one's concerns at shareholder meetings and to the investor relations department, and otherwise be heard as an insider instead of an outsider. Of course, you're not going to single-handedly create a boardroom coup at a multinational corporation just because you bought ten shares, but being a shareholder will allow you to affiliate with other shareholders with similar values and perhaps have an impact. (See p. 263 for more information on SRI.)

THE MIDDLE WAY FOR INVESTORS

If you were given a choice between the following two portfolios, you might think that since they have the same average return in percentage terms, they would yield the same results. Not so. Which do you think would grow your money the fastest?

PORTFOLIO	A'S RETURNS	B'S RETURNS
Year 1:	40%	10%
Year 2:	−20%	10%
Year 3:	10%	10%
AVERAGE:	10%	10%

The answer—despite the 40 percent gain that A experiences in Year 1—is B. In fact, over a three-year period, a $100,000 investment in A grows to $123,200 while the same $100,000 in B grows to $133,100, even though the two have the same 10 percent average return! It's the old tortoise and the hare. The reason is that the smoother ride of B (known as lower volatility in investment lingo) means it has a much higher compound return, which is what dictates how much money you'll have at the end of the period. Who wouldn't want a higher return with lower volatility? Though finding an investment that will make you 10 percent year in and year out without undue risk is rather difficult, the aim is to smooth out the ride (lower the volatility) of our investment portfolio. But how do you do this?

So far we've discussed passive indexing and social screening. These are both contributors to a conscious, holistic approach to investing. But there's another key component to the Conscious Investor program: incorporating classes of investments that don't move in lockstep with each other. This is known as "asset-class diversification"—in simple terms, putting your money into investments that move in different directions at different times.

In 1990, Dr. Harry Markowitz won the Nobel Prize in Economics for his work on portfolio theory. He told me in our interview for this book, "The world is uncertain, and even the insiders don't know if a company is going to succeed or fail. My work has been to use formal math to work out how we should diversify our investment portfolios to get the maximum return at a given point of uncertainty or risk." Markowitz's work showed that investors can do this by acquiring different types of assets. For example, holding a combination of large stocks, small stocks, foreign stocks, and real estate over the long term will increase return and reduce risk compared to a portfolio that only contains one of the four. Interestingly, though Markowitz's work was not based on any spiritual texts, this notion of combining dissimilar asset classes was described in the Talmud, Judaism's ancient text on ethics and law, which says, "Let every man divide his money into three parts, and invest a third in land, a third in business, and a third let him keep in reserve."

In other words, a good asset allocation is 33 percent real estate, 33 percent stocks, and 33 percent bonds, which I consider the three major asset classes.

Investors would be wise to follow this nearly two-thousand-year-old advice, because these asset classes will do well or poorly at different times and to different degrees. (Mathematically speaking, they are not highly correlated to each other.) During the bear market of 2000–2003, for example, a period when the S&P 500 lost 44 percent of its value, real estate (as measured by the National Association of Real Estate Investment Trusts index) rose 45 percent and bonds (as measured by the Lehman Intermediate Government/Corporate Index) rose 28 percent. So, instead of losing 44 percent of his capital (if he only owned the S&P 500), an investor who diversified in this way would have instead *made* 10 percent overall. Not bad for two-thousand-year-old advice!

TRUE DIVERSITY

Many investors mistakenly assume that diversification simply means not having all your eggs in one basket. For some, knowing that they own at least twenty stocks makes them feel adequately diversified. For others, it comes from owning multiple mutual funds or hiring two or more investment advisors.

The problem with both of these approaches is that what really matters is how diverse your *asset classes* are, not how many stocks or managers are involved. I've seen numerous portfolios, put together by reputable and trusted professionals, where there were eight to ten mutual funds or separate account managers, all with different names and containing hundreds of individual stocks, leading the untrained eye to think that there was adequate diversification. However, most of the time when I've done an analysis to see which asset classes these stocks represented, it became clear that more than two-thirds of their assets were in U.S. large blue-chip companies. This is why so many people lost 50–75 percent of their stock investments in the 2000–2003 bear market.

Within the three major asset classes called for in the Talmud—stocks, real estate, and bonds—there are further subdivisions we can make that reduce the risk to the overall portfolio, especially when one invests in these asset classes on a passive, or indexed, basis. These include:

VALUE STOCKS. These are stocks whose total market value (i.e., what the entire business would sell for) is low relative to their annual sales or their book value (an accounting term for the sum of all the assets—e.g., desks, buildings, inventory, and equipment a company owns—net of its debts). This is a class of stocks that are out of favor at a given moment. Their story isn't very glamorous; perhaps their management has been making mistakes, or they are considered "old economy." As a result, the values of these companies have gone down relative to other companies. As an example, as of this writing you'd have to pay about eight times book value to buy Microsoft, but only two times book value to buy Southwest Airlines. It's sort of like having one part of your garden that has begun to receive less water and sunlight because a sprawling tree is taking up all the resources and another part that is thriving, with great sunlight and water. The sunny, hydrated part of the garden is analogous to all the best-managed, fastest-growing companies, which everyone already expects to do well. If you only have a limited amount of resources to distribute—new water and sunlight—where do you think it will reap the most reward? The shady, undernourished part of the garden, of course.

Well, it's the same with investing, except that it's our capital instead of sunlight and water that is the scarce resource we have to distribute as efficiently as possible. If you could buy for $100 a company that had annual sales of $100, or buy for $300 a company that also had annual sales of $100, and you knew nothing more about either company, you'd much rather buy the first company, because chances are very good that you'd be paying substantially less for the right to earn each dollar of net income the company earns. It's kind of like the company is on sale, although what is specifically for sale is the company's stream of future earnings, which is what you are actually buying when you become an owner of its shares.

The point is that just because a business is doing very well, or is well managed, is not a reason to invest in it—*because the rest of the stock market's investors know the story too, and so the price you'll have to pay for the stock already reflects that optimism.* Some of the most famous and successful investors, including Warren Buffett and Benjamin Graham, were value stock investors. Investors' pessimism regarding value stocks is usually warranted when you look at the risks one company at a time. But if one invests a portion of one's assets in a broadly diversified index of value stocks, the risk of the overall portfolio usually declines because those that will rebound and exceed the market's pessimistic expectations will more than offset the few that will continue to languish. And over the past forty years, value stocks have returned about 3 percent more than U.S. blue-chip stocks. This may not sound like a lot. But over a forty-year period, it amounts to an investor having triple the money he or she otherwise would have had.

SMALL-CAPITALIZATION STOCKS. These are stocks whose total market value is low in absolute terms. There are many competing definitions of what small is, but my belief is that the smaller the better because that's where you get the most counterbalance to large-cap stocks, which dominate most people's portfolios. Over the past forty years, small-cap stocks have returned about 2 percent more than U.S. blue-chip stocks.

INTERNATIONAL STOCKS. These often provide risk-reduction benefits during U.S. market declines. Foreign stocks don't necessarily earn more than U.S. stocks, but they tend to earn their returns in different periods (especially when denominated in their local currencies), again smoothing out the ride of the overall portfolio. Foreign stocks can (and should) include large and small companies located in both developed and emerging markets (i.e., developing countries).

REAL ESTATE. The simplest way to own real estate in the United States is through real-estate investment trusts (REITs), which derive their streams of earnings from real estate instead of products and services. As with stocks, it is very important that investors focus on geographic diversification; properties should not all be located within one city or geographic region. This runs counter to how most investors think of real estate, which is generally acquired because they can see it and touch it, or it was inherited from family and is therefore located in one geographic area. The second important type of diversification is property-type diversification, which means that you don't only own one property type, such as office, apartment, retail, or industrial. This would be like only owning one type of stock, such as oil or financial services. The reason for these types of diversification is that most real-estate downturns affect different regions and property types at different times. A regional recession that drives up office vacancies in the Northeast probably won't drive up apartment vacancies in the West. I like to see more affluent clients invest directly in real estate, but you need to have enough so that you can buy at least three separate properties, preferably as different from each other as possible. If your investment portfolio isn't large enough to allow this, a good index fund of REITs will provide adequate diversification.

COMMODITIES. Commodities such as agricultural products, precious metals, and oil behave similarly to real estate in that they are both very different from stocks and bonds. Now, there are very risky ways to invest in commodities, known as futures, where fortunes have been made and lost quite suddenly. I'm not proposing that you try to play in that league. Instead, there are a small handful of commodities index funds that are balanced among many different types of commodities—metals, energy, and agricultural products—and that help reduce overall portfolio volatility, even though commodities may appear quite volatile when viewed in isolation.

BONDS. As you'll read below, increasing one's allocation to bonds is the surest way to reduce downside risk in a portfolio. The general rule of thumb is that over time, you don't get rewarded for investing in junk bonds or for taking on the risk of owning long-term bonds (which are much more sensitive to interest rate changes). Bottom line? *I advise clients to focus the bond side of their portfolios on highly rated corporate and government bonds that will be paid off in five to seven years or less.*

SO HOW DOES A DIVERSIFIED PORTFOLIO PERFORM?

Evaluated on their own, each of these asset classes can seem extreme in terms of volatility, which types of market conditions make it behave poorly or well, and how it comes into and out of favor. Bottom line? *Just as we need to achieve a balance among the different archetypes in ourselves, the key to successful investing is to combine asset classes in such a way that they balance each other out.*

Here, then, is the allocation I recommend for a portfolio that contains no bonds. Of course, if you need a more conservative portfolio, you will include bonds as well. The percentages below apply only to the non-bond portion of your portfolio.

U.S. Large	21%
U.S. Large Value	21%
U.S. Small	9%
U.S. Small Value	9%
International Large Value	8%
International Small	4%
International Small Value	4%
Emerging Markets Portfolio	3%
Emerging Markets Small	3%
Emerging Markets Value	3%
Real Estate	10%
Commodities	5%

BUYING LOW AND SELLING HIGH

Once you've allocated your assets, you must institute a very important ongoing discipline called rebalancing, in which you periodically re-allocate your portfolio back to its originally established targets.

Let's take a look at a simple example: Say your portfolio is allocated 40 percent to a large stock index fund, 20 percent to a small-stock index fund, and 40 percent to a short-term bond fund. If the stock market (including both large and small) goes up 30 percent and bonds stay flat, you're now going to have 66 percent of your assets in stocks and only 34 percent in bonds. Rebalancing mandates that you sell your large stocks (in this example) back down to 40 percent of the new higher-total portfolio value, your small stocks back down to 20 percent of the total, and use the proceeds to buy your bonds back up to 40 percent. This forces you to sell what has just appreciated and buy what has just gone down in value, relatively speaking.

Most investors do just the opposite—they buy more of what's gone up, and often sell what's gone down. Over the long run, this is akin to buying high and selling low, whereas successful investors obviously want to do the opposite. Rebalancing will require you to go against your emotional instincts fairly often, but it is practiced by the majority of the country's most successful investors and is considered a best practice in the investment management industry.

Many investors wonder how long to hold on to their "winners"—the assets that have appreciated most dramatically. Most hold on too long. Rebalancing forces us to sell our winners and reinvest in those asset classes that have appreciated less. You might wonder just how often one ought to rebalance. Most professional investors choose to rebalance at periodic intervals, such as every calendar year, or they pick an acceptable range within which each asset class can move without generating a trade. For example, if your portfolio has a target of 40 percent U.S. large stocks, then you might set an acceptable range of 32 percent to 48 percent so that if that asset class gets below 32 percent, you'll buy more of it, or if above 48 percent, you'll sell some of it. How much? Just enough to get back down to your target allocation.

Most of the ready-to-go strategies I recommend in the appendix starting on p. 246 take care of rebalancing for you.

Here are two sample portfolios. One is security diversified, meaning that there are many different stocks or funds, but substantially all the assets are invested in U.S. large blue-chip companies; the other is asset-class-diversified in accordance with the percentage guidelines discussed in this section. Take a look at the results for yourself:

Value of $1,000 Investment after Thirty-Four Years

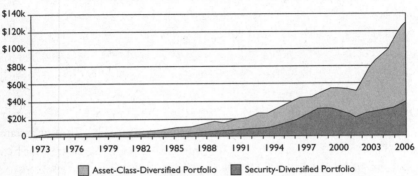

As mentioned earlier, a big part of the reason why the asset-class-diversified portfolio grows so much faster is that there are fewer ups and downs when we combine the extremes (just as an individual benefits when he or she balances archetypal extremes). Consequently, there is actually a lot more wealth at the end of the day (just like a more balanced investor has attained more peace and freedom).

All investors are looking for a free lunch: that next hot tip or sure thing that will bring us big rewards. I believe asset-class diversification is the only true free lunch in investing, in that you can actually reduce your risk and increase your rate of return in a reliable, time-tested manner. Many spiritual traditions stress balance between extremes as a key to growth and progress, and this also holds true in investing.

UNEARTHING THE HIDDEN FEES AND COSTS OF INVESTING

When it comes to the costs and fees charged by the financial services industry, there are definitely no free lunches. To avoid paying more in fees than you need to pay, it is helpful to understand a bit about the history of the investment advisory business. Originally, a corporation would approach a financial services firm to raise capital, the investment banking department of the firm would underwrite a stock offering, and then a team of salespeople, who later came to be known as brokers, would get on the phones and pitch the stock to investors. If you had one client—the corporation—paying you millions of dollars in fees, and thousands of other clients, each paying you perhaps a few hundred or thousand in fees, where do you think your primary loyalty would lie? Probably with the corporation paying you millions to underwrite their stock offering and not with the many individual investors whom you viewed as customers for that stock.

There has been little pressure put on financial services firms to make their fees and charges more transparent to individual investors. As a result, most investors are paying much more in fees than they think they are. (Later in this chapter, I'll show you how to find out just how much more.) In response, many financial advisors would say, "Who cares what our fees are? What you should care about is the performance I'm getting you." This kind of a statement avoids the tremendous body of independent research showing that high fees and costs consistently create poorer performance results for the investor.

John Bogle, founder of the Vanguard Group, determined that persistently high expense ratios (the amount a mutual fund charges its investors for its services) were behind much of the lackluster performance of mutual funds that we reviewed earlier in this chapter. Bogle's analysis of the performance of funds with active portfolio managers (i.e., those who pick and choose which stocks to buy and sell) versus a passive market index (such as the S&P 500) found that expenses accounted for 92 percent of the mutual fund shortfall in performance relative to the market index. This makes sense because whatever the gross return of your investment portfolio, everyone who has their hand in the cookie jar must be paid out of that gross return.

In a perfect world, I would love to see a full and simple fee-disclosure schedule that each investor must sign before any investment is made. This would look much like the gas mileage window disclosure stuck on the window of all new cars, or the nutrition-facts box on all packaged food products. It would say simply,

The total amount of fees and costs associated with this investment, assuming a three-year holding period, is **3.10 %**

Bottom line? *High fees and costs are behind most of the performance disadvantage that non-indexed investment managers have historically exhibited.*

Most investors would be shocked to learn that they're likely giving up between 2 and 5 percent per year of their investment assets (yes, 2–5%) to their brokers and financial services companies. I'm not talking here about certain abusively priced annuities or insurance products, which can go even higher. I'm talking about your run-of-the-mill investment account at a typical broker-age firm, trust company, retail mutual fund, or money management firm.

The other major cost to consider is taxes. They can greatly reduce return, yet most mutual fund and separate account managers are hired and fired based on pretax performance. Therefore, many advisors pay too little attention to the impact of taxes. Based on a recent academic study of the subject, this has led to anywhere from 1.4 to 4.1 percent of gross returns being lost to the IRS, depending on the asset class in question. In contrast, there are tax-efficient portfolios of index funds that typically lose less than 0.50 percent per year to taxes.

> "Wall Street has worked hard to make investing very complicated. That's why they're able to charge a lot of money for giving advice and guidance."
>
> —Joe Moglia,
> CEO, TD Ameritrade

Please don't underestimate the importance of fees and taxes. If you are paying more than you should, it could make a huge difference in your future financial security and choices. For example, a 1 percent increase in costs could require you to work an extra five years before retiring, or to send your child to a college that costs half as much as the one you could have afforded had you reduced your investment costs sooner.

Bottom line: *Know how much your investments are costing you.*

HIDDEN FEES

Because it is so hard to unearth all the hidden fees, I'm including a short list of questions for you to ask your investment provider(s). I'm includ-ing some industry-specific terms that you can use verbatim to get more accurate and truthful answers, even if you don't necessarily understand the meanings yourself. After each question, I've listed in parentheses the standard amounts I believe should be charged. If you're paying more (and you very likely are), you are making a bet that your investments will overcome the extra expense burden through better performance (which, according to the data, occurs only in extremely rare cases). Tell

➤

your advisors or managers to calculate the answers based on the prior twelve months of your relationship with them. If this is a new relationship, have them put together a sample portfolio that they propose to invest in on your behalf, and answer these questions on that portfolio—perhaps using an existing client with holdings similar to what you're going to own. If any of these are flat dollar amounts, have them convert the annual total to a percentage of your assets.

1. *How much am I paying you and your company directly in management fees, transaction fees (for buying and selling securities), financial planning fees, and retainers?*
_____% (0.25%–1.25%; the more assets you're investing, the lower the percentage should be).

2. *How much will the total trading expenses, including spreads between the bid (the price I receive when I sell a security) and the ask (the price I pay to buy a security), cost me as a percentage of my portfolio each year on securities that I buy directly from you or your firm?*
_____% (0%–0.25%)

3. *How much in up-front or deferred commissions (known as "loads") or placement fees will I pay on the mutual funds or other investments you're recommending?*
_____% (0%)
With a few exceptions, this number should be zero, if their answer to question 1 above was greater than 0%. Because a load or placement fee only occurs once, divide it over the expected holding period for the investment. For example, a 5% load over a three-year holding period would be 1.67% per year.

4. *What is the expense ratio (the amount a fund manager charges a client or fund for their services) or ongoing management fee charge for the fund companies or separate money managers I am invested in?*
_____% (0.15%—0.50%, depending on the asset class. In general, the small and international asset classes should be toward the higher end of this range.)

(continued on next page) ➤

HIDDEN FEES *(continued from previous page)*

5. As a percentage of my portfolio each year, what are the costs that you pay for transactions, including bid/ask spreads?

This is a different question from question 2 above. Just like any investor, mutual fund companies and money managers must endure similar spreads between the ask and the bid prices on each security, as well as other transaction expenses on securities they buy on your behalf. For example, if a fund buys a stock for $15.50 but can only sell it for $15.00, that $0.50 cost will ultimately be borne by the fund's shareholders.

_____% (The industry average is between 0.60% and 0.80%, depending on which study you read.)

6. Do you earn any other fees or commissions I haven't asked about? What is the source of those? In what way do they come out of my portfolio's returns? If they are in addition to the charges discussed above, what percentage of my assets do they represent per year?

_____%

When you have your answers, add up all of the percentages from each of the six questions to see what the total is. Assuming the stock market will be kind enough to earn you a gross return of 8 percent in the coming decades, subtract the total percentage from 8 percent and that is the net return you're most likely to earn.

Yes, I am asking you to do a little digging. But once you've completed this assignment, my guess is that you'll find a manager whose charges you can live with over the long run, and you won't need to repeat this exercise very often. And you will very likely save yourself a bundle of money. In the event that your advisor or investment firm is not willing to answer these questions forthrightly, I encourage you to seek a new relationship.

TIME IS ON YOUR SIDE

One of the hardest things for investors to accept is that every investment strategy risks losing money at some point. The potential loss may not be obvious to you; in fact, it may never occur. For example, a lot of people believe that the value of their home has always gone up. But invariably, they only knew the value of their home with any certainty when they bought it, refinanced the mortgage, or sold it. Compared to the information readily available on stocks, there's just a lot less data flowing into one's brain when it comes to home ownership. If the newspaper or TV news told you the value of your home as often as it does your stocks, people would likely exhibit very similar financial behaviors with their homes as with their other assets.

The other retort to my statement about every investment losing money at some point could be that if you invest in CDs, they never lose value. But this leaves out the effect of taxes and inflation. If you earn 5 percent on a CD and then pay 25 percent tax on that return, you're down to 3.75 percent. Higher tax brackets would reduce your after-tax interest rate even further. What's more, cost-of-living increases have averaged 3–4 percent over the long term, depending on which basket of costs you're counting. In the case of our CD investor, then, he might actually be losing real purchasing power, slowly but surely, even though he believes he's in a no-risk investment.

Bottom line? *The more risk you're willing to take in the short term, the greater the chance that you will have enough to fund your long-term goals.* In the last hundred years in the United States, there have been virtually no ten-year periods and absolutely no fifteen-year (or longer) periods in which stocks have underperformed bonds, so if your goal is that far out (and most are), you're taking far less long-term risk by having a portfolio that is tilted to stocks and real estate rather than bonds. To put it another way, would you rather face the upset stomach of seeing your portfolio decline 25 percent next year and staying invested or the emotional distress of running out of money in your eighties or nineties?

The following graph illustrates how both the upside and downside risks decline the longer we are willing to stay in an investment. (Note that for this table, I'm using the S&P 500 for stocks.)

> "There's one interesting piece of research around on behavioral tendencies—it should be put into a little red book and circulated to everybody. This says that people who trade a lot, on average, gross the same amount as everybody else. And net, of course, they do a lot worse, because excessive trading leads to excessive fees and costs."
>
> —Dr. Harry Markowitz,
> Nobel Prize–winning
> economist

S&P 500 Annualized Returns: October 1926 to September 2006

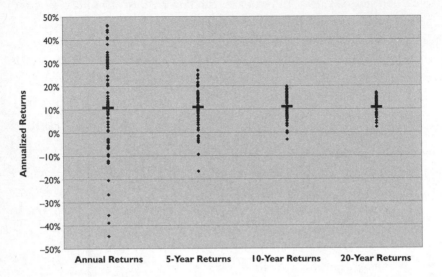

As you can see, if we are only looking at one-year returns (far left), there have been years when people made or lost almost 50 percent on their investments. If we limit our view to only five-year periods, the worst loss was 17 percent annually and the best gain about 28 percent. For ten-year periods, the worst saw losses of 4 percent annually and the best gains of 20 percent annually. Finally, there have been no twenty-year periods with a negative return, and the best return over twenty years was in the high teens annually.

This reduction of risk over time explains why it is so important for investors to cultivate internal discipline. Those who get rewarded—meaning, per the Dalbar study, they grow their $10,000 to $93,050 instead of $23,252—do so because they don't sell when things look the absolute worst, even if everyone is saying, "It's different this time, you can't look at history." They know that there's a different version of that refrain that accompanies *every* market downturn. So they ignore it or, better yet, buy more when everyone else is most pessimistic.

That said, there are certain situations where exposure to stocks and real estate should be avoided. As diversified as the portfolio I've recommended above is, it will still lose money in some years, and if you're relying on this money for a near-term goal, you need to reconsider your allocation. You don't want to be 20 percent in the hole if your kid's college tuition bill is showing up in a couple of years, for example. Use the following chart to determine the maximum safe allocation to stocks and real estate. (A caution: if your goal is retirement or some other long, slow drawdown of your assets that will begin in the short term but be stretched out over a much longer term, you should apply this table using the time when the *average* dollar, as opposed to the first or last dollar, will be withdrawn.)

Time until the average dollar will be withdrawn for your goal	Maximum % in stocks	Maximum % in REITs and commodities	Short-term bonds and money markets
Less than 2 years	0%	0%	100%
2–4 years	25%	8%	67%
4–6 years	50%	16%	34%
6–8 years	65%	20%	15%
More than 8 years	75%	25%	0%

PREPARE YOURSELF

It is very important, especially if you've never before been invested during a bear market, to understand how it will feel to watch your investments lose value. The importance of this depends on which archetype you most identify with. Though the following exercise will benefit all of us, if you are a Guardian, Saver, or Empire Builder, it is especially important. Do this exercise, and you won't bail out when the going gets rough.

WHAT'S THE RIGHT MIX OF STOCKS AND BONDS FOR YOU?

The big question is how much of a reduction in the market value of your portfolio you can stomach. (Even if you only have a couple hundred dollars to invest, you can and should invest, so read on!) The best way to protect yourself from risk is by increasing the percentage of fixed-income investments (e.g., bonds, cash, money markets, and CDs) that are in the portfolio, but that doesn't mean more fixed-income investments are right for everyone.

(continued on next page) ❯

WHATS THE RIGHT MIX OF STOCKS AND BONDS FOR YOU?
(continued from previous page)

First, write down about how much you have in investable assets to-day (include any real estate you don't keep for personal use, net of loan balances, as well as any business or other asset you'll be selling within two years):

$_____(a)

Now, keeping in mind that, historically, a diversified portfolio has always bounced back if you give it long enough, to what dollar amount would you be willing to allow your portfolio to fall without bailing out? Be honest now. Such a decline will occur; it's just a matter of when, not if.

$_____ (b)

Now, (a) − (b) = $_____ (c)

And last, (c) ÷ (a) = _____% (d).

Now find your answer to (d) in the left-hand column of the chart below, and the column on the right will tell you how much of your over-all portfolio ought to be allocated to fixed-income investments (bonds, cash, money markets, and CDs):

Maximum loss you'll accept and stay invested	Minimum percentage to allocate to bonds or money markets
0%	80%
15%	40%
20%	20%
30%	10%
>30%	0%

These allocation targets presume that you'll be employing the principles described in this chapter. If your portfolio is less diversified or more costly in fees and costs than what I'm recommending here, your losses will likely be worse in down markets than those described here, and so your allocation to bonds ought to be a little higher.

➤

If you are an extreme Guardian, you may want to see how your portfolio would have done during the Great Depression. You can do this by going to www.BrentKessel.com, where there is an Excel spreadsheet (entitled "1929") that you can fill in to see the effect the Great Depression had on various mixes of stocks and bonds. This will help you determine which portfolio might be right for you—if you really want to look at what is in my opinion an extreme worst-case scenario. (For the record, I don't believe we'll have another Great Depression, but we will have market corrections of 20–50 percent every few years albeit at irregular and unpredictable intervals.)

Bottom line? *It is very important to ascertain your tolerance for risk in the short term so that you'll stay committed to whichever portfolio allocation you choose. That is the most important ingredient for success, which is why I say it's much more important to study yourself than the markets.*

Investing is an incredibly powerful, positive experience when we approach it from the inside out. This chapter has covered a large amount of material, including concepts that are misunderstood by most investors. This includes passive investing, social screening, lowering your fees and costs, reducing your risks by choosing asset classes that don't move in lockstep, being willing to stay invested for the long term, and handling your emotions when your investments don't go as planned. No matter how you currently invest, try taking at least one step toward conscious investing this month. I could tell you countless stories of small steps clients have taken that paid big. John, a self-proclaimed Guardian, decided to sell his pharmaceutical sector fund (which owned forty stocks) in favor of a much more diversified global growth fund (which owned 650 stocks). Ursula, an Innocent who had been stuffing her unopened brokerage statements into a drawer for five years, asked her broker to answer questions on his fees and costs and was able to negotiate a much more favorable arrangement. Taking the time to align your investments with these time-tested principles grows your financial resources much faster, allowing you to achieve your innermost goals and values sooner and with greater peace of mind.

I'M GOING TO LOSE IT ALL!

At some point, even the most self-aware investors will have a difficult time coping with the vagaries of the market—to the point where they might want to abandon their strategy. If you find yourself in this situation, take heart—and follow these steps. They may seem touchy-feely, but trust me, they are extremely practical and I've used them successfully with many clients through several market corrections, including the worst one since the Great Depression.

- **NOTICE YOUR FEELINGS.** Instead of immediately acting on your tried-and-true methods of getting relief, just look inside and name your feeling state(s). Perhaps you aren't even aware of feeling anything. You just think your current strategy may not be right for you, and you're tired of waiting around for it to do what you want it to. Still, try to sit quietly, even if only for five minutes, and see if you can feel what's underneath your thoughts. Which of these words describe how you feel?

☐ Angry	☐ Sad	☐ Frustrated	☐ Confused
☐ Enraged	☐ Envious	☐ Hopeless	☐ Worthless
☐ Overwhelmed	☐ Greedy	☐ Competitive	☐ Fearful

  See if you can witness the feeling states as they change or stay the same, as they move around your body or get stuck. Do absolutely everything within your power not to make an investment decision while you're feeling an intense emotional charge.

- **IF YOU HAVE AN INVESTMENT ADVISOR, CALL HIM OR HER.** You are paying this person to do what's best for you. If the advisor is fee-only®, there should be almost no conflict of interest here, and he or she should put your needs first. If you have lost faith in your advisor, then visit another fee-only® planner for a second opinion. A good advisor will almost always advise you to stay the course, unless circumstances in your life—not in the stock market or the world at large—have changed.

➤

Speak to friends or business colleagues, but only if they've been successful and disciplined investors (ideally for many years) themselves. Ask them what they're doing in light of current circumstances.

• **IF YOU MUST ACT, WAIT UNTIL THE EMOTIONAL STORM HAS PASSED.** You might do some of the exercises prescribed in the archetype chapters in this book, especially in chapter 3. If your four-year-old self is screaming that you've got to do something right now or you could lose everything, go through the Worst-Case Scenario exercise on p. 56. Then, do your best to engage in a systematic process to establish a new strategy—one that you can now commit to in light of the new information *about yourself* that this experience has given you. Remember, nothing truly new ever really happens in the markets.

In summary, the Conscious Investor:

• owns broadly diversified indexes of stocks instead of trying to pick winning stocks or fund managers,

• processes emotional reactions to investment results internally rather than through external actions,

• insists on a portfolio that is sustainable for both the planet and his own financial future,

• understands that diversifying her portfolio across asset classes is what matters; diversifying among stocks or industries within one asset class or among financial advisors is far less essential to risk reduction or return enhancement,

• keeps costs low, ideally under 1 percent in total, and

• understands his practical and emotional ability to tolerate risk, sets prudent targets for his stock/bond mix, and rebalances to those targets in good times and bad.

CHAPTER THIRTEEN

THE YOGA OF MONEY

"Let us more and more insist on raising funds of love, of kindness, of understanding, of peace. Money will come if we seek first the kingdom of God—the rest will be given."

—MOTHER TERESA

A friend of mine, Bob Patillo, used to own a very successful real estate company but sold it and now devotes his life to helping impoverished people in developing countries. As we sat together in a Boston lounge talking about our children, he told me a story that touched me deeply:

I was driving along with my eight-year-old son, Gus, when we came upon a van parked at the side of the road with its doors open. A group of nuns were walking up and down the sidewalk in front of a grocery store, carrying boxes of packaged foods and produce. I said, "Let's pull over and see if we can help." We parked our car, got out, and went up to the sisters to see what they were doing.

They told us that they ran an orphanage, and that just a week before, three days prior to Christmas, a major fire had broken out in the orphanage and destroyed all of the children's presents. The grocery store had agreed to donate the boxes of food as a helpful gesture, even though it wouldn't replace the lost gifts the children had been so looking forward to.

At the time, I was in the habit of tracking my son's allowance on a small index card that I carried with me. We divided his weekly stipend of $6 into three equal imaginary buckets, the spending bucket, the savings bucket, and the giving bucket. He looked up at me and asked, "Dad, how much do I have in my giving bucket?" I reached into my pocket and removed the three-by-five card and said, "Twenty-six dollars." He looked at me and said, "Can I please give her twenty dollars of it for the children."

Bob's eyes moistened as he retold the story of his son's gesture. "What more could a parent ask for?" he asked.

The Dalai Lama recently said, "Love, compassion, forgiveness, and contentment are at the core of every major religion." Love and compassion are inborn, natural qualities of being human. We all know this by nature, not by law or religious doctrine. And as anyone who has given of himself or herself knows, it is not only the recipient of generosity who benefits. Many new parents express awe at the realization that they alone are responsible for the care and feeding of their infant, and this awe leads to a sense of unity, compassion, and inspiration to do the very best they can for this innocent being. Regardless of whether you're a parent or not, the feeling of being able to give, to make a difference in someone else's life, is a precious experience.

Compassion is a state of being, while generosity is an action. Money can free each of us to find the unique way that we are naturally compassionate, as well as providing a means of doing generous things in the world if we so choose. One of the greatest gifts of a healthy relationship to money is the recognition and experience that we can be satiated materially, even if that sensation is fleeting. Out of this satiation, our inspiration, fulfillment, peace, and compassion grow. When we feel we have enough, we naturally and effortlessly want to give of what we have, regardless of the size of our bank account. The phrase I use for this is the yoga of money. The word *yoga* means "to yoke, to bring together," or simply "unity," so the yoga of money is the act of using money to affirm and enhance our sense of unity, with money itself, with one another, and ultimately with something greater than all physical forms.

> ## WHEN HAVE YOU BEEN
> ## TOUCHED BY YOUR OWN GENEROSITY?
>
> Think back to a time in your life when you gave something or cared for someone and were touched in a positive way. It could be as small as picking up the tab for lunch or as life-changing as volunteering in the Peace Corps. As best you can, recall the effect that your generosity had on your state of mind and perhaps even the peace or anxiety in your body. Take a moment to honor and enjoy the essential part of your heart and soul that wanted to give. Revisit these memories and add to them by remembering other experiences of compassion or generosity in which you felt good giving. This exercise allows you to become more aware of how giving can affect you physically, emotionally, and spiritually.

SELF-CENTEREDNESS

All of us were once children who received care and support from another human being, or we wouldn't have survived. But as we grew older, we came to realize that the world is not always a safe or happy place, that our needs might or might not be provided for, and that ultimately it would be up to us to make our way in the world. This is when the Core Story was formed, which essentially is an answer to the question "How can I be safe and happy in the world?" But as we've seen, the answer to this question varies widely. Some people feel they'll be safest by enjoying their money today or by buying objects that bring them pleasure. Others feel they need to save for a rainy day. Still others feel that by avoiding money, essentially putting their heads in the sand, things will come out all right. Whatever our Core Story is, its position is always extremely self-centered. It wants to make sure that our survival is ensured.

> "My father was a lawyer at that time, and I said, 'You've been doing some law work for Uncle Henry. And I know you charge high fees. You going to charge him the same fee?' And he said, 'Well, don't be silly! It's Uncle Henry.' I said, 'Dad, in my work in the world, everyone is Uncle Henry!'"
>
> —RAM DASS

The irony is that the more self-centered we are, the less likely we are to survive. A medical study of more than three thousand individuals over seven years measured the frequency with which each person spoke the words *I, me,* and *my,* to see if there was any correlation between this self-referencing and coronary heart disease. Amazingly, they found that self-referencing was indeed related to the incidence of heart disease; in fact, it was the strongest predictor of mortality among heart-attack victims.

Beyond the question of whether self-centeredness will kill us or not, we need to understand whether other-centeredness makes us any happier or whether it's simply an externally imposed sense of responsibility to be "a good person." If caring more about others makes us happier, then we have greater incentive to move beyond our Core Story and express generosity for our own good.

> "The most sensible way to look after our own self-interest, to find freedom and be happy, is not to directly pursue these things but to give priority to the interest of others. Help others to become free of their fear and pain. Contribute to their happiness. It's all really very simple. You don't have to choose between being kind to yourself and others. It's one and the same."
>
> —PIERO FERRUCCI,
> TRANSPERSONAL PSYCHOLOGIST

Not to be caught in our Core Story—whether the Innocent's or Idealist's survival struggle, the Empire Builder's or Saver's insatiable ambition and accumulation, or the Star's or Pleasure Seeker's uncontrolled spending—gives us the balance to use money to express our soul's most natural state of being, which I believe is a state of compassion.

But we don't have to wait for complete freedom. If we allow ourselves to be less influenced by our primary archetype for even one hour a day, we can use that time to express compassion. For example, the Guardian can stop worrying, the Pleasure Seeker can say no to an impulse to purchase his own pleasure, and the Caretaker can expand her compassion to a different person or group—or herself—all for an hour a day. There is no set goal we have to reach to be compassionate. We need only liberate ourselves a little bit—to let go of our Core Story's rules and habits one moment at a time.

As previously discussed, my Core Story about money has predominantly been to save and spend prudently so that I could accumulate enough financial freedom to feel safe and not worry. Because I grew up in South Africa, I witnessed a great deal of human suffering caused by other people. I always knew that I wanted to be involved in helping others, but aside from volunteering some time and making token contributions to charity, generosity wasn't a prime motivator for me as I built my business. I felt that I needed to become wealthy first, and I hoped I would then naturally want to be more philanthropic.

But life took an unexpected turn. In March 2002, my older son, Kaden, then two, began urinating excessively. My wife, Britta, and I took him to the pediatrician, with his five-month-old brother, Rumiah, in tow, and learned that Kaden had type 1 (juvenile) diabetes. At that moment, everything changed. We began testing his blood sugar at home eight to ten times a day, measuring every bite of food that went into his mouth, and giving him shots of insulin. After the initial shock had worn off and the adaptation to a new life had set in, we did more research on this illness in order to understand when and if a cure might be coming. We learned that juvenile diabetes is a mysterious disease for which research was being conducted on a variety of fronts. Through the Juvenile Diabetes Research Foundation, a charity started in the 1970s by parents of type 1 children, we also learned that money was key to advancing this research.

So, despite my impulses as a Saver, we became avid fundraisers and donors for our cause. All of a sudden, our charitable contributions went up tenfold. But strangely, instead of feeling impoverished by this, I felt enriched. I felt more secure than I had in my frugal days. This didn't add up. I had thought I needed to be wealthy in order to feel free to express my generosity. But instead, being naturally drawn to express my compassion in a concrete way was making me feel wealthy.

It is important to stress, however, that I had not completely abandoned my most ingrained coping strategy—that of the Saver—to become more generous. I think if I had said, "I've seen the light—it's really about being generous. Then I'll feel wealthy, and I won't need to be as prudent or careful as before," I would not have been moved in the same way. Despite my personal connection to this worthwhile cause, it wouldn't have taken long for my old habits and thoughts to come rushing back: "You idiot! How could you have become so careless and undisciplined? Get back to work, stop this crazy spending and giving, and damn it, make me feel safe again!" Instead of prodding myself to be more generous, I practiced the Middle Way with my giving. That meant calling on the positive attributes of the Saver—prudence, self-sufficiency, and abundance—while cultivating the empathy and generosity that are the hallmarks of a balanced Caretaker.

I have seen many examples of how more generosity leads to more, not less, abundance. In the summer of 2006, I was invited to an event at the Los Angeles Hilton to meet Amma, an Indian woman from a small fishing village who is known as the "hugging saint." This plump, beaming woman draped in a simple white robe sat at the front of a large banquet hall filled with a few hundred people. I had to take a number, like everyone else, and wait four hours in line. As I got closer to her, I saw her hugging handicapped people, wealthy celebrities, and the maids who cleaned the hotel in which the event was being held. Amma, whose name means "mother," is able to hug hundreds of thousands of people a year on very little sleep without her body falling apart. And she seemed to emanate more love than just about anyone else I'd met. When it was my turn to be hugged, I looked into her warm brown eyes, received my hug, and felt a flood of profound peace and well-being.

In meeting her, I had the sense that Amma really does defy gravity in a certain way. My understanding has always been that resources like money and time and bodily energy are finite—irrefutable laws of the universe. If you give more away, you'll have less for yourself. But here was this poor, simple, middle-aged woman who I knew had committed to raising one billion rupees for tsunami relief (about $23 million, half again what the U.S. government committed). How could she make such a pledge? Where would the money come from? She doesn't even charge for her events, much less head a big organized fundraising effort. I'd certainly heard the old adages: "The more you give, the more you get," "Giving is its own reward," and "It is better to give than to receive." But this person was literally creating more money, time, energy, and love by giving.

The student of economics inside my head was baffled. Perhaps scarcity and abundance are not as simple as I thought. It's as though the laws of the universe bend for love. Financial laws bend. Temporal laws bend. Logistical constraints bend. By giving much more than we habitually feel comfortable giving, we might just end up having more.

IT'S NOT JUST FOR SAINTS

There is an old Jewish story that was told to me by Rabbi Harold Kushner. A rabbi is talking to a student and says, "If a man has five hundred dollars and he gives away one hundred dollars, how much does he have left?" The student looks at him incredulously and says, "Why, four hundred, of course."

And the rabbi says, "No, that's not correct. He actually has one hundred. The four hundred he may spend, he may lose, it may be stolen from him, he may invest it badly. The only thing he has permanently is the one hundred that he gave away."

Generous giving is one of the five pillars of Islam. In the following excerpt from Sura 17 of the Koran, we are invited to cultivate our generosity: "And give the kinsman his right, and the needy, and the traveler; and never squander."

In the book of Luke, followers of Christ are commanded, "Give, and it will be given to you: good measure, pressed down, shaken together, and running over will be put into your bosom. For with the same measure that you use, it will be measured back to you."

And in Buddhism, compassion is seen as a primary means of ending our self-centered suffering. In fact, Buddhist teachings describe three types of compassion. The first is when we have a feeling of closeness or empathy for a friend or someone who is nice to us, whom we like. This type of compassion is mixed with our emotional attachment to the person, so there's a bit of a bias. If he or she were to stop being nice to us, our compassion would likely cease. The second type of compassion occurs when we have a feeling of concern for another person, but it's mixed with superiority and separation. With this type of compassion, there is more pity than empathy, and perhaps lack of respect for the other person. Finally there is unbiased compassion, in which we wish that everyone may overcome suffering, regardless of how close we feel to them or how they treat us. This type of compassion does not arise spontaneously for most people. It must be cultivated through training and effort, but it brings immense benefits. When we feel unbiased compassion, everyone seems like a friend, and we experience much less worry, fear, doubt, and jealousy.

> "Generosity breeds an immediate kind of happiness, which is different than other practices, which often have a delayed positive reinforcement. This helps generosity beget more generosity with less and less effort."
>
> —Joseph Goldstein, co-founder, Insight Meditation Society

All these traditions speak of altruism not only as a responsibility or a way to care for others, but really as the primary way to care and create freedom for *ourselves*.

SHARE THE PAIN. SHARE THE GAIN.

There two practices can help you to cultivate unbiased compassion.

1. **LET'S SAY YOU'VE JUST GOTTEN A PIECE OF BAD FINANCIAL NEWS.** Perhaps you expected a tax refund but just got word from your accountant that you're going to owe the IRS several thousand dollars instead, or you just had several medical claims denied by your insurance company, or you just had an important business transaction fall through.

The first step is to realize that other people have this pain too, this very same pain that you're feeling. It might not seem genuine at first, but just admitting that you're not the only one often allows breathing room into the situation.

The second step is to say or just feel inside yourself the wish or yearning to be free of the pain you are feeling.

The third step is to extend your wish out to other people, feeling or saying, "May other people be free of this pain as well." Pema Chodron, renowned teacher of Tibetan Buddhism, offers a variation on this theme: "Seeing as how I'm feeling this pain anyway, perhaps I can feel it for all the others so that they might instead feel relief and happiness."

This whole exercise can take literally a few seconds. Just try it when you're struggling and see what happens.

2. **NOW LET'S ASSUME THAT YOU JUST HAD A WONDERFUL FINANCIAL SURPRISE.** Perhaps you received a much higher bonus or raise than you expected, or you just closed escrow on your first home, or you paid off a credit-card balance that you'd been carrying for a long time.

Make the wish that other people might also experience this joy or pleasure.

I was recently at a wonderful restaurant eating the most incredible-tasting bowl of soup, when I remembered this practice. I said, quietly to myself, "May all people who are hungry in the world right now get to taste something this wonderful and nourishing today."

A cynic might say, "Well, a lot of good your little silent prayer will do for the poor guy who's actually starving somewhere!" But I contend that it does a world of good. First of all, it pulls us out of self-concern, which means we're less likely to be caught up in our conditioned be-

➤

haviors with money, and that in and of itself is likely to lead to more compassionate action. Second, wishing others well actually deepens our enjoyment of the experience. Though not necessarily making us happier in the moment (we may naturally feel a little bit sad as we think of others' suffering), this sort of conscious awareness opens our hearts, and we are less likely to get caught up in repeating our habitual patterns with money. Ultimately, it is generous action that brings the most interconnected experience, and as this book has repeatedly emphasized, lasting change in our outer financial life starts on the inside.

RIGHT MOTIVATION

The mysterious thing about the great reward we get from giving is that it's not something we can simply sit down and logically plan for. It happens best when our giving is as natural as possible, just a part of life, without "shoulds" or "musts."

Still, many people do feel that they should be generous, or more generous than they are. Our motivation is often a mixture of guilt and moralistic compulsion. Examples of this perspective are the statements "It's the right thing to do" and "I want to be a good citizen." But something very important is lost when we approach giving from this place. We are essentially letting our Core Story—our conditioned inner voices about money—tell us how to behave, which is not freedom and doesn't feel very joyful.

When our motivation is to ease suffering or to add to other people's enjoyment of life—as opposed to the need to measure up to some external standard of goodness—our generosity benefits both us and our causes. This is what the spiritual traditions mean when they speak of creating heaven on earth. The point isn't to accumulate merit for an afterlife (although many religious belief systems promise that we will). Rather, it is to give out of compassion and empathy so that we experience more love and compassion today, motivating us in turn to give more, which generates more love and compassion, and on and on. When donors feel good about giving, not only are they likely to give more, but the recipients of their gifts have a sense of connection with the giver and do not feel like charity cases. The line between who is giving and who is receiving begins to blur, and that is when the fun really begins.

OBLIGATION OR INSPIRATION?

If you tend to give out of a sense of obligation rather than joy, I'd like you to recall an experience in which you gave because you felt you should. What did you give and to whom? How did you feel afterward? Do a physical inventory of your body as you recall that experience. How do you feel about that gift today? Now, by way of contrast, think of a time (perhaps from the first exercise in this chapter) when you gave from your heart, out of a sense of empathy or because it gave you pleasure to give. What about that cause or need touched you? How does your body feel as you recall that experience of giving?

In which experience of giving did you feel more of a need for recognition? In which experience did you feel the most satisfaction?

For myself, I recall a time when I used to give to a local homeless mission for their holiday meals, year in and year out. When the "thank you for your past generosity, but we've never needed you more than now" letter arrived each November, I'd get a sinking feeling in my chest. I felt I owed them a similar-sized contribution. But as noble as their work was, my heart wasn't in it anymore. In contrast, recently I have been moved to fund a soup kitchen at an after-school activity center for AIDS orphans in South Africa. Hearing the stories of these kids and their yearning to survive touches me. I find myself smiling, and a contented feeling of peace runs down my spine as I think about them. So I've opted to give to the South African after-school soup kitchen, trusting that others more genuinely moved will take care of the local homeless mission for now.

IF NOT NOW, WHEN?

The key question in determining whether to give is whether you feel a shift in your emotional state now, or are giving in the hopes of a future shift. Giving for a future reward (such as wanting to be recognized as generous) is a setup for disappointment. Giving because it feels good right now will make a much bigger difference in the world.

However, we don't need to have completely pure motivations before we give. Most of us are moved by a mixture of wanting happiness now and future happiness, and that's fine. We merely need to appreciate that some part of us wants good for others, even as we feel compelled by a "should" voice or focus on the recognition we hope will come from our gift. With growing awareness of our inner motivations for giving, we can begin to focus on cultivating positive motivations and letting go of whatever aspects of our Core Story hinder this growth.

In other words, don't beat yourself up if you begin to notice that you often give for tax purposes or because you want others to think well of you. It is much more helpful to focus on the good part of your intention than to criticize yourself for less than pure motives. Criticizing is not being compassionate, least of all to yourself. Encouragement and praise are the approaches that beget more compassion.

HOW MUCH SHOULD YOU GIVE?

Religious and spiritual traditions have historically had a variety of commandments about giving. The most common is the instruction to tithe 10 percent of income. Unfortunately, the writers who came up with these simplistic mandates had probably not studied accounting in much detail. If one person owns $10 million in land that generates no income and receives $5,000 a month in pensions and Social Security, and another person works fifty-hour weeks as an executive chef and earns $15,000 a month but has no savings or other assets, who ought to be giving more? Claude Rosenberg, a former fund manager and author of *Wealthy and Wise,* suggests alternatively that we give away one percent of our net worth each year. Giving away the greater of 10 percent of income or 1 percent of net worth certainly makes the playing field more level.

I contend that the amount we give be decided from inside ourselves, not from externally imposed authorities or cultural mores. If we are earnestly pursuing a self-inquiring relationship to money and our own happiness, we come to realize that giving is an integral part of our fulfillment, and it is appropriate that the amounts we give be different at different times in our lives.

Many people would like to give more money and feel a tremendous amount of compassion, but they hold themselves back because they're afraid of not having enough money for their own needs. Earlier, I discussed the

Wanting Mind and its perspective of "not enough." For the Wanting Mind, every action is evaluated on the basis of whether it will contribute to or detract from our own chances for survival. If we are comfortable enough to not be grappling with survival, the Wanting Mind looks for ways to make things a bit better for us.

Some of us may want to give more and more, and that in turn may cause its own problems. Yes, there are people who give too much! I had a client named Ben, a graphic designer who inherited money in his late thirties. Almost immediately, he began giving money to causes he believed in and to family and friends in need. Ben's imbalanced Caretaker was putting him in real jeopardy. His spending exceeded his income, and what he needed was a dose of prudence and self-concern (from the Guardian, a role he initially empowered his financial planners to play) to rein in his giving.

But most people who are afraid of giving too much are not in Ben's financial position. Instead, their fear of running out of money, even if it is irrational, deprives them of the joy they could have by expressing their generosity.

We all have this fear inside us, to a greater or lesser extent. And we all have a desire to make the world a better place, even if only for ourselves. The question is, "Which part of yourself most needs to grow—the cautious Guardian or the generous Caretaker?" Or, to reiterate a question asked earlier, "What is your deepest desire?" As Thich Nhat Hanh says, "Water the seeds you want to see grow."

When we give, we are subliminally telling ourselves and the world, "I have enough." This is why I felt so enriched after my wife, Britta, and I increased our charitable giving, spurred on by Kaden's diabetes. My prior perspective of "I don't have enough; therefore, I need to earn and save more" shifted to "I have enough to take care of my family and to give money to help find a cure for this disease." Thus, the seeds of enoughness were being watered. And guess what happened? More than enough began to come in. Call it coincidence if you must, but our newfound generosity led to a marked spike in our financial abundance. When one's orientation shifts to "I have enough, I am grateful, and I will use this money well," people sense an energy that they want to be around, buy from, and support—whether they realize it or not.

Be careful, though, that you're not naïvely over-giving in the hopes that it will magically create more income or wealth in the future (like the Innocent might do). As I said earlier, this magic does often occur, but only when it's not a major motivation for our giving. Especially if you are a Caretaker, an Innocent, or even a Pleasure Seeker, temper your generosity with the prudence of the Saver, Empire Builder, or Guardian. But as long as your financial security is objectively not threatened, try pushing the envelope with your giving. Let your heart race a little bit. This means your self-centered Core Story is being challenged to grow and widen its sphere of attention and compassion.

HOW MUCH HAVE YOU GIVEN, AND WHY?

How much did you give away last year? Look at your checkbook register, credit-card statements, and tax return. List the overall amounts you gave, and why:

Recipient or Category	Reason for Gift	Amount
		TOTAL:

Are you content with each gift and the reason you gave it? Go through and put a check next to each gift you still feel good about. Now look at the total amount of your donations. What percentage of your net worth does that number represent? The easiest way to figure this out is to divide your total gifts by your total net worth (the sum of all of your assets minus the sum of your liabilities). Do you think your fulfillment would be enhanced by increasing this amount or decreasing it?

It really is true that no matter how much we have, we can give something. In Buddhism, even the recipient of generosity is asked to give to those less fortunate than he. The amount of the gift is not really the focus. Instead, it's the intention that matters.

GIVE IT AWAY

No matter what state your finances are in, be open to giving something away in the next week, ideally to a person or cause that moves and touches you. Pay attention to the effect it has on you. To avoid continuing an old habit that doesn't feel like a stretch, try to give to a new cause or person, one you've not given to in the past.

THREE BUCKETS

Generosity is a value that can be cultivated from a young age, and indeed, many of my clients ask me how to teach their kids about money. The story at the beginning of this chapter is based on one of the best practices I know: breaking an allowance into three buckets. One is for spending on present purchases, the second is for savings for future purchases, and the third is for giving away. I believe this practice can be started with those as young as four years old. What's more, none of us is too old to learn from it.

For some very wealthy people, the three buckets exercise could lead to putting the majority of their assets into a generosity bucket, as Bill Gates and Warren Buffett have done in recent years. Without this type of exercise, many wealthy people give dollar amounts or percentages of income that are disproportionately small relative to their net worth. Often, they're not experiencing the level of impact that would truly gratify them and bring them the feeling of "enough" and the interconnectedness that comes from generosity. But whether your assets run to three or ten figures, your giving doesn't have to make an apparent change in the world. If it changes you, that is revolutionary.

Mike Murray, a former head of human resources for Microsoft and investor in microloans for impoverished people, tells the following story:

My wife and I looked at the total amount of assets we had accumulated; to a large degree because of our religious beliefs, we chose to take a large chunk of that and create a family foundation. And that did a couple of very good things for us.

First, it prevented us from waking up rich each morning. And what I mean by that is that when you create a foundation and put money in it, that money's no longer yours. You can't use it to buy the new car, to remodel the house, to buy another vacation home, etcetera, etcetera.

So, suddenly, even though it's still kind of part of your whole umbrella of financial influence, it's "hands off" in terms of any personal improvement in your personal life.

And then the second good thing about that, because of the way the U.S. laws work, you're required to take about 5 percent of that amount of money and donate it to charities every year. So suddenly you have a giving budget and you have to decide what's important to you, whether it's going to be poverty alleviation or environmental issues or education issues or health issues—I mean, the list just goes on and on and on—or public works or the opera.

As I hope I have conveyed, there are obviously no hard and fast rules about how much each of us can or should give. But I do want to offer a couple of rules of thumb so that you can see where your current giving stands.

If you are still in your earning or accumulation years, you can safely give:

- As much of your earned income as you don't need for current spending as well as retirement savings. You will likely need to engage a well-trained Certified Financial Planner® professional or other objective advisor (see p. 263) to help you determine this amount.

If you are independently wealthy or retired, you can generally give away some combination of the following:

- As much as 100 percent of your passive income (meaning income earned from investments, rental real estate, or a business in which you don't actively work), as long as it is not required for ongoing expenses.

- As many of your assets as you wish, as long as you are left with income-producing or appreciating assets that are worth about twenty-five times your ongoing annual expenses. If you are still young or your life may see major increases in expenses in the future, be sure to factor these changes into the computation. Also, if the nature of your assets are such that they will generate a rate of return of less than about 7 percent over the long run, you'll need to retain more than twenty-five times your annual spending.

WHAT CAN YOU GIVE?

There is a lovely fable about a man standing on the roadside feeling dejected. A woman walking down the street feels empathy and smiles at him. The man, heartened by the smile, decides to write a letter to a long-lost friend. The friend is so touched to receive the letter that he gives ten dollars to a homeless beggar on the street. The beggar later that day finds a stray puppy shivering in an alleyway, and he uses the money to buy food for the dog and keeps it warm by his fire. The dog follows the beggar, and that night they stop and ask a family if they can spend the night on the porch because it is going to rain. The family agrees. During the night, they are all awakened by the incessant barking of the puppy. They discover that the house is on fire— right near the child's bedroom. They are able to save the child, who grows up to become a famous medical researcher and discovers the treatment for malaria, saving millions of lives. And it all started with a simple smile.

As we free ourselves from the dictates of our own Wanting Mind and Core Story, we are much more likely to offer a smile or other positive energy to those who are suffering. Our sensitivity and empathy naturally increase as our self-concern wanes—no real effort is required. Giving love, energy, and time are all valuable ways to share our compassion. But I am a financial planner, and so I'd like to cover a few more of the practicalities of giving away money and other tangible property.

Financially speaking, there are two sources from which we can give: our income or our assets. Our income is either the reward for the labor we expend in the world or a return on our capital (our investments). If you work as a paralegal and are paid a salary of $6,000 per month, that's your reward for labor. If you also own a portfolio of investments from which you earn $2,000 a month, that's a reward for capital. If that portfolio is your only asset and is worth $400,000, that is the amount of your capital, or your net worth.

So, continuing this example, this paralegal could give any of the following:

1. A portion of his salary,

2. A portion of his investment income,

3. A portion of his net worth, or

4. Any combination of the above.

Usually we think of income alone when we are trying to determine how much to give. But I want to call your attention to the different financial sources from which you can give, and the benefits of giving from your assets rather than giving cash.

In the United States, when you give to an established charity, you can deduct the amount of your gift from your taxable income, up to a certain percentage of your income, depending on what you've given. If a person gave 10 percent of his salary, that amount would likely be a deduction on his tax return. If he were in a 25 percent tax bracket, then 25 percent of his gift would effectively be the government's gift, in the form of a reduction of his taxes. In other words, he gives $1,000 and gets a $1,000 tax deduction, which offsets $1,000 in income, on which he would have otherwise paid $250 in tax. So though he initially parted with $1,000, because of the $250 in tax savings, his net cost is really only $750 ($1,000–$250). If he were to give a percentage of the investment income in cash, the tax treatment would be the same.

If instead he were to give a portion of his investment portfolio to a public charity, then he would get a deduction equal to the fair market value of the contribution, again up to a limit. But let's go a bit further and say that some of the funds in his portfolio had appreciated dramatically, or had been inherited and had a cost basis (the amount paid for the shares) that was much lower than the market value. He would still get a deduction equal to the fair market value, and he would avoid paying the capital gains tax that would have been due had he just sold the investments and donated cash. The following comparison shows just how powerful it was for one of my clients to donate highly appreciated assets instead of cash to her high school alma mater to buy textbooks, allowing her to increase her giving 25 percent at the same net out-of-pocket cost to her:

ASSUMPTIONS

Desired value of gift: $10,000

Cost basis in her assets: $0*

Capital gains tax rate: 15%

Income tax bracket: 25%

	DONATE CASH	DONATE THE ASSET
Sale of asset:	$11,765	N/A
Capital gains tax (15%):	($1,765)	$0
Amount donated:	$10,000	$10,000
Charitable deduction (25%):	($2,500)	($2,500)
Net cost of donation:	**$9,265**	**$7,500**

This shows that it effectively would have cost my client about $0.93 for each dollar had she given cash, but only $0.75 for each dollar of the highly appreciated asset she gave. This means that she could give about 25 percent more in highly appreciated assets than cash with the same net after-tax effect. You might retort that she didn't need to sell the asset, and so she wouldn't have paid the capital gains tax. But she (or her heirs) may well sell one day. And many people will die with highly appreciated assets in their estates. If they're subject to estate tax, the rate will likely be much higher than the capital gains tax rate, making the comparative value of contributing the appreciated asset even greater. If your cost basis is above zero, you will still likely be better off than if you gave cash. Basically, the lower the cost basis the better.

If the asset you own is much more valuable than the amount you'd like to give to charity in one specific year, there is an alternative, called a donor-advised fund. With a donor-advised fund, you are able to donate cash or other assets into the fund, which is usually administered by a local community foundation, and then slowly distribute your charitable funds over time, at a pace that is comfortable to you. This is much more convenient if,

---

* Note: The cost basis is almost never zero for an asset we bought as an investment, but can often be zero for stock inherited or gifted a long time ago or for fully depreciated real estate.

for example, you are thinking of selling a piece of real estate, a business, or another less liquid asset and don't want to donate the whole amount at one time (if, for example, the piece of real estate is worth $500,000, but you only want to give away $25,000 a year). See p. 264 for more.

WHAT'S YOUR CAUSE?

Each of us is touched by different causes, which is why philanthropy takes on such a wide variety of expressions.

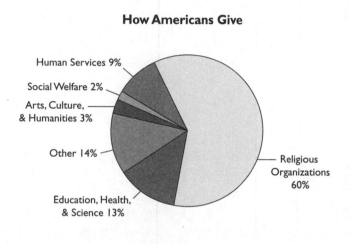

How Americans Give

Human Services 9%
Social Welfare 2%
Arts, Culture, & Humanities 3%
Other 14%
Education, Health, & Science 13%
Religious Organizations 60%

Some of us are most moved to protect the environment. With the United States consuming 26 percent of the world's energy—especially in fossil fuel use—and the average American consuming 270 pounds of meat per year, environmental degradation is rampant.

Some of us are most touched by the arts or music and wish to support those causes. In the past five years, public funding for the arts has declined by over 60 percent, but solid research has shown that arts education greatly enhances learning across the disciplines, especially for children from low-income backgrounds.

Others are moved to help end global poverty. Three billion people in the world live on less than two dollars per day. A full 640 million children do not have adequate shelter, and 400 million children do not have access to safe water.

Still others are moved to give closer to home, either in our own communities or our own families. And as the chart on the prior page shows, the vast majority of giving is to religious institutions, many of which give in turn to such causes as protecting the environment, eradicating poverty, and supporting the arts.

CREATE YOUR PERSONALIZED GIVING POLICY

Whatever our causes are, and no matter how much we have to give, it is often helpful to form a giving policy, which is a written plan that describes the following:

1. To whom you're going to give (including either specific names of charities or general causes to which you'd like to give),

2. How much you're going to give to each one each year (in money or time), and

3. Whether and how you're going to measure the effectiveness of your giving.

As a start, write down all the causes that you've ever given to. In addition, focus on causes or people whom you have felt most touched by in your life. If you "ran the zoo," what would you change in the world?

Make sure to leave some percentage—between 10 percent and 50 percent of your annual giving budget—for spontaneous gifts. If you have Caretaking tendencies, this document will help you instill more discipline in your giving process and not overgive. When new causes or people ask for your help, you can agree to put them on your list for next year, or fund them from your spontaneous giving budget. If you are a Saver and tend to hoard your resources, this document will empower the inner voice that is suggesting you loosen up a bit with a concrete giving plan. (See p. 263 for further information on how to find out what percentage of your gift will ultimately reach the people you want to benefit.)

TEACH A MAN TO FISH

So far, this chapter has focused on charitable giving and philanthropy as the primary means of using money to express our interconnectedness. There is also an important thirty-year-old model, called microfinance, that is improving over one hundred million impoverished lives. It is growing dramatically even as we speak. Instead of a handout, someone who invests in a microfinance fund is actually providing capital to a person with a very small business, usually a woman living in the Third World. The loan might be for her to buy an oven with which to bake bread to sell, or a dairy cow from which to sell milk. The average loan size is under two hundred dollars, and the repayment rate, industrywide, is above 95 percent. The loans are guaranteed by a group of micro-entrepreneurs, instead of just one, to reduce the risk of default.

This section could have easily gone into the chapter on investing, because microfinance lenders often earn both a financial return and a social return. The financial return can be anywhere from one percent to about five percent. For high-net-worth investors, there are a few funds that buy into microfinance institutions (the banks that make the loans). These funds offer a possibility of financial returns even better than those available to investors in stocks in the developed world, albeit with more risk and more uncertainty.

But much more important than the financial returns are the social returns that microfinance investors create. Generally, a two-hundred-dollar loan will provide the capital necessary to create or expand a business that provides the income for a family of five to live on. And better yet, the money doesn't disappear but is paid back and recycled to another micro-entrepreneur in the future, creating more self-sufficiency for others.

At Abacus, we have found this to be a powerful complement to philanthropy and pure financial investing for our clients. But don't think of it as a tool only for the wealthy. I've seen school classrooms and working-class folks make loans as small as a hundred dollars to micro-entrepreneurs a few blocks away or halfway around the world. If you would like to explore microfinance in more depth, please visit my Web site at www. BrentKessel.com.

> **"This is not charity. This is business, business with a social objective, which is to help people get out of poverty."**
>
> —MUHAMMAD YUNUS, NOBEL PEACE PRIZE WINNER AND MICROCREDIT PIONEER, FOUNDER OF GRAMEEN BANK

SO YOU WANT TO LEAVE A LEGACY

Whether Empire Builders or not, many of the people I've worked with over the years want to be remembered. We all would like our lives to have been significant in some way. Too often, however, our wills and estate plans—the documents that govern the tangible results of our life's work—are dictated by societal norms or our Core Story's marching orders.

I have sat in countless client meetings with estate-planning attorneys where everyone simply assumes that the client wants to leave as much money as possible to their children and grandchildren and reduce taxes as much as possible. But planning for what will happen to our money ought to begin with a completely blank canvas, which means we need to identify and then remove the cultural and familial expectations regarding our money before we even start the planning process.

WILL THEY REMEMBER ME?

Do you know the name of any of your great-grandparents?

What do you know about their life stories?

If you're like most people, you had trouble answering these questions. And you likely only have to go back one or two generations further until your ancestors' lives are banished from memory. As important as their lives were, their wants and desires, their Core Stories, are wholly insignificant now.

Most people never realize just how forgotten their own lives will be if they only live out their personal desires and preferences. Even those Empire Builders who would like to build a great business or another legacy and then see it sustained by future generations are fighting an uphill battle. Seventy percent of family wealth is gone within two generations, 90 percent within three. This is because most families leave almost all their money to their offspring, giving them little or no training on how to manage it and having no awareness of what impact this will have on the wider world. Often, the Empire Builder's Core Story has been so overbearing that subsequent generations have rebelled against his values rather than embracing them—adopting, for example, extreme versions of the Star, Caretaker, or Pleasure Seeker, leading to further erosion of wealth.

But there are exceptions to the rule—families like the Rockefellers, who have been able to sustain and grow their legacies, usually by channeling a substantial portion of their resources toward the common good.

Though many factors contributed to families like the Rockefellers maintaining more of their wealth than other wealthy families did, I believe that having a balanced focus on using wealth (or any amount of money) for the greater good plays a critical role in preserving that wealth. I don't believe that this is because God or some other divine power consistently rewards those who do good things in the world. There are just too many examples of good-hearted people who've been tortured, killed, or otherwise lived lives of great suffering in spite of their compassionate natures. I do believe, however, that when we are focused on the greater good, we are not as consumed by our own self-involved Core Story, and hence more is possible.

DON'T WAIT UNTIL YOU'RE DEAD AND GONE

Though tremendous good has been done by those who have left large philanthropic gifts at the time of their deaths, I often wish they'd been alive to experience for themselves the good that their gifts did.

WRITE YOUR OWN OBITUARY

What do you want people to say about you two generations from now? What do you hope your effect on the world will have been? What did you come here to do that you have not yet done? Consider sharing this with your children or other loved ones.

Giving during our lifetimes is a great way to enhance our enjoyment of life right now. In addition, active philanthropy is one of the most powerful ways to teach children the principles of wise stewardship of money. Once you've decided the extent to which you want to incorporate philanthropy into your life, give as much as is prudent before you die so that you can enjoy the experience of seeing your compassion in action and the relationships that form around your giving.

LOVING-KINDNESS MEDITATION

The term *loving-kindness* comes from Buddhism, but I've seen many similar prayers and meditations in other traditions. This quiet contemplation can be done by people from any religious tradition. The only requirement is that you believe in your own potential to be compassionate toward others.

Find a quiet place to sit, where you won't be distracted or disturbed. First, notice your breath. As you breathe in, without any fanfare just say to yourself, "I am breathing in," and as you breathe out say, "I am breathing out." You may shorten it to "in" and "out" if you wish.

As you continue, start to quietly wish for peace and well-being for yourself, perhaps by saying, "May I be happy" or "May I be free of suffering." Do your very best to maintain a soft disposition toward yourself and the areas where you struggle the most in life. Be as gentle as if you were wishing happiness and freedom from suffering for your own children or loved ones, but for now, direct that gentle disposition toward yourself.

After a little while, extend your wish out to someone who is close to you—perhaps your mother, your brother, your spouse, your friend, or someone you just barely know who is going through difficulties: "May he be happy," "May she feel peaceful," "May he have a relaxed state of mind," "May she be free of suffering."

Next, widen your focus even more, perhaps to a whole family or community: "May they all be at peace," "May they all be fulfilled and happy," "May they all be free of suffering."

Continue on to an entire country, to all human beings throughout the world, and finally to all beings everywhere.

Throughout this meditation, notice what changes occur in you as you progress. Do you get more bored or easily distracted when the focus is on others, or is it easier for you to take the focus off yourself? Does anything change in your general level of worry or anxiety as you move through the meditation? Which part felt the best and most invigorating for you? As you do this practice more, you'll likely find that your answers to these questions will be quite different. Appreciate your motivation to be kind, and recognize that you want to help this motivation grow within you.

Using money to express our loving-kindness is paradoxical because we've been taught that the more we give, the less we'll have. But my experience is that, within reason, our giving truly does beget more for us—not just more money, but more relaxation, enjoyment, peace, and freedom to more skillfully choose our relationship to money. No matter where you are in your current expression of generosity, I strongly encourage you to try just one or two of the steps described in this chapter, and check out for yourself what effects they have on your life. I am quite sure you will find yourself a surprisingly fortunate beneficiary of your own good deeds.

CHAPTER FOURTEEN

YOU HAVE ARRIVED

"Freedom isn't a matter of the future. It's a matter of
the present moment."

—Thich Nhat Hanh

After reading this book, you may feel inspired to make sweeping changes
in your relationship to money. On the other hand, you may feel that the
changes you need to make are too daunting and so back off from doing
anything at all. Though both responses are natural, it is very important
that you not exert too much or too little effort in altering your relationship to money, and only you can know what the right amount of effort is.
Ahimsa is a Sanskrit word that means "nonviolence." In ancient yoga texts,
it means not violently compelling ourselves or others to change physically,
emotionally, or spiritually. Good yoga teachers often encourage their students not to strive to achieve some image of a pose but rather to become
more and more aware of the subtleties that exist within the pose, *as it is,*
before making any change. In that spirit, I encourage you to pay attention
to the moments in your daily life when you struggle with money. Realize
that you are, at your deepest core, just fine, even if you never change. Para-
doxically, it is only out of this deep acceptance of your present life that true
and lasting change can arise.

One way I've seen clients and friends harm themselves is by directing
all their attention and energy to what's wrong financially. Examples of this
include finger-wagging advice to themselves, such as, "Don't buy any more

new clothes this month!" or "Stop working on weekends—we don't need the extra money!" This is like the parent who constantly tells a child what not to do. As most parenting educators know, children tend not to hear the "not" or "don't," so these kinds of commands just end up reinforcing the behavior we are trying to discourage. What we need instead is the ability to make financial decisions with less agitation, with a mind at peace.

It may be hard for any of us in modern society—overwhelmed with basic survival concerns, rising health care and college tuition costs, tens of thousands of investment choices, and material temptations everywhere we look— to imagine a truly still mind. But stillness is within our reach.

> "To the mind that is still, the whole universe surrenders."
>
> —LIEH TZU,
> FIFTH-CENTURY CE
> PHILOSOPHER

Most decisions about money are nothing more than reflexive responses to our conditioning. If we had experienced different life circumstances, different conditioning, we would be making different decisions. What I have been trying to convey in these pages is that regardless of your situation or conditioning, there is a new way of making decisions, one that arises out of the profound depth of silence and peace every one of us has within, a way that is creative and chosen instead of constricted and without choice.

BE STILL

If you need to make a financial decision and your mind is far from still, put off making the decision. The anxiety and confusion you feel often masks a deeper set of emotions and beliefs. As Tsoknyi Rinpoche says, "Instead of focusing on the symptoms of our hope and our fear, we must find an 'in' to go into the hope or the fear itself; otherwise we are deluded into believing that the symptom is real." In other words, we think that the decision to refinance the mortgage or sell our investment will lead to freedom or prevent something we dread from occurring. But pinning this responsibility on the symptom instead of the cause just perpetuates hope and fear in the future because we haven't dealt with the root cause.

Sit in a quiet place, with no distractions, and inquire into what's behind the decision you're grappling with. What are you telling yourself will be the internal result of either alternative? ➤

You need to understand the financial facts that affect your decision in order to proceed. Try to collect this information without any expectation of acting on it yet. What are the facts you need to know to make an educated choice?

Write out the worst-case scenario if you decide to go one way, and the worst-case scenario if you decide to go the other. Also write out the best-case scenario for each choice.

Then—and this is the important part—look into how this decision is going to affect your innermost essence, as opposed to your thoughts and emotions. Inquire into what would really change for this most still part of you were you to make the decision one way, then the other. Doing this will likely bring about a certain healthy detachment and a quieter state of being. From that stillness, see what your gut tells you is the obvious next step.

After you've made the decision, don't be surprised if the critical voices arise in your head, second-guessing you. Just return to the best-case and worst-case scenarios through the lens of your essence, your soul, or whatever name you choose to refer to the most wise and still place within you. In this way, you will be able to respond instead of reacting to the money challenges and opportunities you face.

DON'T DO, BE

There are many ways to bring your attention to the essence that animates your existence, and indeed, doing so is a quest at the heart of almost all spiritual traditions. (Various traditions refer to this quality of attention as "realizing your true nature," "awakening," being "born again," or "enlightenment.") For me, being silent and coming to know this awareness, this presence that is beyond any thought or idea of "me," has been my most profound teacher. This is not about adopting any belief system or label. Instead, it is an invitation to directly experience your own life force, an awareness that is always present regardless of what you are doing or thinking.

"WHO AM I?"

What is breathing you right now?

What is sensing through your body, seeing through your eyes, hearing through your ears, feeling the temperature of the air on your skin?

Sit silently for just a few seconds or minutes and get a taste of this most basic awareness within you. Or, like many saints and sages throughout history, you could choose to sit for as long as it takes.

The natural and effortless expression of this force is love and compassion. My direct experience of this essence is that it transcends physical boundaries, so it is naturally loving and compassionate because it is everything and everyone. It has no quarrel with life—with any part of life. That means it doesn't need your Wanting Mind to stop wanting. It doesn't need your Core Story to change. It doesn't need you to be more interconnected with your money. It is only here to experience. And when our attention is focused on it, we feel a tremendous peace, a tranquility, and the most powerful sense of well-being—which is why the world's spiritual traditions have used words like *heaven, paradise, oneness,* and "the peace which passeth all understanding" to describe it.

The mind hears words like these and assumes that this essence is lazy or unmotivated. "If life really felt that good, then why would I want to get up and do anything?" My experience of the people who have most consistently focused their attention on this essence of being is that just the opposite happens. They have more energy and often take more action in the world than before. And that action is aligned with how their essence wants to be expressed in the world. The mind thinks that effective action takes discipline and willpower. But in fact, when our attention rests fully in this presence, the next step, no matter how grand or how small, becomes obvious and effortless for us.

PRESENCE AND THE CONTEMPLATION OF DEATH

To cultivate awareness of this essence, author Ken McLeod suggests the following exercise in *White Paper III*:

Stop reading for just a moment, and imagine that you are going to die in one minute. The last things you are going to experience are reading these pages, sitting in this room, wearing the clothes you are wearing, thinking and feeling what you are thinking and feeling right now. This is it. This is the end of your life. You have no time to do anything about it. You have no time to write a note or make a phone call. Your life is over. You will die in one minute. *All you can do is experience what is, right now.*

The beauty of this exercise is that if you really do it, you stop fighting. You stop wanting. You stop achieving. You stop hoping for a better life. Getting anywhere else becomes meaningless.

What remains? What is that state of awareness within you that is devoid of all actions and thoughts and hopes? That doesn't want for anything?

With any luck, this was just an exercise and you're still alive and reading! If so, can you still access that whole and complete place inside of you, the place that doesn't need anything to change? If not, try the exercise again. Or spend some time meditating or in silence of any type. This part of us is sublime and usually drowned out by the mind's constant scurrying. But in silence, it speaks with unmistakable power and is our most trusted guide.

AS GOOD AS IT GETS

This book has explored many aspects of our relationship to money and has suggested many methods and insights to bring those relationships into better alignment with our spiritual nature. If you get caught up in the superficial aspects of these practices, you may do everything right with money and yet still not experience true freedom. This is because true freedom doesn't reside on the physical or psychological planes of existence. Whatever your spiritual or materialistic persuasion, whichever archetypes you identify with, the more you inquire into this aspect of your being—which was there before you had a name, a story, or even your very first thoughts—the more you will experience true freedom in your everyday life.

Much of this book has been about bringing awareness to the inner seeds of your actions related to money. We suffer when we act in unconscious ways regarding money (or anything else) because we are moving in opposition to how our essence or soul wants to act. When we turn our awareness inward, we are able to ask, "Who is the awareness that's looking?" When people look sincerely within, they realize, "Wow! It's all just conditioning. I don't have to behave like that anymore, unless I choose to." The Core Story no longer holds the same power it once did. And our behavior with money shows a marked, albeit gradual, capacity to change.

Remember, your essence has no problem with your Core Story or conditioning. In fact, it looks on these things with quite an affectionate, amused perspective. We can afford to be amused when we are no longer under the delusion that we *are* our Core Story. This is real freedom.

Think of an ocean storm with gale-force winds and crashing swells, and then think of the stillness just thirty feet below the surface. The part of us I am talking about is much like those deep ocean currents, unaffected by the drama and swirling weather of our daily lives.

You have arrived when you are making financial decisions that support what is most important to your essence. This has to do with satisfying your heart and soul, not ego-gratification. This is not the means but the end. What are the highest priorities of your most unencumbered state of being? Glance through this list and identify the qualities you most value:

Compassion	Faith	Simplicity
Freedom	Creativity	Joy
Fulfillment	Relaxation	Contentment
Inspiration	Generosity	Peace

Which states of being are your highest priorities?
What is your highest potential?
What is your deepest desire?

YOU HAVE ARRIVED

Carve out a day when you do nothing for your future and have no plans whatsoever. Arrange it ahead of time with your family, roommates, or co-workers, so you'll have support to be spontaneous and unplanned. This is a day when you can be completely unstructured and just follow your heart from moment to moment. You have earned this right—the right to just enjoy yourself, your surroundings, your people, being in your body, your life.

The first time I did this exercise, I was shocked by how often my mind wanted to plan the future. True to form, it chanted, "There are so many cool things you could do instead. Write. Read. Organize your iTunes. Listen to music. Play with the kids. Take a nap. Work out. Eat. Call a friend. Come on, there must be something out there for you to do! You'll be happier the more you can fit in."

When the voice comes up that says, "What a great opportunity to get X, Y, or Z done," don't listen to it, unless doing X, Y, or Z will bring you happiness in the doing of it, not the completion of it. On this one day, if you're not enjoying what you're doing in the moment or the next few minutes, move on to something else. In other words, you do not need to have anything to show for this day at the end of it.

If taking a whole day seems too daunting, start with just one hour. You may not be able to do this the first few times you try it, but dedicate yourself to this practice so you can begin to cultivate the experience of having arrived. A day like this is a celebration of your life as it is instead of a struggle to create the life that your mind thinks will make you happy one day.

Being in touch with this aspect of ourselves as we make financial decisions is as good as it gets. Money is a store of life energy, and when we can channel that life energy into an expression of what is most dear to our soul, an exciting alignment takes place between our financial and spiritual lives.

Along with this alignment comes a feeling of always having enough. In fact, our essence always does have enough, even when its physical body is cold or hungry or scared. But more than just having enough, our essence is deeply loving, contented, and grateful, not from any effort but as its most natural expression. We are free when we move from a focus on getting love, abundance, peace, and freedom to being love, abundance, peace, and freedom. In fact, when we are identified with that part of us that already has enough, that has arrived, that feels sufficiency rather than scarcity, impulses of love and generosity arise naturally and without effort.

My most sincere wish for you is that money be a profound teacher in your life, guiding you toward this abiding sense of freedom and fulfillment. None of this is easy, but it is quite simple. Freedom and happiness are your birthright, and no matter what your life situation, nothing outside your own mind can stop you from experiencing them.

May you be happy.

May you be free.

May your life be a full expression of your own unique spirit, in this very moment and all moments to come.

THE NUTS AND BOLTS

In this book, my aim has been to help you cultivate more happiness and peace in your relationship to money. That said, there's no denying that an important component of happiness and peace is found in the outer financial world: cash flow, debt management, retirement planning, tax, insurance, and estate planning, philanthropic advice, and other specifics that I generally share with my clients. What follows is an easy-to-read guide to the practical financial planning strategies and techniques that have been referred to throughout this book. There is also a series of charts that summarize the characteristics of the eight archetypes and offer specific practical recommendations on how to counterbalance one's impulses in each of these categories. This material can help you further your goals, regardless of the size of your bank account.

As you read, I encourage you to draw on the feeling of abundance and bounty you are beginning to cultivate. In dealing with these practical matters, you will naturally notice anxieties or old thought patterns. Treat these feelings as opportunities to pause and return to the practices introduced throughout the book. You will notice that the actions you take when you are in a calmer, healthier state of mind will be easier and make a more lasting impact in your life.

Having gotten to this point in the book, you are progressing toward your goal of understanding your financial life from the inside out. Some of you already have a great working knowledge of financial matters, while others are befuddled by anything having to do with money. Though I hope I've helped you identify the patterns that are specific to you, it's beyond the scope of any book to provide advice tailored to every individual's level of interest and knowledge. Some sound advice does hold true across the board, though, which is why I'm including it here. If you need more help than is provided here, there are many excellent books that go into much more detail about products and strategies. A list of some of my favorites can be found in this appendix. Of course, your financial advisors (if you have them) may have given you advice that conflicts with that offered here, and they may be right for your particular situation. But the following will give you a basis on which to ask informed questions about the advice you've received.

READY-TO-GO INVESTMENT STRATEGIES

If you'd like to implement my Conscious Investor approach, here are some practical steps you can take whether you're a brand new or seasoned investor. A word of caution, however; everyone's financial life and needs are a bit different, and I highly recommend consulting a fee-only® financial planner or Registered Investment Advisor if possible (see p. 263). However, because these professionals often work only with affluent clients, those with less may be forced to use high-cost, nondiversified, tax-inefficient investments. To help you no matter what amount of assets you have, this section provides some ready-to-go tools that you can access and that employ many if not all of the principles espoused in this book.

I'm brand new and have never invested before, or I have less than $75,000.

The key for you is to utilize a disciplined, automatic program, and tax-favored retirement plans are one of the most powerful investment vehicles available. If your job offers a 401(k) or another retirement plan, start by participating in that until you're contributing the maximum. Most plans give you a choice of investment options. Do your best to apply the principles in chapter 12, and select a mix that is diversified across domestic, international, large-cap, small-cap, and value stocks. You'll likely only be given one choice of index fund, perhaps in the U.S. large-asset class. If that's the case, then select that fund, but be sure to allocate assets to the other asset classes, even if you must go with actively managed funds. Try to get as close as you can to the percentages for each asset class listed on p. 196. However, if there are no funds in a particular asset class, then add that allocation to the most similar asset class. For example, if there is no fund for international small-cap stocks, use international stocks; if no U.S. small value-stock fund is offered, use U.S. small-cap stocks.

If you have investments aside from your retirement plan, you can always make up for any diversification shortfalls there. It is much more important that your overall portfolio be diversified across asset classes than that each individual account be diversified. To make sure this is the case, first determine how much of your portfolio belongs in bonds, based on pp. 205 to 207. Depending on your preferences, choose from one of the following:

I prefer a big mutual fund company whose name I recognize.

Call Vanguard at (877) 662–7447 or go to www.vanguard. com and purchase one of their LifeStrategy mutual funds. The funds have a $3,000 minimum, are not socially screened, and come with four different bond allocation amounts:

Fund Name	% in Bonds	Ticker Symbol*
Vanguard® LifeStrategy® Income Fund	80%	VASIX
Vanguard® LifeStrategy® Conservative Growth Fund	60%	VSCGX
Vanguard® LifeStrategy® Moderate Growth Fund	40%	VSMGX
Vanguard® LifeStrategy® Growth Fund	20%	VASGX

If social screening is important to you and you're willing to give up the asset-class diversification described earlier, you can just invest in the Vanguard FTSE Social Index Fund (VFTSX), but you will likely have a bit rockier ride and a lower long-term rate of return.

If you have between $30,000 and $75,000 to allocate to stocks and real estate, and especially if you want to invest in socially screened funds, have Vanguard divide up the nonbond portion as follows:

---

* The ticker symbol will help you communicate to the company exactly which fund you're interested in buying.

Fund Name	Ticker	Allocation
FTSE Social Index Fund	VFTSX	20%
Value Index Fund	VIVAX	20%
Small-Cap Index Fund	NAESX	10%
Small-Cap Value Index Fund	VISVX	10%
REIT Index Fund	VGSIX	15%
Total International Index Fund	VGTSX	15%
Emerging Markets Index Fund	VEIEX	10%

I prefer a bit more customization and automatic rebalancing.

Call TD Ameritrade at (800) 858–9775 or visit their Web site at www.TDAmeritrade.com and open an Amerivest account. They have their own quiz they'll want you to take, but if your goal falls within the time frames I mentioned on p. 205 and their allocation to bonds is different, you can override it and insist on my bond allocation. At the time of this writing, Amerivest does not offer a socially screened portfolio. However, Amerivest does use exchange-traded funds, which are passive like an index fund, combine asset classes that don't all move in lockstep with each other, and are low cost and tax efficient.

I've got more than $75,000 to invest.

The same advice about maximizing retirement accounts applies to all investors, regardless of the size of their portfolio, so read the first paragraph in the section just above this one. With your remaining assets, you can invest at either Vanguard or Amerivest, as described above. If you'd prefer to have a face-to-face relationship with an advisor, go to www.dfaus.com/find_advisor/ for a list of fee-only® registered investment advisors who use only passive, asset-class-diversified portfolios (although many don't employ social screening), or to www.napfa.org/consumer/planners/ to get a list of fee-only® comprehensive financial planners, some of whom use passive indexing (in my view, good), some active stock selection (in my view, bad), and some social screening. I also encourage you to explore my Web site (www.BrentKessel.com) or call 888–422–2287 to see if one of my companies' services is appropriate for you, as they employ the investment principles espoused in this book.

I've got more than $1 million to invest.

As the amount of your investable assets gets higher, there are more interesting choices as far as social screening, passively managed individual stock strategies, and alternative investments with exceptional financial and social returns.

You can look for a face-to-face wealth-management relationship using either of the Web sites listed above, or contact our firm through my Web site (www.BrentKessel.com) or call 888–422–2287 to see if our services might be appropriate for you or if there's a firm in your city to which we can refer you.

CASH FLOW

If I were to guess, I would say that a good 70 percent of all adults couldn't tell you within 10 percent what they spend in an average month. To earn money, most of us use our intelligence and our physical strength—what can be called our "life energy." Cash flow, then, is the expenditure of this life energy. For this reason, it is incredibly important to know where you're spending your life energy so that you can make changes if your priorities are not reflected in your spending. It is also very difficult to stay out of debt, save for the goals you feel are most important, or commit to an appropriately sized philanthropic program if you don't know the numbers.

The trick is to make the observation of what you're earning and spending simple and easy to understand. The most accurate way is to use a personal finance software program like Quicken or Microsoft Money. These programs allow you to pay bills online and easily see how you're spending your money. (If you hate computers, hire someone or barter with a savvy friend. But keep in mind that you and only you should sign the checks and have withdrawal privileges on your accounts.) A simpler method is to use an online budgeting calculator (see Resources, page 284).

Whether you use software or not, keep separate accounts for business and personal cash flow. This makes keeping track of what you spend, as well as tax preparation, infinitely easier. Don't commingle your savings/investment and personal spending accounts. Have one account that is just for paying bills. This way, you can always look at your year-to-date withdrawals and know what you're spending. Have recurring paychecks automatically deposited into these accounts.

If you have any nonrecurring bills (less than monthly) that take you by surprise (like taxes, vacations, or once-a-year obligations), create an automatic monthly transfer into a separate account. First, make a list of all significant nonrecurring items you spend money on. Then, estimate what you spend on those items in a year. Total up the list and divide by twelve: this is the amount you ought to be transferring into your Big Bills account each month. (The budgeting calculator mentioned previously will calculate this amount for you.)

If you tend to receive big, irregular cash inflows (gifts from parents, commission checks, or other income from your vocation), have this income deposited into a savings or money market account that is separate from your regular spending account. Then set up an automatic monthly transfer into your spending account for an amount that will cover your spending.

Even though this might all seem complex, once you've got things set up, it is the simplest way to see if you're spending more or less than you estimate. If it's more, and if living within your means is an important objective to you, you'll need to trim back your lifestyle (see exercises on pp. 18, 67, and 116). If, on the other hand, you find you have more income than you're spending, you can reflect on what use of the surplus will give you the most lasting fulfillment.

DEBT AND MORTGAGE MANAGEMENT

If going into debt is a pattern for you, you won't create financial freedom for yourself unless you first get an understanding of what you're earning and spending. Then you will be able to make a plan to pay off the debt. Don't consolidate your debts onto one credit card or take out a home equity line of credit until you've established what your cash flow actually is. To pay off a debt, you need to know the numbers so that you can make transfers methodically and automatically.

Once you've done the math, if your credit allows, consolidate your debts into the option with the lowest interest rate you can find. If you must keep your debts separate, do not be tempted to pay off the smallest balance first. Instead, pay off the debt with the *highest interest rate* first, and only pay the minimum on the others until you've paid off the balance on the highest rate card or loan. Then move to the next highest. Most important, never ever use a card for spending that you're trying to pay down; you'll have no idea how much progress you're making, and you won't have any psychological momentum. Use a debit card or a new card that you pay off each month, or if your problem is chronic, use only cash and money orders. If you have persistent debt problems, please contact Consumer Credit Counseling Services (CCCS); more information is available in the Resources section of this appendix.

Keep in mind that loans (up to $1 million) secured by a residence you live in are almost always tax-deductible, making the effective interest rate lower than it appears. Consider the following example:

	Credit Card	Mortgage
1) Loan amount	$25,000	$25,000
2) Interest rate	8%	10%
3) Monthly interest cost	$167	$208
4) Tax bracket	30%	30%
5) Mortgage interest tax deduction (#4 x #3)	N/A	$63
6) Net interest cost (#3 – #5)	$167	$145
7) Net interest rate (#6 x 12 ÷ #1)	8%	7%

This means that borrowing on your property in order to pay off higher interest debts that offer no tax deduction is generally a good approach. However, if you're trying to pay debts down, don't get an equity line that you can keep increasing in the future. Instead, get a one-time equity loan with fixed payments that you can build into your budget. Most big banks offer these with little or no closing costs and very competitive interest rates.

Many people have the notion that they will be financially more secure if they pay down or pay off their mortgage, and there's been an increase in the popularity of programs that charge several hundred dollars per year to convert your monthly payments into biweekly payments, resulting in your thirty-year loan being paid off in approximately twenty-one years. What proponents of these programs don't tell you is that by paying half your monthly payment every two weeks, you're paying twenty-six times a year, which is merely the equivalent of making thirteen monthly payments instead of twelve. That thirteenth payment is, for the most part, what accelerates the payoff of the loan. In other words, if you have the discipline—or, better yet, set it up automatically with your checking account and your mortgage company—you can accomplish much the same result (getting the mortgage paid off in twenty-one years instead of thirty and avoiding excessive interest), while saving several hundred dollars per year in fees. If you can't set it up automatically, go ahead and enroll in a program if paying your mortgage off early is important to you.

However, the best way to determine if you'll be financially better off by accelerating payback of your mortgage is by doing a comparison between the after-tax cost of the loan and the after-tax rate of return of other investments. The challenge here is that it's hard to know for certain what you will earn on your investments. When trying to decide whether to pay down a mortgage, first calculate the after-tax cost of your mortgage, using the same approach as we used in the previous table.

Mortgage

1) Loan amount	$25,000
2) Interest rate	10%
3) Monthly interest cost	$208
4) Tax bracket	30%
5) Tax deduction (#4 x #3)	$63
6) Net interest cost (#3 − #5)	$145
7) After-tax interest rate (#6 x 12 ÷ #1)	7%

Now ask yourself, "Can I invest to earn a guaranteed after-tax return greater than my result in line 7?" If the answer is yes, then you shouldn't be accelerating payment on your mortgage.

Another way to look at this is if other investments are likely to earn more after taxes than the interest rate of your mortgage over its remaining life (usually fifteen or thirty years), then rather than paying off that mortgage or holding a property debt-free, you're better off borrowing at a lower interest rate and investing at a higher one. If this makes you nervous, keep in mind that there has never been a fifteen-year (or longer) period in which the stock market has lost money. The longer your timeline, the safer stocks and real estate are and the more unsafe bonds are (because of inflation). When we do financial planning calculations for our clients, we assume that a globally diversified, passive portfolio with no bonds should earn about 8 percent after tax. This is a very conservative assumption, given that such a portfolio has actually averaged in the mid-teens over the past thirty years. For this reason, if your after-tax mortgage cost is less than the return you think your portfolio can earn, don't rush to pay down your mortgage more quickly. The money you spend to pay it off is better invested in the stock market. (If it truly increases your anxiety to follow the advice in this paragraph and you don't need to do it in order to gain a necessary financial advantage, then by all means, don't create unnecessary stress.)

RETIREMENT PLANNING

These days, the most secure way to plan for retirement is to find work you love so much that you never want to retire. With the advances in medical technology, most people are going to live much longer than they think. Some medical doctors I've spoken with believe that by 2020, those who are alive, healthy, medically insured, and under the age of seventy will live past age 130. That's almost twice the life expectancy most people plan for at present. For all but the wealthiest people, paying for six decades of expenses with entirely passive income will be impossible, and generally speaking, only during the final years of this period will people be physically unable to work. Most retired people I work with thrive on making a contribution to society, be it through part-time work, volunteering, grandparenting, or other philanthropy. Start to plan now for what your contribution will be, whether you'll be paid for it or not, and have your financial planner factor that into your projections.

And speaking of projections, many financial advisors are still doing retirement plans that assume the same rate of return every year. This is not realistic. It has therefore become a best practice in the financial planning industry to do what is called a Monte Carlo analysis, in which rates of return are randomized around an average. Thousands of future scenarios can be run using your income, spending, and asset levels, each with a different series of possible rates of return. In this way, the probability of having a successful outcome, depending on your life choices, can be calculated. For example, if you continue working in the job you don't like and then retire in ten years, you may find that you have a 75 percent likelihood of never running out of money, whereas if you go into the freelance consulting work you love, and do that for twenty more years at 60 percent of your current pay, give 15 percent of your annual income to your favorite charities, and cut your spending by 10 percent when you're age eighty, you'll have a 92 percent chance of never running out of money. Used correctly by a trained professional, this type of analysis gives a much more robust answer than the traditional methodology, which assumes a static rate of return. (A word of caution: it's easy to misinterpret or otherwise abuse this type of analysis. These studies merely illustrate the existence of risk and steps that can be taken to reduce the risk; they do not guarantee a result.)

As suggested earlier, take full advantage of your employer's 401(k) if one is available to you, as it is effectively the same as the U.S. government giving you an interest-free loan. This is because Uncle Sam lets you keep and invest the portion of your salary that would have gone to taxes had you not put it in the retirement plan. If your employer matches your contributions at all, taking advantage is even more beneficial to you as the effective rate of return on this investment is astronomical. Almost everyone drastically underappreciates the power of these vehicles (401(k)s, 403Bs, IRAs, SEP-IRAs, and profit-sharing plans), with or without employer-matching.

Last, if you're over forty, own your own business, and earn at least 25 percent more than you need to spend, it might behoove you to set up what's known as a defined benefit pension plan. Though these plans are being phased out by the larger corporations, they can be incredible savings vehicles because they don't impose the usual contribution limits that all other retirement plans do (typically 25 percent of compensation or a dollar limit—$45,000 in 2007). I have some clients who have been able to contribute well into six figures each year on a tax-deductible basis, even if that contribution represents three-quarters of their income! As with other plans for the self-employed, you can invest the plan's assets in stocks, bonds, or even real estate and trust deeds if your plan administrator allows such investments in the plan document. (If you have employees, you will have to contribute to their accounts as well, depending on their age, years of service, and salary level. Many employees place great value on these contributions once they understand them.)

TAXES

The retirement plan contributions described above are among the best tax-savings vehicles around. Charitable contributions are another. As mentioned, many people forget about taxes when they're comparing rates of return on bank deposits and CDs to other options. Interest income (unless from a tax-free municipal bond) is taxed as ordinary income, meaning that depending on the state where you live and your other income, you could be paying into the 40 percent range in tax on interest generated by money you have in CDs, for example. Capital gains taxes, which are assessed against any type of asset that has appreciated, be it real estate, a stock, a mutual fund, or even a bond, are currently 15 percent federal, leading to a tax rate that is about half the ordinary rate for most taxpayers. Also, with appreciating assets like stocks and real estate, you don't pay tax until you realize your gain (i.e., sell the asset), which provides the added financial benefit of tax deferral.

Finally, I strongly suggest that you not prepare your own taxes. Almost everyone I know (including myself) who once prepared their own taxes and then began to get them prepared by a professional saved money (and aggravation) by making the switch. If you really enjoy preparing your own taxes and are confident that you're maximizing all your deductions, then by all means keep doing it. But if not, you'd likely be well served to hire someone else to do it for you and put your energy into something you love doing.

ANNUITIES

Annuities are investment vehicles that are not taxed on their growth or interest until you withdraw money. They are usually offered by large insurance companies. There are two kinds of annuities: fixed annuities, which offer an interest rate much like a bank account, and variable annuities, which allow you to invest in stock, bond, and real estate funds. In my opinion, annuities should only be used as a savings vehicle after you have maximized all other retirement plan options available to you (including possibly switching to a solo 401(k) or defined benefit pension plan if you're self-employed). And even then, they rarely work out to your benefit. If you are in one of the highest tax brackets and you want to consider buying a variable annuity, make sure that it has no up-front or deferred load, it has a very low annual total expense ratio (under 0.50 percent for all administrative charges), and it gives you access to good, passive, low-cost investment options. If you select a fixed annuity, in which a fixed interest rate is offered, compare the rate to that of corporate bonds of similar quality. Remember, though, that the annuity will have the benefit of deferring taxes until you withdraw money. With either type of annuity, there should be no surrender charges (a penalty for taking your money out early, usually in less than seven years).

Indexed annuities are sort of a combination of a fixed and variable annuity, and provide limited participation in a stock market index (such as the S&P 500) with a limited downside (indexed annuities essentially promise that if you keep your money invested for a minimum number of years—often five or seven—you are guaranteed not to lose principal). While on their face these seem to offer the best of both worlds—stock market returns with no risk—they are a much better deal for the insurance company than the owner. This is because over such time periods, markets almost never lose money, and the price of having what I firmly believe is unnecessary protection is usually very high. For example, one indexed annuity I recently analyzed would only credit its owner's account with up to 15 percent in any given year. Between 1926 and 2005, the S&P 500 went up more than 15 percent in thirty-nine out of the eighty years. If you remove all the performance in excess of 15 percent per year, even after removing every single losing year, instead of a $1,000 investment growing to $1,663,337 over those eighty years, in an indexed annuity it only grows to $333,079. In my view, that's too high a price to pay for a relatively small amount of protection.

But annuities are good for some purposes. One way I like to use them is to create a lifetime stream of cash flow. For example, I have a client in his seventies who wanted to put a portion of his assets into a charitable fund. However, he was concerned that if the stock and real estate markets crashed, he and his wife might not be able to afford their ongoing living expenses. They had Social Security income of $1,780 a month, and they spent $6,000 a month. So we went to an insurance company and asked the company how much we would have to pay in a lump sum (known as a single premium in the insurance world) to guarantee the couple $4,220 of monthly income, increasing with inflation, until the second of them died. The answer was $1 million. When I crunched the numbers, this meant that if the second of them died at age ninety, the stream of monthly income would be the equivalent of a 6 percent guaranteed return. If the second of them lived longer than that, the payments would continue and the effective rate of return would be even higher. Conversely, if the second of them died before age ninety, the return would be less. For these reasons, fixed annuities are best for people who expect to live longer than the actuarial averages, which as I stated above, will likely be most healthy people under the age of seventy. Also, one must be careful only to buy from a reputable company because if something adverse were to happen to the annuity provider, it could turn out to have been a very poor financial move.

INSURANCE

Insurance is an emotionally laden area because it requires us to ask, "What happens if things go wrong?" This is something many don't want to face. (Others, of course, obsess about that possibility.) But for just a moment, think about what would happen to your family's quality of life if you died and your spouse and kids had to fend for themselves using your family's current assets. Or what might happen if you became permanently disabled and were unable to work? Where would you all live? What aspects of your life would no longer be affordable? These questions are immensely important, because the best budgeting, investing, and tax planning in the world will not help if your planning hasn't taken into account the possibility that some kind of tragedy might befall you.

LIFE INSURANCE should be used, in almost all cases, to cover the needs of those who are financially dependent on you. There are many trustworthy insurance agents; if you have one, please buy your insurance through her. However, I believe in reducing conflicts of interest wherever possible, which in this case means having someone who is not going to receive a financial benefit from your purchase (thus ideally not an insurance agent) help you calculate your insurance needs. Any Certified Financial Planner® professional or accountant should be able to help, and there are also Internet calculators that do a pretty good job. After you have assessed your need, you can certainly still buy insurance through the agent. To take care of your dependents, buy term insurance in which the premiums are fixed (known as level-premium term in the insurance world), with a term equal to the time period over which the beneficiaries would have been financially dependent on you. For example, if your youngest child is twelve years old and you assume that he or she would be financially dependent no longer than age twenty-five, then level-premium term insurance of at least thirteen years is sufficient.

What I'm about to suggest is controversial and there are some exceptions, but most of the time, life insurance should not be used as an investment vehicle. If you invest in a truly diversified, tax-efficient manner, the cost savings and performance advantages of your investment strategy will likely outweigh the tax-deferral benefits offered by a permanent insurance policy (also known as whole variable, or universal life insurance, which combine the tax-deferred savings benefits of an annuity with the insurance coverage offered by term insurance). If you do decide to buy permanent life insurance, try to locate a low-load or no-load insurer through the Internet. (A load is an up-front or back-end commission that the company takes out of your premium.)

DISABILITY INSURANCE is in many ways more important than life insurance; at age forty, for example, you are three times more likely to become disabled (not necessarily permanently) than you are to die. Though this likelihood does decrease with age, the average duration of the disability increases.

First, make sure you're taking whatever disability insurance your employer offers, because it will be the cheapest (although the benefits, should you ever need them, will be taxed just like your salary). Often, though, employer-provided disability insurance isn't adequate to cover your prior take-home income and keep up with inflation, throughout retirement. If this is the case and if your other assets are not sufficient to provide adequate interest and growth to cover your spending, you ought to buy private disability insurance. Additionally, many employer-provided disability insurance plans only cover employees to age sixty-five. But if you have been disabled for a number of years, you will not have been contributing to your retirement plan, and the employer-provided disability insurance disappears just as you need retirement income. As with life insurance, you might be well served to have an objective third party analyze your needs before committing to a policy.

LIABILITY INSURANCE is an underutilized but crucial type of insurance. Let's say that you own a house in California worth $800,000, have an IRA worth $250,000, and other investments worth $400,000, for a total net worth of $1,450,000. One evening, after having three martinis at dinner, you are driving home and you run over an investment banker crossing the street. A jury awards his survivors $3 million. California has a very limited home-owner's exemption (the portion of your home equity you're allowed to keep even if creditors are awarded the rest of your assets), and so you'll lose virtually everything. You might respond, "Well, I don't ever drink and drive." But that's not the only thing you can get sued for. Perhaps you live in a city where many people are driving $80,000 imported cars, and you rear-end one of them, and four others behind you are in the pile-up as well. There are a myriad of ways in which a judgment could be entered against you.

These are awful scenarios, but there's a very inexpensive way to protect yourself. For a few hundred dollars a year, you can obtain umbrella liability insurance. This is usually bought through the same agent who sells your car and homeowner's (or renter's) insurance, and it kicks in where the liability limits of those policies leave off. If you don't have any assets you want to protect, then you probably don't need to buy this type of insurance, although you may end up filing bankruptcy if a judgment is entered against you. It is important to note that just buying enough umbrella liability insurance to cover your net worth may not be sufficient. If the judgment is greater than the policy limit, the insurance will pay first and then your assets will pay. Therefore, we generally counsel clients to buy as much liability insurance as they can afford.

HOMEOWNER'S INSURANCE. Most people are underinsured for the replacement cost of their homes. Construction costs have risen so much in the last few years that in some neighborhoods the cost to replace a suburban single-family home without any particularly opulent finishes has topped $300 per square foot. Most policies written in the past few years cover $150–$200 per square foot. Check with a reputable builder, then confer with your insurance agent if you want to be doubly sure you could replace your home, then have your policy updated.

RENTER'S INSURANCE is something that most renters should have. It covers the theft of your personal property (both from your residence and away from it) as well as providing some liability coverage for you personally. Very few renters go to the trouble of getting renter's insurance, which is usually available through your auto insurance broker.

AUTO INSURANCE. Make sure that you have coverage adequate for the value of your car and the types of cars that could be in an accident with you, as well as a deductible that you can afford in the event your car is damaged.

LONG-TERM CARE INSURANCE. People over sixty-five face at least a 40 percent lifetime risk of entering a nursing home. Ten percent will stay more than five years. LTC insurance, as it is known, covers the cost of an extended illness either in a nursing home or, with many policies, in the home. It is most important for a couple whose assets and income are (or will be) just enough to cover their joint living expenses, or for someone who wants to leave their home to heirs no matter what happens with their health and who doesn't have sufficient assets to cover both their current living expenses and the costs of in-home or nursing-home care. For example, let's say a couple has $475,000 in total investments and a home worth $300,000 with a $50,000 mortgage balance. Their expenses are $35,000 per year, which are covered by Social Security and withdrawals from their investments. If one of them were to have an extended illness, and the care averaged $40,000 per year in 2006 (this number could easily be double that in some regions), they would be forced to sell their home and would likely deplete their assets in about thirty years. LTC insurance would protect them.

If you do buy LTC insurance, the best policies:

- are issued by a company rated by A.M. Best at A- or higher that hasn't ever raised its premiums on a class of insureds (A.M. Best is an agency that rates insurance companies),

- are tax qualified, which means you may be able to deduct the premiums if they exceed 7.5 percent of your adjusted gross income (the bottom line on your federal tax return Form 1040),

- have benefits that increase with inflation, and

- are guaranteed renewable, which means that as long as you pay your premiums on time, the policy cannot be canceled.

As with all insurance, always get more than one quote and compare the costs and benefits of each.

ESTATE PLANNING

If you take only one thing away from this section, please let it be that you need to sign and prepare a will (and possibly more estate-planning documents) that reflects your wishes. You are going to die. Many of the people you currently know may well live longer than you. What do you want their experience to be in the days and weeks after you're gone? As stated earlier, if you don't decide, the government will.

A caveat: I am not an attorney, and estate planning requires one, so the following should all be discussed with and implemented by a qualified estate-planning attorney.

Estate planning is rarely irrevocable. You can change a will, a living trust, or a power of attorney anytime prior to incapacity or death. Just get something signed, because anything you come up with will reflect your wishes better than what the government will do.

If you have a will but nothing else, you ought to consult with someone about whether other documents might be in order for you. A revocable living trust is often a significant improvement over just having a will because it keeps your affairs private and avoids probate delays and costs after your death. Powers of attorney for health care and financial decisions that become effective upon your incapacity are also extremely important, regardless of how much or how little money you have.

I'm not a fan of trying to use estate plans to control children or others from the grave. If you haven't parented them in such a way that they have financial values you like, then it's probably too late anyway. The exceptions to this are children who have problems with addiction or other special needs. In these instances, receiving too much money can do tremendous harm, and these kids should get their money in small doses. If they're still minors, try to pick guardians who will help them become healthy adults, financially and otherwise.

I generally recommend that the guardians of your children not be the same people as the executors of your will or the trustees of your living trust. This provides a system of checks and balances where the people controlling the money are not the same people spending the money. Try to make sure they're not people who already have an adversarial relationship, and of course, those in control of the money should have no conflict of interest; for example, if they are going to inherit whatever's left in the trust after the kids are grown, they might try to curtail spending from the trust.

I favor estate plans that leave assets to children in three installments. You can pick the appropriate ages, but essentially the first installment ought to occur when they're in their early to mid-twenties. These funds will probably be used for lifestyle purchases like a car, a nicer place to live, or perhaps more impermanent things, like a vacation or shopping expedition. The second installment might occur when they're in their late twenties or early thirties and will probably be used to start a business, buy a first home, or have kids. And the final installment might occur when your children are in their mid-thirties. This money will generally be earmarked for long-term goals, such as retirement or investment. Still, the inheritors should be allowed to spend the money as they see fit. If your children don't have special needs and they still blow all three installments, I'm not sure there's much you could have done differently.

Parents have to make their own choices with respect to how much to leave to kids and how much to leave to charity. But don't just walk into an estate planning attorney's office without having thought carefully about the effect of your money on your offspring. Many people automatically assume that the right thing to do is to leave all their assets to their children, less any estate taxes (which under current law, for wealthier people, can take away around 45 percent of the assets). Getting everything, though, is not always the best outcome for your children. First, think about how much annual income you'd like your kids to receive from you, as opposed to how much you want them to earn on their own. Then multiply that number by twenty if they'll invest according to the principles espoused in this book, or as much as thirty if they'll be more conservative or less diversified in their approach. This is the approximate principal you want to leave to each child. You may need to adjust this number for inflation by either revising your plan every few years or including a self-executing formula in your estate-planning documents. (A self-executing formula might mean having your attorney draft language that would leave your children a specified sum today, but would increase that number by inflation [CPI] so that they'd be getting the same inflation-adjusted amount of money even if you die in thirty years. Language such as this means that even if you don't update your plan every five years, as you should, you won't have unintentionally left your heirs much less money than you originally intended.) Make an informed and thoughtful choice rather than just going with what you perceive as a cultural norm.

If you own life insurance in your own name, and your children are your beneficiaries (or contingent beneficiaries), then the proceeds of that life insurance will be included in your estate and possibly taxed. There is a relatively simple solution to this: have your attorney set up an irrevocable life-insurance trust that will effectively buy the insurance instead of you personally owning the policy. You can also transfer your existing policy to such a trust. The rules around this are complex and go beyond the scope of this book, so be sure to speak to an estate-planning attorney about whether a life insurance trust might be appropriate in your situation.

Consider carefully the role you'd like philanthropy to play in your estate plan. For many more affluent people, asset disposition at death comes down to a choice between voluntary and involuntary philanthropy. In other words, you either decide to allocate a portion of your estate to philanthropy (by using a family foundation or donor-advised fund) or the government takes it in taxes (involuntary philanthropy).

Though it is controversial, I'm a big fan of discussing your estate plans with your children and any other heirs before you die. Many parents are uncomfortable with this, because they're afraid the feelings that arise will be difficult to deal with. My question is, "Would you rather have those feelings come out after you're dead?" For some, the answer is yes. But if it's not, arrange a family meeting and discuss your plans while you're alive. Others can suggest changes; you're under no obligation to accept their ideas, but they might have some good suggestions. There are also good professional facilitators who can be brought in to smooth out awkward or tense family situations. It might be easier for you to wait until after you're gone, but it's almost never easier for the people your money is going to impact.

FINANCIAL PLANNERS

My favorite places to get access to well-trained, independent, objective advisors are the following:

- www.napfa.org is for those looking for an ongoing relationship with a competent fee-only® planner, likely including investment management. All of NAPFA's planners must provide comprehensive financial planning, have taken a fiduciary oath to treat their clients' money as they would their own, and are subject to double the continuing education requirements of most CFP® professionals.

- www.garrettplanningnetwork.com is for those looking for objective, independent, hourly financial planning without investment management help. Garrett's planners focus on what's called the "middle market," meaning that they don't have the high minimum asset levels of most financial planners.

- www.kinderinstitute.org is for those who are specifically looking for a relationship with a life planner who can help navigate both the emotional and financial aspects of life.

You can also find links to these groups of planners at my Web site: www.BrentKessel.com.

SOCIALLY RESPONSIBLE INVESTING (SRI)

Social Investment Forum (www.socialinvest.org) has many resources for SRI investors. They also have another Web site (www.sriadvocacy.org) that provides good information on shareholder activism, as does Co-op America (www.coopamerica.org/socialinvesting/shareholderaction).

SMART PHILANTHROPY

When looking for the best nonprofit to give to, you might focus on what percentage of your gift will ultimately reach the people you want to benefit. Information like this can be found at www.guidestar.org or www.charity-watch.org.

DEBT REDUCTION SERVICES

Consumer Credit Counseling Services (CCCS) is a national network of non-profit credit counseling agencies that examine a client's income, expenses, assets, and liabilities and offer a range of possible options and solutions, giving clients the tools to better manage money going forward. In approximately 25 percent of the cases, CCCS ends up establishing a Debt Management Plan, whereby they try to help clients get their payments and finance charges reduced and consolidate the payments so that the clients can send them a monthly deposit for disbursement to their unsecured creditors. No matter how bad your situation is, CCCS has likely seen worse (www.nfcc.org or 800–388–2227).

DONOR-ADVISED FUNDS

Donor-advised funds are similar to a charitable foundation, except that they are much easier to set up and maintain. These funds, generally run by community foundations or financial services organizations, allow you to donate cash or securities today but give the money to the end-recipient charities over time. Let's say you have $10,000 in stock you inherited from your late grandmother that you're not attached to keeping. However, you're not quite ready to give away $10,000 this year. A donor-advised fund will allow you to effectively fund in advance several years (or decades) of your charitable giving and receive the tax deduction today. You can generally give your fund any name you wish (for example, the Fillmore Family Charitable Fund), and some give you a choice of how the funds are invested. Go to www.BrentKessel.com for more information or check out the Schwab Charitable Fund (www.schwabcharitable.org/scf) or the Giving Back Fund (www.givingback.org).

CHARACTERISTICS OF AND PRACTICAL RECOMMENDATIONS FOR EACH ARCHETYPE

The Guardian

CASH FLOW AND BUDGETING Some Guardians keep meticulous records of their spending, keeping track of what categories have gone up or down. They are analytically astute, which leads them to live within their means. Other Guardians use "retail therapy" to calm their nerves, allowing short-term relief to take precedence over long-term sustainable well-being.

To relieve yourself of the hyperalertness you think is compulsory, set up a system to alert you if your situation deteriorates. If things get to a point where action might really be required, you will be alerted; until then, you need not concern yourself. For example, hire a bookkeeper (or buy a bill-paying program like Quicken or Microsoft Money) so you can be alerted by an outside party when you are not meeting predefined goals (i.e., when your expenses exceed your income in a calendar quarter). If you can't afford these measures, write down the major thresholds that you feel will require you to take action. For example, you might feel that if your investments have underperformed a major index (like the S&P 500) over the past three years or have had negative returns for two years in a row, it's time to make a change; or if you accumulate more than $10,000 of debt to get through job training, you'll get a night job to supplement your income. These types of rules, along with the internal practices recommended in the Guardian chapter, will allow you to focus your time and energy on calming and rejuvenating activities. Schedule these activities so that they also become automatic!

INVESTING Many Guardians tend toward ultraconservative investing, or they bounce around between different investment vehicles in an attempt to avoid losses. For these reasons, they often earn a subpar return, which ironically increases the chance that they might really have something to worry about in the future.

Follow the recommendations in chapter 12 about long-term investing. The best investment program for the Guardian is one that requires no intervention or monitoring. For example, buy a collection of index funds or exchange-traded funds that track the market year-in and year-out, and just keep adding to your investment *no matter what*. Alternatively, go through a very careful process of selecting a financial advisor you can trust and then *trust your advisor!* Why? Because she is more objective than you can be. You'll have to summon up a healthy dose of inner discipline to pull it off, but if you're willing to do that up-front, you'll have much more inner peace over the years, as well as a strong likelihood of much better results than if you continue making investment changes in an attempt to alleviate your emotional distress. If you can't afford a paid advisor, there are free financial-literacy and credit-counseling services (see p. 264) that can give you objective, helpful advice.

INSURANCE Guardians in general have too much insurance. They are focused on catastrophes of all kinds, which unfortunately makes them easier targets for overcovering themselves. Alternatively, some Guardians get so consumed by particular risks that they don't pay attention to other risks that might be more significant.

Some Guardians have no insurance. This is one of the surest ways of putting yourself in a situation that justifies your worry, and for a long time! Buy the minimum you need to be secure.

Allow a trained, objective professional to worry for you. Insurance is a wonderful tool when used appropriately. However, you need to be quite careful to select an agent who has integrity and who asks questions about your needs before recommending an amount of coverage or type of policy. Be wary of agents who make generalized statements like "You ought to have X times your annual salary in life insurance" or "Let's select the highest amount available from this company to make sure your needs are covered." These statements appeal to the Guardian's yearning for peace, but they're likely to provide either too much or too little coverage. If you want a completely unbiased opinion, hire a fee-only® financial planner through www. napfa.org or www.garrettplanningnetwork.com to do an insurance-needs analysis for you.

TAXES Guardians avoid putting the money they should into retirement plans, because they worry about not being able to touch their money until age 59½ without a penalty. Also, Guardians are more likely than those in other archetypes to prepare and file their own tax returns. Though this gives them a feeling of control, they don't have the professional training and continuing education requirements that CPAs and enrolled agents do, leading them to miss out on legal tax-saving strategies.

Delegate, delegate, delegate. Unless you're a CPA yourself, have someone else do your tax work. In fact, even if you are a CPA, barter with another tax professional. Chances are that if you're a Guardian, you can't be objective about your own situation. With very few exceptions, you should contribute the maximum amount permitted by law to retirement plans and rely on other means for your emergency funds. The economic benefits are just too great.

GIFTING AND ESTATE PLANNING Often worried about how the next generation will handle money, Guardians try to control from the grave. Many Guardians just can't get themselves to sign their wills or other estate-planning documents because they believe the people they've chosen as executors, trustees, or guardians of their kids won't be as careful as they themselves are.

Get an estate plan signed. You can always change it later. Yes, no one will be as good as you, or know your situation as well, but if you don't have an estate plan, the state will decide who plays these roles, which is far worse than any decision you could make. If you don't have the money to hire a lawyer, use a free legal service or buy forms from a stationery store or Quicken Willmaker Plus.

PHILANTHROPY AND GENEROSITY Most Guardians do relatively little philanthropically, commensurate with their level of income or assets. Their focus is on themselves, which unfortunately exacerbates their worries.

Start inquiring into how you might do something philanthropically now, no matter how insignificant in your mind. Volunteer time or money. What causes or people are dear to your heart, and how might you support them? Each time you write a check or volunteer, you send a subliminal message to yourself that there's nothing to worry about, because you have enough to help others.

The Pleasure Seeker

CASH FLOW AND BUDGETING Pleasure Seekers often spend on credit cards with high interest rates.

Don't buy *anything* on credit, period, unless your net worth has been growing more than 4 percent per year.

INVESTING Pleasure Seekers' investments are often concentrated in lifestyle assets, such as a nicer home than might be financially prudent. For the more affluent, investments might include second homes, country-club memberships, boats, and other assets that bring pleasure.

Because this archetype is more impulsive than most, if you do have stocks, bonds, or mutual funds, you are more likely to be plagued by frequent changes of investment vehicles or advisors, leading to drastic underperformance.

Only own assets that appreciate. Rent or lease assets that have a pleasure component to them (like cars or boats), as they often depreciate. Most people should rent rather than buy vacation homes because there are better financial assets in which to invest. Also, most Pleasure Seekers, when trying to justify the purchase of a second home, don't include, as they analyze the true cost of their purchase, the interest they would have earned on their down payment had they put it in higher-yielding investments.

Set up an automatic investment program that you don't change, or empower someone else to make investment decisions for you.

INSURANCE This archetype may not have sufficient insurance for highly valuable collectibles such as art, jewelry, electronics, cars, or boats, or may be engaged in risky hobbies with inadequate liability insurance (drinking alcohol, motorsports, entertaining).

Make sure your insurance agent is aware of the assets you own (including all valuables) as well as the hobbies you engage in and that your insurance is sufficient to cover them both.

TAXES Most pleasure purchases are not tax-deductible, so Pleasure Seekers often pay a higher percentage of their income in taxes than do other archetypes.

Start a self-employed business in an area you enjoy so that you can write off more of your pleasure spending against income (assuming that you are engaged in a for-profit enterprise).

GIFTING AND ESTATE PLANNING Some Pleasure Seekers try to control from the grave, teaching their children or grandchildren to live a more prudent financial life than they themselves lived, through the use of incentive trusts, which give heirs more money for starting a business or getting a college degree, for example. Sometimes, the "live for today" attitude leads to no will or estate planning.

At a minimum, get a will signed. Incentive trusts rarely have the desired outcome because your heirs will most likely react to what you do, not what you say—whether in person or in legal documents. Live the way you hope they will live.

PHILANTHROPY AND GENEROSITY Usually little or no philanthropy arises out of the Pleasure Seeker archetype itself. If there's overlap with the Star or Caretaker, then there may be a philanthropic impulse.

Give sensory pleasure to others who haven't ever experienced it at the level you do. Ask yourself whether this brings you more or less pleasure than spending on yourself and whether there's a difference in how long it lasts.

The Idealist

CASH FLOW AND BUDGETING Idealists sometimes don't know how much they're spending or earning. Their focus on areas other than money can lead to late payments, finance charges, bad credit, and so on. They are more likely to be receiving financial help from others (spouse, family) or to be in debt than are other archetypes.

Some Idealists, by contrast, pride themselves on how little they need to get by. Subsisting on the bare minimum, they often don't have emergency funds for unexpected expenses.

Look at the numbers. Pay a bookkeeper or barter with a friend to help you, because it probably makes your skin crawl to crunch numbers. Set up as many bills as possible to be paid automatically, thus reducing late payments and finance charges.

Create a rainy day fund. If you have a job with a regular paycheck, aim for three times your monthly living expenses. If your income is irregular, aim for six times monthly spending.

INVESTING If there are any savings or investments, investments deemed to be socially progressive and creative have been given higher priority than those with higher financial returns. Investments will often be hodge-podge, such as a tract of land in a beautiful place, a few stocks gifted by family, some expensive artwork, and perhaps a few orphan mutual funds bought on the advice of a friend ten years ago. Create an investment plan, either with the help of chapter 12 in this book or with a trusted professional advisor you already know. Then stick to the plan. Your values can be incorporated into the plan, but do so systematically rather than impulsively. To create more resources to pursue your art, social activism, or spiritual path, make your savings and investment program automatic, so that a set amount of money is automatically moved from your checking account into your investment account each month. At a bare minimum, automatically transfer a predetermined amount into a Roth IRA each month.

INSURANCE Idealists are often uninsured or underinsured. This can be a result of disdain for large bureaucracies (like insurance companies), a willingness to take risks and buck the system, or avoidance of financial matters in general. Many have been told, "You're not responsible with money" for so many years that lack of adequate insurance has been programmed into them. Others may favor alternative health care and use this as a justification not to carry traditional health insurance.

Ask yourself whether being underinsured is really serving your artistic, social, or spiritual goals. If not, obtain at least the lowest levels of insurance. Ask friends in a similar situation who they're insured with. Often, there are plans designed for specific vocational groups or people with similar life-styles. Check with an association to which like-minded colleagues belong. See p. 256 for a list of the basic types of insurance coverage that every person should have and p. 263 for planners who can help you get your risks and needs assessed and covered.

TAXES Idealists often don't pay taxes because of a declared income below the minimum required to file a tax return, financial disorganization, or con-scientious objections to the government's use of tax money. If paying taxes, Idealists often declare less than actual earnings or they look for potentially audit-attracting loopholes because of a disagreement with how the govern-ment spends tax dollars.

Don't do anything illegal, but pay as little in tax as you legally can. This requires focus and attention instead of avoidance. Hire an inexpensive tax preparation service or barter with a friend, but file and pay your taxes. The more your vocation earns and the more assets you have, the more benefit you'll receive by hiring tax-planning help, such as a CPA or tax attorney.

GIFTING AND ESTATE PLANNING Idealists are attached to leaving tangible as-sets, such as a home or a piece of real estate or artwork, to specific heirs. This desire to hang on to certain prized possessions can lead to a lack of liquid funds that your heirs could use to pay estate taxes (if your estate is valuable enough to be taxable). It can also lead to self-deprivation or giving less than you'd like during your life. Or you may lack any assets to leave heirs and hold on to a vague hope that your work will one day be worth something financially.

Have a will or estate plan, regardless of how much or little money you have. Without it, the state will decide who cares for your minor children, there will be no privacy as to what you had and who gets it, and your heirs will have to wait longer and pay more before they receive the assets you want them to inherit. If your estate is large enough, understand that when you die, as a U.S. citizen or resident, you either participate in voluntary or invol-untary philanthropy, meaning the U.S. government takes up to 45 percent of your estate, and Congress decides how it should be spent. In voluntary philanthropy, you gift your assets to a charity, a donor-advised account, or a family charitable foundation that will further your creative, social, or spiritual legacy, thus allowing you to decide how the money should be spent. Seek the counsel of a good estate-planning attorney, or at the very least use a legal-aid service to create your basic will and powers of attorney.

If you have work that will need to be managed after your death, do not leave it to your heirs to oversee that process without discussing it with them first. Many children end up having to unwind the artistic affairs of their deceased parents without remuneration.

PHILANTHROPY AND GENEROSITY For Idealists, charitable giving is either nonexistent or impulsive and unplanned. They may not give to large organizations, distrusting fundraising and believing that the best cause is their own work. There are some Idealists who are very organized and effective as fundraisers themselves, but they're usually not the starving-artist variety.

Define your charitable mission (see p. 230). Don't give more than you can afford, but do donate something. Allow a high percentage of your overall giving to be for unplanned gifts, perhaps 50 percent, but don't exceed that amount (unless you revise your plan). If you're like most Idealists, you'll get more fulfillment from giving your time and talent than money.

The Saver

CASH FLOW AND BUDGETING The Saver likely knows exactly how much they earn, spend, and save. A high percentage of their income is being saved. They spend much less of their income than other archetypes do, to the point of excessive frugality or even deprivation. Savers are unlikely to be generous with family, friends, or charity. They also sometimes place too much emphasis on paying off mortgage or business debts early.

What additional spending or charitable giving would fulfill and inspire you? How might you add to your life or the lives of those you love? If you don't know, ask others. Move money for these purposes out of the main accounts you're used to looking at to count your treasure (i.e., put the charitable portion into a donor-advised account in a lump sum, then do your giving out of that).

INVESTING Savers tend to review their investment performance too often and thus make changes too frequently. Disciplined Savers often are less than disciplined investors, earning poor returns due to overly active trading, stock-picking, or an overly risk-averse orientation (e.g., too high a percentage of assets in bank CDs or bonds).

See chapter 12 for advice on investing or use one of the ready-to-go strategies shared at the beginning of this appendix and set your portfolio up to earn market rates of return without micromanaging by you. Review your investment returns no more than once a quarter and create an overall investment plan that you can stick to. If you are a very conservative investor, consider having your planner or financial advisor show you what would happen to a more aggressive portfolio even if the Great Depression were to occur tomorrow. If your financial security would still be fine, consider increasing the risk, and thus reward, of your investments. Use the excess for more fun and generosity.

INSURANCE Savers are sometimes underinsured in the name of saving money on premiums. More often Savers are overinsured because they are afraid of loss, and their savings and insurance are there to protect them from loss.

Have an independent insurance agent or fee-only® financial planner conduct a thorough review of your needs and present coverage.

TAXES Savers are good with tax reduction, especially the use of tax-favored retirement plans (which are also savings vehicles).

Explore the ways in which charitable gifting can reduce your tax burden while still providing you with income (charitable remainder trusts, annuity trusts, gift trusts). In looking for investments, focus on after-tax returns, not just nominal returns. Make sure you have the optimal tax-deferred retirement plan set up and are doing as much prudent saving as you need to do into these retirement accounts first.

GIFTING AND ESTATE PLANNING Because of their focus on accumulation during life, Savers often have wills and estate plans that encourage their heirs to save, as opposed to spending or charitable giving. There is a resistance to estate planning that takes any assets out of their direct control.

Have a Certified Financial Planner® or estate-planning attorney help you calculate how much of an estate you're likely to die with. If it's going to far exceed what you can spend, and is likely to be taxed at close to 45 percent, consider increasing your family and charitable gifting, enjoyable spending, and irrevocable estate planning while you're still alive. Chances are this will be the best financial move, and you and your loved ones will receive much more fulfillment.

PHILANTHROPY AND GENEROSITY Charitable giving as a percentage of income or assets is often extremely low or nonexistent for Savers. Savers are wired to protect themselves, so it's not uncommon to see minimal charitable gifts from Savers who have tens of millions themselves. What looks like greed from the outside is actually fear.

Use your discipline and research skills to make your philanthropic giving as effective as possible. Experiment with giving money, time, and appreciated assets. For one month, try giving away the same amount you save and see how it feels. Ideally, target an annual giving goal of at least 1 percent of your net worth, which for Savers is often a better metric than a percentage of income.

The Star

CASH FLOW AND BUDGETING Stars usually spend most or all excess cash flow on purchases that enhance image (cars, clothing, hair, jewelry, furniture, home theater, entertainment, art, fitness, plastic surgery, etc.). Stars avoid budgeting or looking at where money has actually been spent.

Create and look at a report that shows what you've been spending your money on. If you don't have the skill to do this, pay a bookkeeper to produce a report for you, or use software like Quicken or Microsoft Money. Look for spending categories and items intended to enhance the image you want to project. Are you comfortable or happy with your spending in these areas? If not, set spending goals that feel right to you, and continue to track your spending at least once every three months. If you're constantly spending more than you earn, consider paying cash for everything for three months.

INVESTING The Star's investments are often selected to keep up with the latest trend, such as technology stocks in the late 1990s and early 2000s, or real estate in 2004–2006. Sometimes, a Star's portfolio is symbolic of the image he wants to project, be it socially responsible funds, hedge funds promising high returns, initial public offerings, or trophy real estate. The common theme is that the story is more important than the economic substance. More often than not, this leads to rather dismal investment returns compared to other investment options within the same category of assets.

Go to an independent, fee-only® financial planner or Registered Investment Advisor and allow them to construct a low-cost, diversified investment plan for the bulk (at least 80 percent) of your investments. As you've read, most successful investing is actually quite boring—nothing that you'll really want to discuss at a cocktail party until a few years down the line, when you have grown your money two or three times as much as the people you're talking to have grown theirs. And you don't have to sacrifice your values: the portfolio can be built with social screening or with an emphasis on particular asset classes you favor. If you really enjoy having an investment story to tell, put 5–10 percent of your total assets into what I call the "cocktail party" account, and do what you want with it.

INSURANCE Stars are often underinsured on cars, art, electronics, jewelry, collectibles, and homes. They may have bought expensive insurance from best-of-breed companies instead of finding a better product for less from a perfectly reputable company. Liability insurance may be too low for risky lifestyle activities (entertaining, boating, swimming pool, fast driving, or four-wheeling).

Obtain a full insurance review from a reputable independent brokerage firm. Make sure to provide a complete list of all valuables and lifestyle activities.

TAXES Stars usually pay higher taxes than necessary because a higher percentage of income must be taken home in order to fund lifestyle expenses.

Learn from Empire Builders and Savers that wages and bonuses are the worst kind of financial income because they're taxed today at the highest rates. In contrast, income that comes in the form of growing your investments or being paid with stock options, deferred compensation, or other equity ownership is almost always taxed later and at lower rates, leading to more money in your pocket after taxes.

GIFTING AND ESTATE PLANNING Stars often seek recognition for charitable gifts to be made by their estate. They are less likely to have thought through the risks of leaving large sums of money to heirs at younger ages. This is by no means limited to Stars, but multiple marriages may have created complex and inequitable wills and estate plans.

Make sure that the charitable giving in your plan accomplishes the tangible, measurable goals you want it to because you're not going to be able to feel people's admiration from the grave. If you have children from a prior marriage, consider carefully how they'll be taken care of (or not) under your current will. When in doubt, discuss it with them while alive or, at a minimum, write them a separate letter to be opened at your death that describes to them what you want them to know about your wishes.

PHILANTHROPY AND GENEROSITY For Stars, the appearance of philanthropic generosity is often given greater weight than the substance of it. At times, little or no money is given because it is believed that lending one's name or social position is just as valuable.

Lead by example. Give the same percentage of your income or net worth that you would like others to give. Focus your giving where you are most touched and moved, which is where you'll get the most lasting benefits. Try doing something out of character. If you never make anonymous gifts, for example, try just one in the next month and see how it feels.

The Innocent

CASH FLOW AND BUDGETING Innocents are usually spending everything they earn, and more. If there are no earnings, then they are dependent on other people or government assistance.

Look at the numbers. Get help from a friend or professional if you don't know how to look at the numbers yourself. Live within today's means as though there were going to be no increase in future income. If you have insurmountable debts, make an appointment with Consumer Credit Counseling Service (CCCS), which can probably negotiate a manageable debt-repayment program for you. Try to reduce or eliminate cash flow surprises by having monthly (instead of quarterly or annual) payments for all your expenses. For example, have your mortgage company impound your property taxes and insurance if you own your home (which means you'll effectively pay them monthly), have a fixed-rate mortgage rather than an adjustable so the payment is predictable, or buy extended warranties to avoid costly repairs.

INVESTING Innocents are more likely to be in debt than to have investments. If there are investments, principal is being spent down such that the money will run out before needs do. There's little or no sophistication and knowledge about investing. Innocents often know more about credit-card companies than investment companies.

Begin an automatic investment program. Add up the amounts you've spent on lottery tickets and get-rich-quick schemes and begin putting that into an investment account on a monthly basis. Have your bank move the lesser of $400 or 10 percent of your income into a Roth IRA account each month. No amount is too small. Just get started with something. Invest your Roth in either a diversified basket of index funds or a single socially responsible index fund. Unlike many financial planners, I believe it is best to start investing even before you've paid all your debts off. Work with a planner or CCCS to help you decide how much to direct to your debts and how much to your investments.

INSURANCE For Innocents, there are sometimes late payments that lead to cancelled policies. There is no disability insurance and possibly no health or auto insurance. Their liability limits are often too low on auto policies to cover an accident they cause with even a typical mid-priced luxury sedan. Sometimes Innocents are suckers for expensive insurance products they don't really need (e.g., buying a variable annuity within an IRA or other retirement plan, or mortgage-payoff insurance in the event of their death).

Get a comprehensive-needs analysis performed by a reputable independent insurance agent. On your auto policy, make sure you've got at least $100,000 of liability coverage and that your deductibles are as low as possible. Set up all insurance policies to be paid with monthly premiums automatically deducted from your bank account. If at all possible, get health insurance. If you have dependents, get a needs analysis done by someone other than the agent you'll buy your insurance through. (There are good Internet calculators available for this, or use an hourly financial planner.) Then buy term life insurance with a fixed premium for as long as those people will be dependent on you (e.g., at least twenty years for newborn children). Pay the premiums monthly.

TAXES Depending on earnings, Innocents may not pay taxes or file. If they do have a job, they're often having too much withheld from each paycheck, such that they receive a tax refund once a year, which makes ongoing cash-flow planning more difficult. In some cases, there are late filings, under-reporting due to avoidance or disorganization, or tax liens. Innocents often pay more as a percentage of their income than people who make more money than they do, because they don't own their own homes and so don't get the benefit of itemized deductions.

File and pay your taxes. You probably hate dealing with finances, so outsource this to an inexpensive tax-preparation service. Reduce your monthly tax withholding at work so that it equals 1/12 of your annual tax bill. If you're self-employed and pay estimated taxes quarterly, open an account at your bank just for tax payments and have them automatically transfer 1/12 of the annual total into that account each month, then write your quarterly checks from there. (You can use this account for all other irregular expenses as well.)

GIFTING AND ESTATE PLANNING Innocents usually have no will and no term life insurance to cover dependents' needs. In the event of death, the state decides who the children's guardians will be.

Use a legal-aid service to get your basic estate-planning documents done. In picking the best guardian for your children, think about how they handle money and what your kids will learn from them. If there will be life insurance proceeds, it might make sense to have a separate executor or trustee for that money rather than the guardian of your children, to be sure that the money will be best used for their well-being.

PHILANTHROPY AND GENEROSITY Innocents are more likely to be a recipient of philanthropy than a donor. Some Innocents do give a lot to charity even though they aren't self-sufficient themselves.

There's always someone worse off than you. When you can help another person, you begin to switch your unconscious beliefs about money from scarcity to abundance. Use giving as one of the incentives to inspire you to make more money. Once you've transformed your inner and outer financial scarcity into abundance, you can help others do the same.

The Caretaker

CASH FLOW AND BUDGETING Caretakers' expenses are unpredictable because other people's needs are unpredictable. Caretakers find it difficult to say no, so if they have the money on hand or, in extreme cases, even if they don't, they cover others' shortfalls, making budgeting almost impossible.

If possible, put those who are dependent on you on an allowance, and make it automatic. For example, transfer $1,500 every month into your dependents' bank accounts to help them out, rather than paying their bills directly. Have them get basic financial training through a local community college, financial literacy program, or Consumer Credit Counseling Service.

INVESTING Most Caretakers don't have much to invest. Those that do tend to keep a disproportionate percentage in assets that can be liquidated quickly if some unforeseen need should arise.

Once you've created budgets or boundaries you're willing to stick to, keep as little of your money as possible in short-term liquid assets to cover your pledges. With the rest, create an investment plan that secures *your* future. If possible, direct some portion of your gifting to other people for their retirement savings or their charitable giving.

INSURANCE Caretakers tend to go to one extreme or another with insurance. Either they are overinsured with life or disability insurance for fear of leaving dependents in financial strain if something were to happen to them or they have almost no insurance because of the grandiosity that surrounds their Caretaking ("No one will ever be able to take care of you the way I do").

Get a thorough review of your life and disability insurance needs by an independent agent or financial planner, preferably one who does not also sell insurance products (to reduce conflicts of interest). If you're giving money to people who have high medical expenses, consider adding them to your health insurance policy or funding a Health Savings Account if possible (and advisable per your tax advisor).

TAXES Most Caretakers are helping others with after-tax earnings, meaning that for each dollar you give, you typically have to earn $1.50–1.80 pretax.

Make sure your tax preparer is fully appraised of the amount of your financial support to others so that she can take advantage of dependent tax deductions and any credits available. Find out if any of your giving can be channeled through a nonprofit charity or through your self-employed business so that you get a tax deduction for it.

GIFTING AND ESTATE PLANNING Caretakers' wills and estate plans often leave too much too soon or attempt to control heirs from the grave (in the case of wealthy matriarchs and patriarchs). Their gifting is done on an ad-hoc basis rather than being strategically designed to help create self-sufficiency. In many cases, Caretakers are unwittingly exceeding the annual limits on tax-free gifting, subjecting themselves to a possible gift-tax audit.

Instead of ad-hoc gifts, set up recurring monthly transfers to the people you're supporting. Define boundaries that will create successful outcomes, but only verbalize them if you're willing to stick to your word! If you'll be leaving an inheritance, make sure that your estate plan gives your heirs the best chance for *their own* success. One formula I often recommend is giving an inheritance in equal thirds at five-year intervals. This way, an heir can blow the first third, perhaps on impulsive purchases like a new car or a fancy vacation. Figuring out that they may want to have more to show for their inheritance down the line, they might use the second third to buy a home or start a business. When the final third comes through, they know there won't be any more coming, and will be more likely to channel it into the areas where it will provide the most fulfillment or security.

PHILANTHROPY AND GENEROSITY In some cases, Caretakers exhibit higher than average giving, but it's disorganized and impulsive. In others, the philanthropy is closer to home, supporting family or friends who are in need.

Write a Giving Policy (see p. 230) that details who you're going to give to and in what percentages. This can include sons and daughters or distant charities.

The Empire Builder

CASH FLOW AND BUDGETING With Empire Builders, a disproportionate amount of cash flow is usually being channeled into the growth of the empire, leaving relatively little for regular spending. Empire Builders can live both within their means and beyond them.

Take profits out of your company and spend, invest, or give them to other causes. If your enterprise requires more capital, raise it from other people. If your business strategy isn't good enough to attract outside capital, it's probably not good enough for you to risk your own capital either. Start to pay yourself a market-rate salary from a start-up business as early in the process as possible.

INVESTING Empire Builders tend to have more than 75 percent of their net worth tied up in their empire, be it a single company, a real-estate portfolio, or collectibles. Other investments tend to get far less attention than they need because all hopes for growth rest on the empire.

Andrew Carnegie said, "Put all your eggs in one basket, and watch that basket." But this is bad advice for most people because no matter how closely you watch, there are risks you cannot see. If it's not possible to sell part of your privately held business, try to find ways to reduce the risk of a major company decline leading to personal financial ruin. This can include building up your outside net worth, hedging (if your company is public), or doing a sale over time to management or employees. Don't assume that just because you know your business better than any other company, it is the most prudent investment. Think of yourself as the head of an endowment fund that has 100 percent cash to invest. Would you choose to invest as high a proportion of the endowment in your business as you currently have invested of your personal net worth?

INSURANCE Empire Builders may not have key-man insurance on most important team members or a buy-sell agreement to allow for a smooth transition of the business without devastating company cash flow.

Have an attorney draft a good buy-sell agreement and fund it with life insurance so your heirs won't be forced into a business they might not understand. If the success and value of the business rests on your shoulders, make sure you have adequate disability insurance to protect your family in the event you're disabled.

TAXES Empire Builders generally do good tax-planning in order to minimize taxes paid and channel more profits into future growth.

Maximize contributions to tax-deferred retirement plans. If you're older, depending on the salaries and ages of your employees, a defined-benefit pension plan may allow you to put away a much higher amount of your income than other retirement plans.

Consider donating part or all of your ownership interest to a charitable foundation and allowing it to sell your interest, which will have significant tax benefits. Note that the profits from the donated interest won't be available for you to spend.

GIFTING AND ESTATE PLANNING Often heirs are unprepared to assume the responsibility of managing the empire.

Talk to your family about what you want to have happen with your company after your death, in addition to putting your wishes into your legal documents. Have a succession plan in place. Don't put people in charge because you think they should be, but rather because they want to be in charge and are qualified. Consider family limited partnerships, charitable foundations, and other attorney-recommended vehicles to reduce taxes and ensure a lasting legacy.

PHILANTHROPY AND GENEROSITY During empire-building phases of life, Empire Builders are often not very involved in major philanthropy, but later in life, may use philanthropy as a substitute for the power and control they used to exercise in business.

One of the best ways to create balance if you are an extreme Empire Builder is to begin giving one percent of your net worth (not your income) to charity each year. (This may or may not be the right number for you, but do ask yourself what percentage of your net worth you want to give away. What percentage would allow for maximum fulfillment and well-being?) This amount should be sustainable for a long time and will likely be a huge increase in your giving. This behavior begins to shift the focus from the self to the wider world, which in itself usually creates greater balance and inner peace.

RESOURCES

SUGGESTED READING

I update a list of my favorite books periodically at www.BrentKessel.com. Here are some of my favorites.

Investing

Bogle, John C. *The Little Book of Common Sense Investing: The Only Way to Guarantee Your Fair Share of Stock Market Returns.* Hoboken: Wiley and Sons, 2007.

Ellis, Charles. *Winning the Losers Game.* New York: McGraw Hill, 1998.

Gibson, Roger. *Asset Allocation.* New York: McGraw Hill, 1990.

O'Shaughnessy, James P. *How to Retire Rich.* New York: Broadway Books, 1998.

———. *What Works on Wall Street.* New York: McGraw Hill, 1998.

Swedroe, Larry. *The Only Guide to a Winning Investment Strategy You'll Ever Need.* New York: St. Martin's Press, 2005.

Temkin, Bruce. *The Terrible Truth About Investing.* St. Petersburg, FL: Fairfield Press, 2000.

Tobias, Andrew. *The Only Investment Guide You'll Ever Need.* San Diego, CA: Harcourt, 2002.

Children of Affluence

Gallo, Jon, and Eileen Gallo. *Silver Spoon Kids: How Successful Parents Raise Responsible Children.* New York: McGraw Hill, 2002.

Owen, David. *The National Bank of Dad.* New York: Simon & Schuster, 2007.

Rottenberg, Dan. *The Inheritor's Handbook.* New York: Simon & Schuster, 2000.

Philosophy and Personal Growth

Berg, Adriane G. *Financial Planning for Couples.* New York: Newmarket Press, 1993.

Chilton, David. *The Wealthy Barber.* Toronto: Stoddart Publishers, 2002.

Clason, George S. *The Richest Man in Babylon*. New York: Penguin, 2007.

Kinder, George. *The Seven Stages of Money Maturity*. New York: Random House, 2000.

Mellon, Olivia. *Money Harmony: Resolving Money Conflicts in Your Life and Relationships*. New York: Walker, 1994.

Needleman, Jacob. *Money and the Meaning of Life*. New York: Doubleday, 1991.

Nemeth, Maria. *The Energy of Money*. New York: Ballantine, 2000.

Financial Planning Basics

Dominguez, Joe, and Vicki Robin. *Your Money or Your Life*. New York: Penguin, 2002.

Quinn, Janet Bryant. *Making the Most of Your Money*. New York: Simon & Schuster, 1997.

Ramsey, Karen. *Everything You Know About Money Is Wrong*. New York: ReganBooks, 1999.

Schwab, Charles. *Charles Schwab's Guide to Financial Independence: Simple Solutions for Busy People*. New York: Crown, 1998.

Tyson, Eric. *Personal Finance for Dummies*. Foster City, CA: IDG Books, 2007.

USEFUL WEB SITES

Obviously Web sites are created, updated and changed much faster than books are published. For the most up-to-date list of my favorite sites, please visit www.BrentKessel. com.

Stock and Market Information

MSN Money: *www.money.msn.com*

Google Finance: *http://finance.google.com/finance*

The Wall Street Journal: http://online.wsj.com/home/us

Yahoo Finance: *http://finance.yahoo.com*

BigCharts allow you to look up historical prices on almost any security: *http:// bigcharts.marketwatch.com/historical*

Zacks.com: *http://www.zacks.com*

Calculators

How much are you spending? *http://www.youcandealwithit.com/budgeting_tools/ budget_calculators.shtml*

BankRate: *http://www.bankrate.com/brm/rate/calc_home.asp*

Financial Planning Industry

The National Association of Personal Financial Advisors, the largest association of Fee-Only® financial advisors in the U.S. (NAPFA): *http://www.napfa.org*

The Financial Planning Association: *http://www.fpanet.org*

The Certified Financial Planner Board of Standards: *http://www.cfp.net*

The Chartered Financial Analyst Institute—CFA's are highly trained investment specialists but generally don't focus on other aspects of financial planning or comprehensive advice: *http://www.cfainstitute.org*

College Planning

The West Virginia Smart 529 is my favorite because of its investment choices and the ability to select age-based portfolios which adjust the asset allocation on your child's ninth, fourteenth, and nineteenth birthdays: *http://www.smart529.com*

Tuition Finder allows you to find out the costs at any U.S. college or university: *http:// www.nces.ed.gov/ipeds/cool/Search.asp*

College Savings Plan of Nebraska: *http://www.planforcollegenow.com/* and Utah Educational Savings Plan: *http://www.uesp.org/*
(Both of the above have investment options from Vanguard, which I like.)

General

Social Security: *http://www.ssa.gov/*
Find a Lawyer: *http://www.martindalehubbell.com*

INTERVIEW PARTICIPANTS' BOOKS AND WEB SITES

ADYASHANTI Meditation teacher based in the Zen and advaita (non-dualism) traditions. Selected books: *Emptiness Dancing, My Secret Is Silence, True Meditation, Impact of Awakening;* http://www.adyashanti.org

A. H. ALMAAS Master teacher of spiritual self-inquiry. Selected books: *The Inner Journey Home, The Pearl Beyond Price, Brilliancy;* http://www.ahalmaas.com

AMMACHI Known as the "hugging saint." Selected books: *Messages from Amma: In the Language of the Heart;* http://www.amma.org

KEN BLANCHARD Teacher, author, and business consultant. Selected books: *The One Minute Manager, Leading at a Higher Level, Lead Like Jesus;* http://www. kenblanchard.com/about/bios/ken_blanchard

JOHN BOGLE Founder of Vanguard Group. Selected books: *The Little Book of Common Sense Investing, The Battle for the Soul of Capitalism;* http://www.vanguard. com/bogle_site/bogle_home.html

DAVID BOOTH CEO of Dimensional Fund Advisors. Selected books: *Trading Costs and Tracking Error;* http://www.dfaus.com

HIS HOLINESS THE DALAI LAMA The head of state and spiritual leader of Tibet. Selected books: *The Art of Happiness, The Wisdom of Forgiveness;* http://www. dalailama.com

RAM DASS Former Harvard professor who became a leader of an Eastern spiritual movement for millions. Selected books: *Be Here Now, The Only Dance There Is, Still Here;* http://www.ramdass.org

DAVID DEIDA Focus on a nonreligious spiritual practice to create a connection between spirituality and sexuality. Selected books: *The Way of the Superior Man, Blue Truth, Instant Enlightenment;* http://www.deida.info

EUGENE FAMA Robert R. McCormick Distinguished Service Professor of Finance, University of Chicago Graduate School of Business. Selected books: *The Theory of Finance, Foundations of Finance;* www.chicagogsb.edu/fac/eugene.fama

CHRISTINA FELDMAN Co-founder of Gaia House in England and a guiding teacher at Insight Meditation Society in Barre, Massachusetts. Selected books: *Beginner's Guide to Buddhist Meditation: Practices for Mindful Living, The Buddhist Path to Simplicity;* http://www.gaiahouse.co.uk

GIL FRONSDAL Zen and Vipassana teacher. Selected books: *The Dhammapada: A New Translation of the Buddhist Classic;* http://www.insightmeditationcenter.org

GANGAJI Freedom and inner peace inquiry based on teachings of H. W. L. Poonja, a disciple of Ramana Maharshi. Selected books: *You Are That, The Diamond in Your Pocket;* http://www.gangaji.org

JOSEPH GOLDSTEIN Vipassana teacher and co-founder of Insight Meditation Society in Barre, Massachusetts. Selected books: *Insight Meditation: The Practice of Freedom, One Dharma;* http://www.dharma.org/ims/joseph_goldstein.html

JERU KABBAL (DECEASED) Spiritual teacher and author. Selected books: *Finding Clarity;* http://www.jerukabbal.com

BYRON KATIE Creator of a body of self-inquiry work designed to help people end their own suffering. Selected books: *A Thousand Names for Joy, Loving What Is;* http://www.thework.com

RABBI HAROLD KUSHNER Rabbi and best-selling author. Selected books: *When Bad Things Happen to Good People, Living a Life that Matters;* http://www.tiofnatick.org

HARRY MARKOWITZ Nobel Prize–winning economist behind modern portfolio theory. Selected books: *The Theory and Practice of Investment Management;* http://rady.ucsd.edu/faculty/directory/markowitz

JOE MOGLIA CEO of TD Ameritrade. Selected books: *Coach Yourself to Success: Winning the Investment Game;* http://www.tdameritrade.com

MIKE MURRAY Venture philanthropist committed to economic and social empowerment of the poor. http://www.unitus.com/sections/aboutus/aboutus_board_mmurray.asp

THICH NHAT HANH Vietnamese Buddhist monk and leader of peace movement; nominated by Martin Luther King Jr. for Nobel Peace Prize. Selected books: *The Art of Power, Peace Is Every Step, The Miracle of Mindfulness, Living Buddha, Living Christ;* http://www.plumvillage.org/

WES NISKER Vipassana meditation teacher. Selected books: *Crazy Wisdom, The Big Bang, the Buddha, and the Baby Boom;* http://www.wesnisker.com

CARRIE SCHWAB-POMERANTZ Senior Vice President and Chief Strategist, Consumer Education, Charles Schwab & Co., Inc. and President, Charles Schwab Foundation. Selected books: *It Pays to Talk: How to Have the Essential Conversations with Your Family About Money and Investing;* http://www.schwab.com/public/schwab/research_strategies/market_insight/1/3/ask_carrie.html

MEIR STATMAN Glenn Klimek Professor of Finance, Leavey School of Business Santa Clara University. Selected books: *Behavioral Finance and Decision Theory in Investment Management;* http://www.scu.edu/business/finance/faculty/profiles/statman.cfm

TSOKNYI RINPOCHE Tibetan meditation teacher in the Dzogchen tradition. Selected books: *Carefree Dignity, Fearless Simplicity;* http://www.pundarika.org

DAVID WHYTE Brings the insights of poetry to bear on the world of work. Selected books: *River Flow: New and Selected Poems 1984–2007, Crossing the Unknown Sea;* http://www.davidwhyte.com

ACKNOWLEDGMENTS

There are so many people without whom this book would not have been written—literally hundreds who have provided enthusiasm and encouragement along the way. I'm not able to name them all, so I instead offer this incomplete but critical list of acknowledgments. First and foremost, I would like to thank Robert Strock, my mentor since age nineteen and my stepfather for most of the last two decades. Robert is a unique catalyst to help people actualize their soul's full potential. His ability to approach unconscious conditioning with the utmost compassion, while at the same time supporting and eliciting the still small voice of wisdom, is the very heart of the Middle Way. I never could have written that chapter without his life-changing guidance and profound insight. Rob contributed to many of the concepts presented in this book, especially the archetypes, several of which were influenced by insights gleaned over his three-decade career as a psychotherapist and spiritual counselor.

My literary team has been phenomenal. My agent, Linda Chester, believed in me and this project based on a short dinner conversation. Kyra Ryan contributed tireless editorial work—filling in the gaps, asking the difficult questions, fleshing out the exercises, and tackling a subject rife with emotional and creative complexity. Mindy Werner brought her sensitive but sharp scalpel to a bloated first draft. And Eric Brandt, Mark Tauber, and the entire HarperOne team embraced the potential of this book a full three years before I did.

None of this would have been possible without the experiences I've had at Abacus and Kubera, and for this I am deeply indebted to my partner and dear friend Spencer Sherman for co-creating businesses that have inspired and significantly enriched the lives of our employees, clients, and the greater community, for sharing his inner life, his family and his generous spirit with me and my family, and for being an essential catalyst for my spiritual, professional, and creative growth since 1999. Many of the stories and lessons contained in these pages would not exist had my clients not opened their hearts and minds to me with the courage to share their fears and vulnerabilities, an invitation most financial consumers would sooner avoid accepting. Spencer and I are fortunate to work with an extraordinary group of people who care so deeply about our clients and each other: Our partner, Jason Cole; Angela Spirrison, JJ Sweeting, and Nadia Fernandez, who coordinated many of the logistics involved in traveling to the interviews; and many other Abacus and Kubera team members: Tom O'Connor, Suzanne Lawrence, Karen Reibel, Jesse Seaver, JD Bruce, Greg Aloia, Laura Giordano, Carleen Gazabat, Robert Barrimond, Pat Jennerjohn, Mike Weiner, Barbara Wolf, and Barrett Porter.

For their invaluable advice to a first-time author, including the introduction to my agent, the late Richard Carlson and his dear friend and writing partner, Benjamin Shield. For their support and encouragement, and for allowing me to write in one of the most beautiful places in the world, Sting and Trudie Styler. For their tremendous enthusiasm and spirit, Tom Nadeau and Cary Granat; and for bringing my work to the public eye for the first time, Alissa Bushnell. For all the 6:00 a.m. dialogues about yoga philosophy, freedom, and money, my Ashtanga yoga teacher of fifteen years, Chuck Miller. Colin Horowitz and Louis Kessel, my fathers, for supporting me in their own unique ways, and for modeling different versions of financial freedom and flexibility. And to Victoria Moran for first suggesting the title.

There were many who made significant efforts to introduce me to spiritual teachers, business leaders, and authors for the interviews that informed this book, including Robert Strock, Gina Thompson, Bryce Skaff, Gene Fama Jr., Jade Kirdain and Giles Martin, Brother Phap Lai, Patty Botari, Greg Wendt, Johanna Hollomon, J. P. Azar, Asiff Hirji, Bobby Sager, Marc Pollick, and Mark Haddad. This group went out on a limb for me at a very early stage in the process. And, of course, I have debts of gratitude to the spiritual teachers, professors, and business leaders who so generously volunteered their time and candor in the interviews.

In addition to Kyra, Mindy, and Robert, a number of people read early drafts of this manuscript, particularly the archetype chapters, and provided extremely valuable feedback. These include Donna Cashell, Pete Kovner, Vicky Schiff, Molly Rhodes, Jens Koepke, Maty Ezraty, Stephanie Solomon,

Jennifer Bruce, and Paula Rochelle. Additionally, Adam Bendell provided helpful rephrasing of several key Buddhist concepts, Pat Jennerjohn proofread the appendix for accuracy, Pam England provided masterful feedback on the Core Story and archetype chapters, and Jay Totten, Danielle Anderson, Kim Weisberg, and Jui-Fu Wang provided ancillary research. Stephanie Ptak and Lou Harvey at Dalbar generously provided their QAIB® study on investor performance. Mike Powell provided his terrific talents as a photographer.

Parts of this book recount my own spiritual journey, and there are many teachers who have challenged and inspired me to grow. My mother, Marilyn Levine, was my first teacher, a true spiritual wise-woman who has traveled through both good times and bad with strength and grace. The many meditation and other personal growth teachers, most of whom are quoted in these pages, have also had an unmistakable impact. George Kinder and Dick Wagner were my early and influential mentors in the financial planning industry, and Carolyn Dellúomo and Dave LaRue have provided invaluable personal and business coaching. I am deeply appreciative of the writing teachers and coaches I have had: Nancy Bacal, Hal Zina Bennett, Dorianne Laux, Joe Millar, and Ellen Bass, and all of the other writers who were compassionate and encouraging with my writing.

Last but certainly not least, I thank my wife, Britta Bushnell, for encouraging me unwaveringly while offering her exceptional intuition at pivotal moments, for improving the writing with her keen sensitivity and experience as a workshop facilitator, and for being an incredible mom to our sons, Kaden and Rumiah, when I was immersed in the writing, on retreat, or traveling to conduct the interviews for this book.

May you all be blessed.

INDEX

Abacus, 231

adolescence, 42, 52

Adyashanti, 20, 51

AIDS, 121, 220

alcohol, 74, 75, 80

Almaas, A. H., 177

ambition, 137, 138, 139

ambivalence, 81

Ang, Brother Phap, 74–75

annuities, 255–56

anti-Semitism, 53

anxiety, 23, 24, 25, 45–49; of Guardian, 45–51; of Saver, 94, 96

appetite loss, 51

archetypes, financial, 39–148; Caretaker, 119–33; characteristics and practical recommendations for, 264–81; dominant, 153–54; Empire Builder, 135–45; finding your, 146–48; Guardian, 45–59; Idealist, 77–88; Innocent, 109–18; introduction to, 39–43; Middle Way and, 165–76; Pleasure Seeker, 61–76; quiz, 146–48; Saver, 89–97; Star, 99–108

art and artists, 9, 79, 80, 81, 82, 83, 85, 110, 229

asset-class diversification, 198

attention, 237, 240; desire for, 99–108; paying, 75, 237

awareness, 239–41; of Star, 106–107

back pain, 51

balance, 65, 196; Middle Way, 151–79

banking fees, 111

bankruptcy, 11, 23, 24, 71

beauty, 99, 101–104

beginner's mind, 12

being, 239–41

Bernays, Edward, 68

Bible, 123, 217

big business, 80, 84

Blanchard, Ken, 139

boats, 72

Bogle, John, 187, 199

bonds, 193, 196; mix of stocks and, 205–207

bookkeeper, 87, 97

Booth, David, 187

breathing, 75, 234

Buddha, 125, 151, 152

Buddhism, 5, 12, 25, 74–75, 80, 123, 124, 130, 144, 151, 152, 155, 165, 217, 218, 224, 234

buen pobre, 93

Buffett, Warren, 188, 194, 224

buy now, pay later attitude, 68–72

California Public Employees Retirement System (Cal-PERS), 190

capitalism, 78

Caretaker, 40, 41, 119–33, 153–54, 222;
action plan, 132–33; beliefs of, 121–22;
caring for, 131–33; characteristics and
practical recommendations for, 277–79;
Core Story of, 120–21; dark side of,
125–28; female, 126; healthy caretaking,
128–33; male, 126; Middle Way and,
173; not doing, 128; payoff, 123–25;
seeds of, 122–23; truthfulness of, 127
Carhart, Mark, 185
Carnegie, Andrew, 138
cars, 4, 10, 20–21, 48, 72, 94, 100, 101,
104, 107; repossession of, 113
cash flow, 249–50; characteristics and
practical recommendations for archetypes, 264–81
CDs, 203, 254
celebrities, 24, 101
cell phones, 101
CEOs, 102
Certified Financial Planner, 96, 117, 144,
225, 263
charity, 27, 80, 99–100, 104, 107, 121,
122, 215, 254; causes, 229–30; how
much to give, 221–24; what to give,
226–29; yoga of money and, 212–35
checkbook, balancing, 114
Chekhov, Anton, 61
childbirth, 52
children, 30, 52, 57–58, 70, 86, 213;
caretaking of, 119, 120, 122; Core
Story and, 30, 31; generosity and, 224;
marketing to, 101; money experiences of, 29, 30, 31, 52, 66, 69, 94,
102–103, 111, 113, 114, 120, 122,
156–58; need for attention, 103; in
poverty, 30, 229; spoiled, 92; wealthy,
63; worrying, 58
Christmas, 66, 67, 211
clothes, 10, 30, 94, 99, 100
co-dependence, 32, 125, 126; of Caretaker, 125–33
college, 13, 48, 204; Ivy League, 63; saving for, 13, 65

comfort zone, stepping out of, 107–108
commodities, 195–96
compassion, 85, 121, 212, 213, 214,
217, 221, 226; types of, 217; unbiased,
217–19
connectedness, 9–10, 182, 184, 231;
investing and, 184–87
Consumer Credit Counseling Services
(CCCS), 58, 117, 250, 264
Core Story, 25–35, 151, 154, 176,
213, 214, 242; archetypes, 39–43; of
Caretaker, 120–21; of Empire Builder,
137–38; of Guardian, 49–50; of
Idealist, 78–80; of Innocent, 110–11;
looking within, 29; Middle Way and,
151–79; of Pleasure Seeker, 62–64;
of Saver, 90–93; seeds of, 30; of Star,
100–101; understanding, 31–35
credit cards, 118; debt, 71, 250–52

Dalai Lama, 155, 181, 212; *The Art of
Happiness at Work*, 20, 152
Dalbar, Inc., 17, 188, 204
debt, 11, 17, 32, 64, 70–72, 111, 112,
118; credit-card, 71, 250–52; management, 250–52; payment, 87; Pleasure
Seeker and, 70–72; reduction services,
264; statistics, 71
Deida, David, 107, 176
depression, 51, 165
desires, *see* wanting
detaching, 9
diabetes, 215, 222
Dimensional, 187
diminishing returns, 12
diversity, investing, 193–98
divine nature, 178–79
divorce, 24, 31, 47, 70, 79, 111,
119, 175
Dominguez, Joe, *Your Money or Your Life*,
118, 184
Domini, Amy, 190
doomsday scenarios, 50
Dyer, Wayne, 124

economy, 4, 91; market, 184–85
empathy, 121, 123, 220
Empire Builder, 40, 41, 42, 135–45,
    153–54, 232; beliefs of, 137–38;
    characteristics and practical recom-
    mendations for, 279–81; Middle Way
    and, 174; payoff, 139–40; removing
    the blinders, 141–45; treat yourself like
    you treat your business, 140–41; Want-
    ing Mind and, 138–39
Employee Benefit Research Institute, 71
emptiness, 65, 105
Enough for Life bucket, 144–45
environment, 121, 229
envy, 33
Epicurus, 67
equality, 85
estate planning, 260–62; characteristics
    and practical recommendations for
    archetypes, 264–81
evil, money as, 81, 88
expectations, 12

Fama, Eugene, 183
family, 4; caretaking of, 119, 120, 122,
    123; wealthy, 63
fear, 29, 31, 32, 49–50, 52, 222; of
    Empire Builder, 142–44; of Guardian,
    49–53; investing, 208–209; of Pleasure
    Seeker, 66–68; of Saver, 91–92, 94, 96
Feldman, Christina, 7, 18; *Soul Food*, 18
feminine-masculine money roles, 176
Ferrucci, Piero, 214
financial archetypes, *see* archetypes,
    financial
financial planners, 96, 117, 144,
    225, 263
financial planning, 13–16, 96, 97, 189,
    263; goals, 14–16; Wanting Mind and,
    16–17
fixed annuities, 255
flow, in the, 9–10
food, 6, 12, 65, 90, 94
forgiveness, 212

four-year-old self, and money,
    156–58, 164
France, 74, 75
Francis, Saint, 125
Freud, Sigmund, 68
friends, 5, 90; caretaking of, 120, 122, 129
Fronsdal, Gil, 72
Frost, Robert, 152
frugality, 28, 32, 69, 91; of Saver, 91–96
futures, 196

Gandhi, Mahatma, 125
Gangaji, 39, 77, 155
Gates, Bill, 224
gender and money roles, 176
General Electric, 187
generosity, 33, 97, 101, 121, 125, 145,
    212–35; of Caretaker, 121–25, 129;
    how much to give, 221–24; right mo-
    tivation, 219–21; yoga of money and,
    212–35; *see also* charity; philanthropy;
    yoga of money
Gladwell, Malcolm, *Blink,* 102
goals, 14–15, 142; of Empire Builder,
    142; financial planning, 14–16; heart-
    felt, 14–16; investing, 14–16, 203–204
Goldstein, Joseph, 151, 217
Graham, Benjamin, 194
Great Depression, 69, 91–92, 96, 207
Greenspan, Alan, 47
Guardian, 40, 41, 42, 45–59, 153–54,
    207, 264–67; breaking death grip of,
    57–59; characteristics and practical rec-
    ommendations for, 264–67; Core Story
    of, 49–50; creating safety for, 58–59;
    feelings of, 51; Middle Way and, 167;
    money mantras, 55; payoff, 55–57;
    survival mode, 51–54; thinking of, 55
guilt, 72, 79, 82, 92, 121, 125, 219

Hafiz, 45
hair, 101
happiness, 5, 10–11, 21, 63, 95, 130,
    162, 163, 234

health care, 71, 120
heart disease, 214
heartfelt goals, 14–16
hedonism, 64, 67
Hinduism, 123
hippies with money, 84–85
Hold Both practice, 163–64, 166
holiday spending, 66, 67
house, 4, 64; mortgage, 46, 250–52;
    remodeling, 72; value of, 202–203
human nature, 178–79

Idealist, 40, 41, 77–88, 153–54; breaking
    free, 86–88; characteristics and practi-
    cal recommendations for, 269–71;
    Core Story of, 78–80; heads in the
    sand, 82–83; hippies with money,
    84–85; Middle Way and, 169; money
    hated by, 81–82; payoff, 85–86; seeds
    of, 80–81
if only, 7–8
illness, 111, 130, 214, 215
income, 226–27
independence, 79
indexed annuities, 255–56
indexing, 187–88, 191
inflation, 137, 203
inheritance, 63, 65, 78, 79, 82, 84,
    111, 222
innate financial wisdom, 161–62, 164
inner conflict, 17–18
Innocent, 40, 41, 109–18, 153–54;
    beliefs of, 111–13, 116–17; character-
    istics and practical recommendations
    for, 275–77; Core Story of, 110–11;
    freeing the, 116–18; getting comfort-
    able with money, 115–18; Middle Way
    and, 172; money mantras, 112; payoff,
    114–15; seeds of, 113–14
instant gratification, 109
insurance, 4, 256–60; auto, 259; char-
    acteristics and practical recommenda-
    tions for archetypes, 264–81; disability,
    257–58; homeowner's, 259; liability,

258; life, 257; long-term care, 259–60;
    renter's, 259
intelligence, 103
intuition, 110
investing, 13–16, 46, 64, 92, 101,
    122, 181–209, 226–27; bonds, 196,
    205–207; buying low and selling high,
    197; characteristics and practical rec-
    ommendations for archetypes, 264–81;
    commodities, 195–96; connectedness
    and, 184–87; costs and taxes, 198–202;
    definition of, 183–84; diversified
    portfolio performance, 196–98; diver-
    sity, 193–98; doing good and doing
    well, 190–91; emotions, 208–209;
    of Empire Builder, 140–41, 144–45;
    goals, 14–16, 203–204; hidden fees,
    200–202; Middle Way, 191–93; mix
    of stocks and bonds, 205–207; passive,
    187–88, 192, 199; preparation, 205–
    209; ready-to-go investment strategies,
    246–49; real estate, 195; rebalancing,
    197; of Saver, 92, 95; stocks, 186–98,
    203–207; time and, 202–205; wanting
    better returns, 16–17
Islam, 123, 217

Japan, 4
jewelry, 101, 105
Judaism, 53, 123, 192, 216

Kabbal, Jeru, *Finding Clarity*, 52, 156
karma yoga, 123
Katie, Byron, 116; *Loving What Is*, 87
kindness, *see* loving kindness
Koran, 217
Kornfeld, Jack, 18
Kushner, Rabbi Harold, 74, 140, 216–17;
    *When All You've Ever Wanted Isn't
    Enough: The Search for a Life That Mat-
    ters*, 74

Latino cultures, 93
lawyers, 13

legacy, 232–33
letting go, 18–19
Lieh Tzu, 238
Los Angeles, 99–100, 105–106
lottery, 24, 111, 112
love, 212; money and, 102, 105
loving kindness, 130, 234–35; meditation, 234
Loving Life bucket, 145

marketing, 101, 112
Markowitz, Dr. Harry, 192, 203
marriage, 117; financial tensions in, 64,
  69–70, 82, 86, 175–76
martyrdom, 125
Marxism, 84
masculine-feminine money roles, 176
mask, money, 159–60
McLeod, Ken, *White Paper III,* 241
media, 100, 105
Medicare, 71
meditation, 8, 20, 74; loving-kindness,
  234; Zen, 20
memory, 29
microfinance, 231
Microsoft, 136, 194, 224
Middle Way, 151–79, 215; archetypes
  and, 165–76; divine nature and human
  nature, 178–79; going slowly, 177;
  holding both, 163–64, 166; innate
  financial wisdom, 161–62, 164; for investors, 191–93; letting the four-year-
  old speak, 156–58, 164; money mask,
  159–60; opposites attract, 175–76;
  playfulness, 178; think more, 154–56
mind, 3–35, 240; in the flow, 9–10; of
  Guardian, 45–59; nature of the, 3–35;
  still, 238–39; think more, 154–56; unconscious, 23–35, 156; Wanting, 4–5,
  6, 10, 11, 62, 68, 95, 110, 138–39,
  175, 222
Moglia, Joe, 57, 200
money wounds, 51–52
Monroe, Marilyn, 101

mortgage, 46; management, 250–52
Murray, Mike, 224–25
musicians, 80, 82
mutual funds, 17, 182, 186–91, 199; subsequent performance of top thirty, 189

Nagarjuna, 152
Native Americans, 123
Nisker, Wes, 6
"not enough" theme, 3–22

obituary, 233
obsession, 51
overspending, 32

pain, 6, 81; sharing the, 218–19
passive investing, 187–88, 192, 199
Patanjali, 10
Patillo, Bob, 211–12
pessimism, 51
philanthropy, 138, 215; active, 233;
  causes, 229–30; characteristics and
  practical recommendations for archetypes, 264–81; how much to give,
  221–24; smart, 263; what to give,
  229–30; *see also* charity; generosity
plastic surgery, 99, 102, 103
playfulness, 178
Pleasure Seeker, 40, 41, 42, 61–76,
  153–54; characteristics and practical
  recommendations for, 267–68; Core
  Story of, 62–64; dark side of buy now,
  pay later attitude, 68–72; debt and,
  70–72; fears of, 66–68; Middle Way
  and, 168; motivations for shopping,
  67–68; payoff for, 65; redefining pleasure, 72–74; seeds of, 64–65
Plum Village, France, 74–75
Presence and the Contemplation of
  Death, 241
procrastination, 109
property taxes, 49
psychotherapy, 89
public image, 99–108

QAIB, 17, 188

race, 102
Ram Dass, 79, 124, 213; *Be Here Now,* 124
ready-to-go investment strategies, 246–49
real estate, 192, 193, 195
real-estate investment trusts (REITs), 195
rebalancing, 197
relaxation, 53
religion, 74, 85, 110, 165, 212, 234; giving and, 123, 216–17, 221
restaurants, 12, 90
"retail therapy," 64
retirement planning, 253–54
retirement savings, 17, 46, 71, 84, 183, 205, 253–54; lack of, 48, 71; statistics, 71
Rinpoche, Tsoknyi, 89, 238
Robin, Vicki, *Your Money or Your Life,* 118, 184
Rockefeller, John D., 3
Rockefeller family, 3, 233
"root of all evil," money as, 81, 88
Rosenberg, Claude, *Wealthy and Wise,* 221

safety, 59; for Guardian, 58–59
sainthood, 125, 216–17
Saver, 40, 41, 42, 62, 89–97, 153–54, 215; breaking the death grip of, 95–97; characteristics and practical recommendations for, 271–73; Core Story of, 90–93; dark side of, 93–94; fears of, 91–92, 94, 96; Middle Way and, 170; money mantras, 92; payoff, 95
saving, 13, 24, 27, 81, 118; lack of, 64; Saver archetype and, 89–97
Schor, Juliet, *The Overspent American,* 5
Schwab, Charles, 109
Schwab-Pomerantz, Carrie, 109
security, 34, 91
self-centeredness, 213–16
self-esteem, lack of, 103, 105

sensory enjoyment, 62, 63, 103
sex, 74, 75, 102; withholding, 86
shareholder activism, 191
Sherman, Spencer, 144
shopping, 32; buy now, pay later attitude, 68–72; motivations, 67–68; Pleasure Seeker, 64, 65, 66–72
skeptic's lens, 83
small business, 80
socially responsible investing (SRI), 190–91, 192, 263
Social Security, 48, 49, 59
social work, 120
Socrates, 64
Soros, George, 26
spending, 81; of Pleasure Seeker, 61–76; of Saver, 97; of Star, 101
spirituality, 79, 83, 85, 110, 152, 165, 234; giving and, 123, 124, 125, 216–17, 221
sports, 9
Standard & Poor's 500 index, 17, 187, 188, 190, 203, 204; Annualized Returns: October 1926 to September 2006, 204
Star, 40, 41, 99–108, 153–54; as attention seeker, 99–108; awareness of, 106–107; characteristics and practical recommendations for, 273–75; Core Story of, 100–101; emptiness of, 105; freeing the, 105–108; Middle Way and, 171; payoff, 103–104; seeds of, 101–103
Statman, Dr. Meir, 185
stillness, 238–39
stock market, 16–17, 46, 182, 186–95, 252; crashes, 53–54, 91; Great Depression and, 91–92; of 2000–2003, 193; Wanting Mind and, 16–17
stock-picking, 185, 190
stocks, 186–98, 203–207; international, 195, 196; mix of bonds and, 205–207; small-capitalization, 195, 196; value, 194–95, 196
stomach queasiness, 51

Strock, Robert, 166
suffering, 6, 64, 234; compassion and, 217; easing, 217, 219; of Innocent, 109–18; of Pleasure Seeker, 64–65
survival, 34, 51, 79, 111, 222; mode, 51–54

Talmud, 123, 192, 193
taxes, 80, 86, 200, 203, 218, 227, 228, 232, 251, 252; characteristics and practical recommendations for archetypes, 264–81; planning, 254–55
TD Ameritrade, 57, 200
television, 62
Templeton, Sir John, 190
Teresa, Mother, 211
Thich Nhat Hanh, 25, 30, 74, 135, 222, 237
Third World, 231
three buckets exercise, 224
tobacco, 80
Trump, Donald, 26
trust-fund kids, 63, 78, 126
truth, seeking the, 108
truthfulness, 127

Ugly Duckling syndrome, 102
unconscious, 23–35, 112, 156, 165, 242; Core Story, 25–35; expectations, 24–25
unemployment, 24

vacations, 5, 11, 12, 13, 61, 62, 65, 103
Vanguard fund, 190–91, 199
variable annuities, 255
victimization, 114
Vietnam, 75, 106
Vietnam War, 84
vulnerability, 85

Wal-Mart, 136
wanting, 3–22, 32, 72; absence of, 20–22; financial planning and, 16–17; financial toll of, 11, 16–17; impulses, 19; inner conflict and, 17–18; letting go, 18–19; list, 22; more and more, 12; "not enough" theme, 3–22
Wanting Mind, 4–5, 6, 10, 11, 20, 62, 68, 95, 110, 175, 222; desires of, 4–17; Empire Builder and, 138–39; financial planning and, 16–17; not wanting, 20–22
war, 81
"Who Am I?" exercise, 240
Whyte, David, 119, 159
wills and estates, 84, 232, 260–62; see also estate planning
Woodward, Bob, Maestro, 47
workaholism, 32, 62
worry, 45–49; child, 58; Guardian, 45–59; as warning sign, 47; worst-case scenario and, 56, 58
worst-case scenario, 56, 58, 239
wounds, money, 51–52

yoga, 182, 237; sutras, 10, 127
yoga of money, 211–35; assets and amount given, 226–29; choice of cause, 229–30; how much to give, 221–24; legacy, 232–33; personalized giving policy, 230; right motivation, 219–21; self-centeredness and, 213–16; three buckets exercise, 224–26; unbiased compassion, 217–19
You Have Arrived, 243
Yunus, Muhammad, 231

Zafon, Carlos Ruiz, 23

SPECIAL OFFER FOR READERS OF
It's Not About the Money

Brent Kessel believes strongly that your financial future and the world's future are interconnected. To this end, he's created an unprecedented offer:

- **STEP 1:** Open an account with Abacus Portfolios, the fee-only® sustainable Registered Investment Advisor Brent co-founded
- **STEP 2:** Select your favorite from a list of participating charities
- **STEP 3:** Keep your account open and invested for at least six months
- **STEP 4:** Abacus will donate $250 to your favorite charity

If you agree with the investment philosophy espoused by Brent and many other financial experts in chapter 12 of this book, and also want to help fund an important cause at no additional cost to you, go to

www.AbacusPortfolios.com/offer

You can fund your account with:

- a 401k from an old job that you never got around to rolling over to an IRA
- excess savings that you've accumulated in a low-interest bank account or CD
- stocks or mutual funds that aren't invested sustainably or in low-cost index funds
- proceeds from the sale or refinance of real estate or business assets

NOTES

NOTES

NOTES

NOTES

NOTES